SOVIET NATIONAL INCOME
AND PRODUCT, 1940–48

A RESEARCH STUDY BY THE RAND CORPORATION

SOVIET

NATIONAL INCOME

AND PRODUCT

1940–48

By **ABRAM BERGSON**

PROFESSOR OF ECONOMICS AND STAFF MEMBER
RUSSIAN INSTITUTE, COLUMBIA UNIVERSITY
CONSULTANT, THE RAND CORPORATION

and **HANS HEYMANN, Jr.**

ECONOMICS RESEARCH STAFF
THE RAND CORPORATION

1954

COLUMBIA UNIVERSITY PRESS, NEW YORK

THE TRANSLITERATION SYSTEM

USED IN THIS SERIES

IS BASED ON THE

LIBRARY OF CONGRESS SYSTEM

WITH SOME MODIFICATIONS

ACKNOWLEDGMENTS

THE WRITERS acknowledge first their indebtedness to Miss Faye Goldware for invaluable aid in reviewing the calculations and editing the Appendices. The study, part of a program of research by The RAND Corporation for the United States Air Force, has benefited at numerous points from comments and criticisms of fellow economists at RAND, especially Dr. Joseph A. Kershaw and Mr. Norman Kaplan. Mr. Marvin Hoffenberg provided valuable help in compiling national product data for the United States that might be compared with ours for the Soviet Union. RAND research memoranda have been cited with the kind permission of the authors.

Citations have been made from *Soviet National Income and Product in 1937,* by Abram Bergson (Columbia University Press, 1953), with the permission of the publishers and of the Russian Institute of Columbia University, which has also facilitated the study in many other ways.

ABRAM BERGSON
HANS HEYMANN, JR.

January, 1954

CONTENTS

CHARTS

TABLES

SOVIET NATIONAL INCOME
AND PRODUCT, 1940–48

A RESEARCH STUDY BY THE RAND CORPORATION

vailing rubles, the revaluation undertaken here is at *current* Adjusted Factor Cost rather than, as might possibly be the case, at an Adjusted Factor Cost that refers to some one year taken as a base. Hence, our procedure is not at all the same thing as deflation or the expression of the national income for a series of years in terms of the prices of some one base year. There is a corresponding difference in applications. Revaluation at Adjusted Factor Cost provides a basis to appraise "real" phenomena of a structural nature. Thus, different aspects of the allocation of the national product, e.g., its disposition between consumption, investment, etc., are measured in terms of resource costs or input. Deflation provides a basis to appraise changes over time in "real" national product and its components.[2] We are concerned in this study only with valuation at current Adjusted Factor Cost, so measurements are made of resource allocation but not of changes over time in "real" national product and its components.

In the present study, as in *Soviet National Income,* we rely to a great extent on statistical data from Soviet sources, particularly budgetary and other financial statistics. So far as reliability is concerned, these data in current rubles appear to be on an entirely different plane from the Soviet official national income statistics in "1926/27 rubles." As students of Soviet economics generally agree, the official national income statistics must be rejected because they are subject to serious deficiencies, particularly the incorrect valuation of new commodities introduced after the base year at the prices prevailing at the time of their introduction. Budgetary and financial statistics in current rubles generally do not appear to be subject to any distortions of this sort. On the other hand, there are many uncertainties regarding the procedures used in their collection and processing, and for this and other reasons the budgetary and other financial data probably are also subject to

[2] This very broad formulation of the nature of the applications of the two types of national income calculations will suffice, it is hoped, for present purposes, but it may be well to note that valuation at Adjusted Factor Cost, in a sense, logically precedes deflation. In any event, data on national income in constant prices may or may not measure changes in "real" national income over time in any meaningful sense, depending on the degree to which the constant prices selected allow measurement of structural aspects in the base period. For the nature and theoretic limitations of the Adjusted Factor Cost standard, the applications of national income data in these terms, and the relation of these applications to those based on deflated data, see *ibid.,* Chap. 3.

I. INTRODUCTION

Purpose and limitations of this study. In a previous study, to be referred to here as *Soviet National Income,*[1] one of the writers presented some data he had compiled on the national income of the USSR for the year 1937. The data are of two types. First, there are calculations in terms of prevailing ruble prices. These take the form of a series of national economic accounts, i.e., sector and global accounts of incomes and their disposition. Second, for some aspects of these accounts, an attempt is made to appraise, and where possible to correct for, divergencies between prevailing ruble prices and a standard of national income valuation referred to as Adjusted Factor Cost, i.e., broadly speaking, unit cost at factor prices corresponding on the average to relative factor productivities in different economic sectors. In effect, then, the accounts are revalued, insofar as is feasible, to approximate Adjusted Factor Cost. Valuation in these terms is considered to be preferable to valuation in terms of prevailing rubles where the concern is to appraise underlying "real" as distinct from purely "monetary" phenomena.

The present study attempts to compile data comparable to the foregoing for several more recent years. A series of national economic accounts of the type previously compiled for the year 1937 is now set forth for the years 1940, 1944, and 1948; and for each year considered, we try also to appraise and correct for divergencies between prevailing ruble prices and Adjusted Factor Cost.

The Adjusted Factor Cost standard is itself something less than ideal from a theoretic standpoint; accordingly, a revaluation in these terms can at best provide only a partially satisfactory basis to appraise underlying "real" phenomena. Furthermore, while we reject pre-

[1] A. Bergson, *Soviet National Income and Product in 1937.* In the Bibliography we cite both a monograph and two journal articles under this title. Reference here and elsewhere, unless otherwise indicated, is to the monograph. For the date and place of publication of monographs cited in this and subsequent footnotes, see the Bibliography.

error.[3] Accordingly, the accuracy of our calculations may be impaired on this account.

Furthermore, again as in the 1937 study but now to a greater extent, the famous Soviet policy of withholding information necessitates frequent resort to estimation and guesswork. The size of this volume, which is devoted in good part to explaining the sources and methods used to compile our national economic accounts, might be viewed as a testimonial chiefly to the formidable difficulties encountered in this connection. It is hoped that it will also be viewed as a testimonial to the writers' concern to achieve as reliable a result as possible under the circumstances, but it would be idle to pretend that anything like precision has been realized. Among the years studied, the limitations of the available information are greatest for the year 1944. Accordingly, the margin of error in our calculations is widest for this year. But there are limitations also for 1940 and 1948, and the figures for these years are also subject to error at numerous points.

Almost inevitably, there is also a difference regarding reliability between our calculations in terms of prevailing rubles and those involved in the revaluation in terms of Adjusted Factor Cost. The latter standard is hardly attainable with statistical accuracy in any circumstances. With the limited information available here, this part of our inquiry can only be viewed as in some measure an attempt to raise questions rather than answer them.

But while our calculations must leave much to be desired, they may be of interest nonetheless as the results of a systematic attempt to compile and put into coherent form the available information on an important topic and one, moreover, that hitherto has been notably obscure. The writers venture to think that the data, with all their limitations, are broadly illuminating on the dimensions of the Soviet economy in the period considered. But with the detailed explanations that are provided, the reader will be able to appraise for himself the results achieved.

Soviet economic developments, 1937–48. In *Soviet National Income*, a few facts were presented on the state of the Soviet economy and

[3] For further comment on the quality of Soviet statistics generally and of the national income, budget, and financial statistics in particular, see *ibid.*, pp. 4 ff.

economic organization in 1937, the year studied.[4] These facts must now be brought up to date for the years covered in this study.

The period under consideration witnessed a sizable enlargement of

TABLE 1

TERRITORIAL CHANGES IN THE USSR, 1939–45[a]

DATE	REGION	SIZE (SQ. KM.)[b]	POPULATION (THOUSANDS)
Nov., 1939	Polish provinces (excluding Vilna district)	194,800	12,500[c]
Mar., 1940	Finnish provinces	35,100	420[c]
Aug., 1940	Rumanian provinces (Bessarabia and N. Bukovina)	50,400	3,700
Aug., 1940	Lithuania (including Vilna)	59,800	2,925
Aug., 1940	Latvia	65,800	1,951
Aug., 1940	Estonia	47,500	1,122
Total gain, Nov., 1939–Aug., 1940		453,400	22,618[c]
Sept., 1944	Petchenga Raion (Murmansk)	10,480	5
Sept., 1944	Tuva Autonomous Oblast	150,000	70
Oct., 1944	Memel territory	2,850	150
Aug., 1945	Kaliningrad Oblast (Koenigsberg area)	9,000	400
Sept., 1945	Transcarpathian area	12,620	800
Sept., 1945	Karafuto (S. Sakhalin)	36,090	420
Sept., 1945	Kurile Islands	10,100	5
Aug., 1945	Byalistock-Suwalki area— lost to Poland	(−)11,000	(−)600
Aug., 1945	Przemysl area—lost to Poland	(−) 3,200	(−)250
Net gain, Sept., 1944–Sept., 1945		216,940	1,000

[a] Sources: *Statistical Yearbook of the League of Nations, 1940/41*, p. 20; Theodore Shabad, "Political-Administrative Divisions of the USSR, 1945," *The Geographic Review*, No. 2, 1946, pp. 303–6. The information in these sources was supplemented with the advice of Mr. Shabad.

[b] One square kilometer = .3861 square miles.

[c] The cited figures do not take into account concomitant losses. Following the partition of Poland, an exchange of populations between Germany and the USSR resulted in a net loss of 260,000 persons from the Soviet-annexed Polish provinces; similarly, from the Soviet-incorporated Finnish areas some 415,000 Karelians were evacuated to Finland. See J. B. Schechtman, *European Population Transfers, 1939–45*, pp. 389, 484–87.

[4] *Ibid.*, pp. 9 ff.

Soviet territory. From 1939 through 1945 areas were incorporated in the USSR which before the war had a population of some 23 million, or about 13 percent of the Soviet population within the pre-1939 boundaries. The gains were realized at various dates, but almost entirely in the period of November, 1939, through August, 1940. Within that time the USSR annexed parts of Poland, Finland, and Rumania and all of Lithuania, Latvia, and Estonia. The different changes in boundaries that have occurred since 1939 are listed in Table 1, together with the size of the territory and population involved.

In addition to these territorial changes, which were due to boundary revisions, the Russians experienced further changes in the area under their control, albeit only temporary ones, as a result of the Germans' wartime conquests. At one time or another during the war the Germans occupied some 700,000 square miles of Soviet territory (within the 1941 boundaries). At the beginning of 1944, however, the Red Army had regained about two-thirds of this area, so that the Soviet government at that time controlled a territory which before the war had a population of 145 million, or about four-fifths of the prewar total for the whole USSR (Chart 1). Taking into account the wartime migration to the East and also the losses in the invaded areas, the population of the free area as of the beginning of 1944 must have been an appreciably larger fraction of the total than it had been before the war. By the end of 1944 the entire prewar territory had been regained, except for a small corner of the Latvian and Lithuanian republics, and the Red Army was pursuing the Axis forces across Poland and into the Balkans.

As with the years preceding 1937, those immediately following it saw an expansion of output. According to the official statistics, the national income of the USSR increased from 96.3 billion "1926/27 rubles" in 1937 to 128.3 billion "1926/27 rubles" in 1940, or by 33 percent. The deficiencies in the official statistics referred to previously generally lead to an upward bias. Accordingly, the increase in total output in the period 1937–40 probably was appreciably less than the official statistics indicate. On the other hand, it must have been greater than might be suggested by the various data on production in different lines compiled in Table 2. The years after 1937 saw a sharp increase

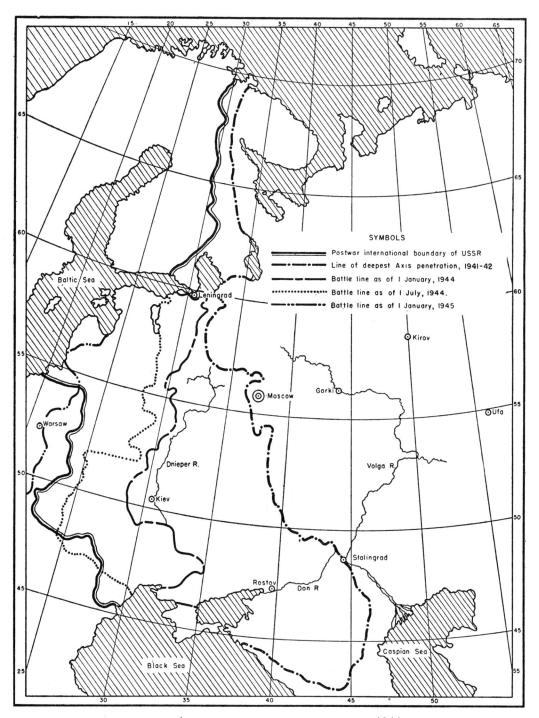

SYMBOLS

———————— Postwar international boundary of USSR
—·—·—·—· Line of deepest Axis penetration, 1941-42
— — — — Battle line as of I January, 1944
·········· Battle line as of I July, 1944.
—··—··—·· Battle line as of I January, 1945

CHART 1. BATTLE LINES OF THE USSR IN 1944

TABLE 2

SELECTED INDICATORS OF ECONOMIC ACTIVITY, USSR, 1937–50[a]

ITEM	UNIT	1937	1940	1945	1948	1950
Fuel and power						
1. Coal and lignite	mil. metric tons	127	166	148	208	261
2. Petroleum (crude)	mil. metric tons	28.5	31.0	19.5	29.3	37.8
3. Electric power	bil. kw.-hr.	36.4	48.3	45.0	66.0	90.3
Metallurgy						
4. Pig iron	mil. metric tons	14.5	15.0	8.9	13.9	19.4
5. Steel ingots	mil. metric tons	17.7	18.3	12.3	18.7	27.3
6. Rolled metal	mil. metric tons	13.0	13.1	8.5	14.1	20.8
Building materials						
7. Cement	mil. metric tons	5.5	5.8	1.8	6.5	10.4
8. Window glass	mil. sq. meters	60.0	44.4	28.4	66.8	84.3
9. Commercial timber delivered	mil. cu. meters	111	119	75	134	162
Chemicals						
10. Mineral fertilizer	thous. metric tons	n.a.[b]	2,608	1,100	3,270	5,100
11. Synthetic dyes	thous. metric tons	35	35	17	43	52
Machinery and vehicles						
12. Tractors	thous. units	51.0	31.1	7.3	53.7	96.0
13. Autos and trucks	thous. units	200	147	83	214	410
Livestock herds (end of year)						
14. Cattle	mil. head	50.9	54.5	47.0	n.a.	57.2
15. Sheep and goats	mil. head	66.6	91.6	69.4	n.a.	99.0
16. Hogs	mil. head	25.8	27.5	10.4	n.a.	24.1
Crops and foodstuffs						
17. Grain	mil. metric tons	120	119	66	115	124
18. Cotton, raw	mil. metric tons	2.6	2.7	1.2	n.a.	3.8
19. Sugar beets	mil. metric tons	21.9	20.9	8.9	n.a.	23.4
20. Sugar, granulated	thous. metric tons	2,421	2,150	465	1,663	2,515
21. Butter	thous. metric tons	185	207	110	285	325
22. Vegetable oil	thous. metric tons	495	724	262	515	775
23. Fish (catch)	mil. metric tons	1.6	1.4	1.1	1.5	1.8

TABLE 2 (*Continued*)

ITEM	UNIT	1937	1940	1945	1948	1950
Industrial consumer goods						
24. Cotton cloth	mil. meters	3,442	3,886	1,605	3,098	3,815
25. Woolen cloth	mil. meters	105	120	60	136	167
26. Leather shoes	mil. pairs	164	205	61	135	205
27. Paper	thous. metric tons	831	812	335	836	1,194
Housing						
28. Urban housing	mil. sq. meters	215	270	205	260	290
29. Rural housing	mil. sq. meters	365	405	350	380	390
Total	mil. sq. meters	580	675	555	640	680
Freight turnover						
30. R.R. traffic	bil. ton-km.	355	415	314	448	601
31. All traffic	bil. ton-km.	418	487	356	525	708
Employment						
32. Hired workers and employees	millions (yearly average)	27.0	31.2	27.3	34.2	38.2

ᵃ For the most part, the data in the table were obtained as follows:

(i) For 1937, from Gosplan, *Tretii piatiletnii plan razvitiia narodnogo khoziaistva Soiuza SSR (1938–42gg.) (proekt)*.

(ii) For 1940, from A. Bergson, J. H. Blackman, and A. Erlich, "Postwar Economic Reconstruction and Development in the U.S.S.R.," *Annals of the American Academy of Political and Social Science,* May, 1949, pp. 56–57.

(iii) For 1945 and 1948, from data in the table for 1950 and figures on percentage changes, 1946–50, in I. Kuz'minov, "Nepreryvnyi pod"em narodnogo khoziaistva SSSSR—zakon sotsializma," *Voprosy ekonomiki,* No. 6, 1951, p. 30.

(iv) For 1950, *Results of the Fulfillment of the Five-Year Plan of the USSR for 1946–1950,* together with data in the table for 1940.

Reference is made below to a number of items which call for special comment:

2. *Petroleum (crude)*: As derived from the foregoing sources and methods, the figures for 1937 and 1940 exclude natural gas. The figures for other years are projected from the 1937 and 1940 figures on the basis of data on percentage changes which may or may not exclude natural gas.

6. *Rolled metal*: 1940, from United Nations, *Economic Survey of Europe in 1951,* p. 127.

8. *Window glass*: For 1937, we cite a figure for 1938 given in TSUNKHU, *Sotsialisticheskoe stroitel'stvo Soiuza SSR, 1933–1938gg.,* p. 67.

9. *Commercial timber delivered*: 1940, 1948, and 1950, from United Nations, *Economic Survey . . . 1951,* p. 128. The figure for 1945 was calculated from the figure cited in this source for 1946 and a corresponding percentage figure in *Pravda,* January 21, 1947.

10. *Mineral fertilizer*: For 1940 and 1950, from United Nations, *Economic Survey . . . 1951,* p. 128.

11. *Synthetic dyes*: For 1937, 1940, 1948, and 1950, from *ibid.,* p. 128. It is believed the figure cited from this source for 1937 refers instead to 1938; this may also be true

for the figure cited for 1940. The figure in the table for 1945 is obtained from that cited in *ibid.*, p. 128, for 1946, and the data on percentage changes in Kuz'minov, p. 30.

12. Tractors: The figures for 1945 and 1948 are from Bergson *et al., Annals . . . ,* pp. 56–57. The figure for 1950 is an estimate of Harry Schwartz, New York *Times,* August 21, 1952.

13. Autos and trucks: 1945 and 1948 are from Bergson *et al., Annals . . . ,* pp. 56–57. The figure for 1950 is obtained from that for 1948 on the basis of data on percentage changes in Kuz'minov, p. 30. Kuz'minov's percentage data are given separately for autos and for trucks but not for these two items together. We assume that as of 1948, 85 percent of the total output of autos and trucks together consisted of the latter item and 15 percent of the former.

14. Cattle; 15. Sheep and goats; 16. Hogs: 1945, from Bergson *et al., Annals . . . ,* pp. 56–57. The figures for 1950 are from *Pravda,* January 26, 1951.

17. Grain: 1945 and 1948, from Bergson *et al., Annals . . . ,* pp. 56–57. The figure for 1950 is from *Pravda,* January 26, 1951. The figures represent the "biological yield," including harvesting and threshing losses, which vary from year to year.

18. Cotton, raw; 19. Sugar beets: 1945, from Bergson *et al., Annals . . . ,* pp. 56–57; 1950, from *Pravda,* January 26, 1951.

20. Sugar, granulated; 21. Butter; 22. Vegetable oil; 23. Fish (catch): 1937, 1940, 1948, and 1950, from United Nations, *Economic Survey . . . 1951,* p. 128. The figures for 1945 are calculated from data in this source and from figures on percentage changes in Kuz'minov, p. 30.

24. Cotton cloth; 25. Woolen cloth; 26. Leather shoes: The derivation is the same as for items 20, 21, 22, and 23.

27. Paper: 1937, 1948, and 1950, from United Nations, *Economic Survey . . . 1951,* p. 128; 1945, from Bergson *et al., Annals . . . ,* pp. 56–57.

28. Urban housing; 29. Rural housing: The figures for 1940, 1945, and 1948 are from the present study, Appendix Table 10, p. 132. We cite here for 1945 figures given in Appendix Table 10 for 1944. The figure for urban housing for 1937 is from the present study, Appendix A, p. 132. The figure for rural housing for 1937 is calculated from this figure and a figure for total housing, both urban and rural, in *Soviet National Income,* p. 108. The figure on urban housing is projected from 1945, assuming normal losses of 16 million square meters and new or restored housing of 100 million square meters, as stated in *Results of the Fulfillment of the Five-Year Plan of the USSR for 1946–1950.* The figure on rural housing for 1950 is projected from 1945, assuming the new construction or rebuilding of 2.7 million homes of 15 square meters each. The number of rural homes restored or newly built is given in *ibid.*

30. R.R. freight traffic; 31. All traffic: J. Blackman, "Transportation," in A. Bergson (ed.), *Soviet Economic Growth: Conditions and Perspectives.*

32. Hired workers and employees: Warren Eason, "Population and Labor Force," in *ibid.*

[b] n.a. = information not available.

---

in Soviet military production, but military end items are not covered in Table 2.

The increase in production, however, was due partly to the territorial annexations. Soviet sources are not altogether explicit concerning the territorial coverage of data published for 1940, but it is believed that those set fourth in Table 2 reflect the territorial gains not only of 1939 but also, in large measure, of 1940.[5] The resultant increases in output were general, but chiefly important in the case of agriculture. According to Table 2, the grain harvest of 1940 is about the same as that of the bumper year 1937. Without the new territories, the 1940 figure would have been of the order of 15 to 20 million tons less.

Total output continued to expand up to the Nazi attack, but subsequently it declined. The year 1942 probably marked the lowest point, but production generally was still well below the prewar level in 1944. From scattered information, such as the figures on production in individual industries in 1945 shown in Table 2, the writers think in terms of a reduction of perhaps as much as one-fourth in "real" national income. Again, we bear in mind here that Table 2 includes no military end items, the production of which increased greatly during the war.

The recovery from the war proceeded far more rapidly than many western commentators expected. According to the Soviet official statistics in "1926/27 rubles," the national income in 1948 amounted to 149.1 billion rubles, or 16 percent more than in 1940. The physical output series in Table 2 suggest that the 1948 national income may have been no larger than that of 1940, and possibly somewhat smaller.

As we have already implied, the trends in production over the years studied differed markedly in different sectors. Among other things, the output of consumers' goods declined during the war far more than production generally and in 1948 was still well below the prewar level. Furthermore, in considering the supplies available to civilian consumers, account has to be taken not only of production but also of stockpiles and military subsistence. Even before the Nazi attack a small but increasing share of the output of consumers' goods was absorbed in these latter ways, and during the war, of course, military subsistence became a major feature.

Understandably, then, the period considered also witnessed important changes in the organization of the consumers' goods market. Rationing, which had begun with the inauguration of the First Five Year Plan, had been replaced by an open retail market in 1935 and

[5] See Appendix E.

1936. The open market continued in operation until after the outbreak of war, but then rationing was again introduced: at first (July, 1941) in a few cities, and subsequently for the entire urban population. This system of distribution continued in operation until December, 1947. In connection with the monetary reform of that date, the government reinstituted an open market and this has continued in effect up to the present time.

The wartime rationing, like that of the early thirties, was of a differential character. The highest rations were provided to the army, to workers in defense industries, and to certain priority categories of workers in heavy industry generally. The rationing system was not formally extended to the farm population, but presumably the small amounts of goods made available to them were subject to some degree of restricted distribution nevertheless.[6]

Throughout the period considered, the Soviet consumer bought goods at retail not only from state and cooperative retail shops but also in some measure in the collective farm market, where the peasants were allowed to dispose of their farm surpluses after meeting their obligations to the state. In the immediate prewar years, however, with the acceleration of the defense program, deficiencies appeared in supplies available at established prices in the state and cooperative shops, and goods in the collective farm market—the one completely free market—tended to go at a premium.[7] The collective farm market continued to operate during the war. In view of the acute shortages that then developed, however, prices inevitably soared to astronomic levels compared with the fixed prices of rations disposed of by the government. In April, 1944, the government itself introduced still another source of supply, the "commercial shops." In these shops, limited supplies of goods were put on sale without ration coupons, but at prices which, like those in the collective farm market, were far above those prevailing for rationed goods.

The collective farm market continued in existence after the war and

[6] For a description of the wartime rationing system, see *Bulletins on Soviet Economic Development* (University of Birmingham), Bulletin No. 4, September, 1950, pp. 1–2.

[7] According to *Soviet National Income*, pp. 63 ff., supplies in the state and cooperative shops were broadly adequate to meet demand at established prices around 1937. Correspondingly, collective farm market prices approximated those in state shops.

still operates at the present time. As of 1948, however, there probably was again only a relatively limited margin between collective farm market and state shop prices.[8] The commercial shops lost their special identity in December, 1947, when the open market for consumers' goods was restored generally.

The period studied witnessed also a major reorganization of the labor market.[9] Under the prewar five year plans, as during the NEP, the government relied to a great extent on an open market in recruiting labor. While various restrictions were instituted at different times, these were of relatively limited importance; in large measure the Soviet worker was free to choose for himself his occupation and place of work.

This, however, was the situation only up to 1940. In that year the government introduced a variety of controls, including the decree on Labor Reserve Schools, providing for the drafting of urban and farm youths for a limited period of vocational training and subsequent administrative assignment to industrial work; legislation suppressing, on penalty of criminal prosecution, the voluntary departure of a worker from his place of work; and further legislation providing for the administrative transfer of engineers, foremen, skilled workers, and various other employees from one enterprise to another.[10]

This legislation of 1940, it has been suggested, represents an emergency program. Just what considerations prompted its adoption it is not possible to inquire here,[11] but it should be observed that in contrast to rationing, which was abandoned in December, 1947, the 1940 labor laws as far as is known are still on the Soviet books. Under the Fourth Five Year Plan, which was completed in 1950, the Labor Reserve

[8] On the relation of collective farm market and state shop prices during the years studied, see Appendix D, Section C.

[9] On the organization of the labor market under the five year plans, see A. Bergson, *The Structure of Soviet Wages*, pp. 143 ff., 234 ff.; P. R. Lever, *The State Labor Reserve System of the Soviet Union;* H. Schwartz, "Soviet Labor Policy 1945–1949," in *Annals of the American Academy of Political and Social Science,* May, 1949; H. Schwartz, *Russia's Soviet Economy,* pp. 445 ff.; V. Gsovski, "Elements of Soviet Labor Laws," United States Department of Labor, Bureau of Labor Statistics, Bulletin No. 1026; G. R. Barker, "Soviet Labor," *Bulletins on Soviet Economic Development,* Bulletin No. 6, June, 1951.

[10] For texts of the pertinent legislation, see Bergson, *The Structure of Soviet Wages,* pp. 234 ff.

[11] See, however, the brief discussion in *Soviet National Income,* pp. 71 ff.

School System graduated 3.4 million youths. These must have constituted a major part of the new semiskilled and skilled recruits to Soviet industry in the period covered by the plan.

Furthermore, the measures enacted in 1940 represented only part of the wartime program which the government ultimately adopted. After the Nazi attack, additional laws were enacted. These provided among other things for virtually general mobilization of the able-bodied urban population for work in war industries. Some of these measures, too, remained operative after the war. The law of April 15, 1943, subjecting railroad workers to military discipline was still on the books in 1948. Similarly, certain other restrictive measures applying to special sectors have continued in effect.

It was said above that under the Labor Reserve School System youths are subject to a draft for vocational training and subsequent assignment to jobs. According to Soviet claims, some youths volunteer, and if one may speak meaningfully of a voluntary career decision for youths of ages fourteen to nineteen years,[12] this may be so. For many, an incentive to attend may be provided by the free tuition and subsistence. Since 1940, students in secondary schools generally and also those in universities who are unable to obtain scholarships have had to pay tuition as well as pay for their own upkeep. On the other hand, while there are some volunteers, there is little question that most of the youths are drafted, and on this account, as well as because of the subsequent administrative assignment to jobs, the Labor Reserve School System represents an important reorganization of the labor market toward administrative allocation.

If the Labor Reserve School act has been somewhat less restrictive than it might seem to be, this is no doubt also true of the other new measures referred to. Thus, for a time after the war large numbers of workers undoubtedly moved about on their own, despite the legal prohibition on such activity, and according to many indications such voluntary movements have persisted on some scale in more recent

[12] According to the decree of October 2, 1940, establishing the Labor Reserve System, male youths of ages fourteen to seventeen years were subject to the draft. During the war the draft was extended to girls of ages sixteen to eighteen, and then by a decree of June 19, 1947, it was made applicable to boys of fourteen to nineteen years as well as to girls fifteen to eighteen.

years. But while the enforcement of the new measures may have been lax, it seems necessary to conclude that here too there was a significant change in the labor market organization toward direct controls.

The Soviet collective farm system underwent no major change in the period studied, and arrangements concerning procurements and income distribution are still today essentially the same as they were in the mid-thirties. Now as then, the farmers deliver their produce to the government partly on an obligatory basis at very low prices and partly on a more or less voluntary basis at higher prices. Surpluses remaining after deliveries to the government are available for sale on the collective farm market at still higher prices and for distribution to the collective farm membership on a "labor-day" basis. After the money expenses of the collective farm are met, the money income derived from the sale of farm produce is also distributed on a "labor-day" basis. Finally, the members have at their disposal, in addition to receipts from the collective farm, the produce of their own homestead. Out of this, too, deliveries must be made to the government, but the remainder of the produce is available either for sale on the collective farm market or for consumption.[13]

Collective farms, together with the so-called state farms owned and operated by the government, represented in 1937 practically all of Soviet agriculture. Subsequent to the annexations of 1939 and 1940, a minor part of the enlarged agricultural economy was operated by private peasant farms. While some collective farms were organized in the incorporated areas soon after they came under Soviet rule, collectivization did not become general until after the war, and possibly not until after 1948, the last year of concern in this study.

The arrangements regarding the financial status of the state enterprise have also remained in more recent years broadly the same as they were before the war. The so-called *khozraschet* system[14] involves

[13] Since 1950 the collective farm system has been subject to a major reorganization, including especially a comprehensive consolidation of small farms into larger ones. The arrangements concerning procurements and income distribution, however, are still essentially the same as those described in the text.

[14] On the Soviet *khozraschet* system as it operated in the years studied, see *Soviet National Income*, pp. 13 ff., and further information in the references cited there, p. 15, note 17; also, D. Granick, *Plant Management in the Soviet Industrial System*, particularly chap. ix.

among other things the maintenance for the enterprise of independent financial statements. Relations with the government budget are on a net rather than gross basis, i.e., instead of including all revenues and expenditures of state enterprise, the government budget includes only taxes and allocations from profit on the one hand and grants for fixed capital needs and other special requirements on the other. Finally, the state enterprise is expected to make its own way financially insofar as current operations are concerned, covering its expenses from sales or temporarily by loans from the state banks.

These financial arrangements, while general, have not been universal. For one thing, the government, from the early years of the five year plans, has applied a policy of maintaining low prices for many industrial goods through the granting of subsidies from the budget. The amounts of these subsidies, however, have been of varying importance in different years. We comment further on this at a later point. Also, different economic organizations at one time or another were attached fully to the government budget, rather than only partly as was the case under the *khozraschet* system. The most outstanding example in the period studied is the government-owned and operated machine-tractor stations (MTS) which were attached fully to the government budget in 1938. Even prior to that year these organizations had to be subsidized because of the undervaluation of the income in kind received from the collective farms for services rendered. But beginning in 1938 they ceased altogether to be *khozraschet* organizations. Curiously, this meant among other things that the income in kind received by the MTS from the collective farms became a revenue item in the government budget.

Choice of years studied. In determining the years to be covered in the present study, it can now be explained, consideration was given in the case of the year 1940 to the fact that this was the last Soviet prewar year, and accordingly of special interest from many standpoints. The year 1944 commands attention as a war year of high military output, and also one during which the Russians had regained control of most of their prewar territory. Furthermore, while the Russians have been notably secretive concerning the entire war period, they have released more information of the type needed in our calculations for the year

1944 than for any other war year. The year 1948 was selected as a late postwar year when the study was begun. As it turns out, it also happens to be a relatively favorable one in the postwar period to date, insofar as the volume of information is concerned.

The accounts that have been compiled in terms of current rubles are set forth and explained in the chapter immediately following (II). In Chapter III, we survey briefly the relation of ruble prices to Adjusted Factor Cost in the years studied, and attempt on this basis to appraise and correct for the effects on our accounts of the more important divergencies. In the last chapter (IV), we discuss some of the more interesting economic implications of the calculations.

II. NATIONAL INCOME
IN CURRENT RUBLES

METHODOLOGY; TERRITORIAL COVERAGE

THE VARIOUS ACCOUNTS that have been compiled in terms of current rubles are shown in Tables 3–7. For purposes of comparison we include here, along with the data now compiled for 1940, 1944, and 1948, the figures previously published for 1937. Methodologically, the calculations for all years are modeled largely after the national income data published for the United States by the Department of Commerce. This includes the form and scope of the accounts as well as the income concepts used. The nature of the methodology used and its relation to that of the Department of Commerce have been explained in detail in *Soviet National Income;*[1] we shall comment here only on several special features that come to the fore in the years now studied, namely, the treatment of Lend-Lease and reparations, the treatment of military subsistence, and the valuation of farm income in kind.

Lend-Lease; reparations. According to the Department of Commerce concepts, custom duties are included along with indirect taxes generally among the charges comprising the gross national product. In the present study, in the interest of consistency, we treat in this same way revenues realized by the government from the transfer to economic organizations of Lend-Lease and reparations imports. Apparently such imports were made available to economic organizations at a price rather than free of charge. This price, it is believed, was in excess of the usual custom duties levied on ordinary imports, but the budgetary revenues from such transactions are in no way distinguishable from custom duties generally, and accordingly have been treated here in the same way as such duties.

On the other hand, this treatment of custom duties means in effect

[1] Pages 17 ff.

TABLE 3

INCOMES AND OUTLAYS OF HOUSEHOLDS, USSR, 1937, 1940, 1944, AND 1948[a]

(Billions of rubles)

A. INCOMES	1937	1940	1944	1948
1. Net income of households from agriculture				
a. Wages of farm labor (on state farms, MTS, etc.)	5.6	7.8	6.4	14.7
b. Money payments to collective farmers on labor-day basis; salaries of collective farm executives; premiums	7.3	11.3	9.8	10.8
c. Net money income from sale of farm products	14.2	35.0	44.0	50.5
d. Net farm income in kind	32.5	54.0	31.0[b]	56.0
e. Total	59.6	108.1	91.2	132.0
2. Wages and salaries, nonfarm				
a. As recorded in current statistical reports	77.0	116.3	n.a.[c]	n.a.
b. Other	21.1	25.6	n.a.	n.a.
c. Total	98.1	141.9	149.6	269.8
3. Incomes of artisans; other money income currently earned	13.7	20.6	13.0	34.8
4. Imputed net rent of owner-occupied dwellings	4.0	6.0	8.0	10.5
5. Incomes of armed forces				
a. Military pay	1.5	4.1	14.2	14.0
b. Military subsistence	2.5	8.0	31.0	19.0
c. Total	4.0	12.1	45.2	33.0
6. Statistical discrepancy	4.3	7.9	11.2	20.4
7. Total income currently earned (1-6)	183.8	296.6	318.2	500.5
8. Pensions and allowances	6.1	7.1	19.7	26.1
9. Stipends and scholarships	2.2	2.4	2.1	3.0

	1937	1940	1944	1948
10. Interest receipts	.9	1.4	3.3	1.8
11. Total transfer receipts (8–10)	9.2	10.9	25.1	30.9
12. Total income	192.9	307.5	343.3	531.4

B. OUTLAYS

	1937	1940	1944	1948
1. Retail sales to households				
a. In government and cooperative shops and restaurants	111.5	162.0	113.2	305.2
b. In collective farm markets	16.0	35.0	50.0	48.0
c. Total	127.5	197.0	163.2	353.2
2. Housing (including imputed net rent of owner-occupied dwellings); services	19.9	27.7	21.9	39.5
3. Trade-union and other dues	1.1	1.6	1.8	3.1
4. Consumption of farm income in kind; army subsistence	35.0	62.0	62.0	75.0
5. Total outlays on goods and services (1–4)	183.5	288.3	248.9	470.8
6. Net savings				
a. Net bond purchases	2.9	7.7	26.2	20.6
b. Increment of savings deposits	1.0	.2	4.8	1.5
c. Other, including increment in cash holdings	1.5	.5	14.6	1.0
d. Total	5.4	8.4	45.6	23.1
7. Direct taxes	4.0	10.8	48.8[d]	37.5
8. Total transfer outlays (6–7)	9.4	19.2	94.4	60.6
9. Total outlays	192.9	307.5	343.3	531.4

[a] Data for 1937 are from *Soviet National Income*, p. 18. Minor discrepancies in these data between calculated sums of items and indicated totals are due to rounding. Sources and methods for the figures for 1940, 1944, and 1948 are set forth in Appendix A.

[b] In terms of average farm prices of 1940.

[c] n.a. = information not available.

[d] Includes net lottery subscriptions amounting to 4.6 billion rubles and cash donations to patriotic funds amounting to 3.3 billion rubles.

TABLE 4

CONSOLIDATED NET INCOME AND OUTLAY ACCOUNT OF GOVERNMENT, SOCIAL, AND ECONOMIC ORGANIZATIONS, USSR, 1937, 1940, 1944, AND 1948[a]

(Billions of rubles)

A. INCOMES	1937	1940	1944	1948
1. Net income retained by economic organizations				
a. Retained income in kind of collective farms	2.0	..[b]	2.0	4.0
b. Retained money income of collective farms	2.0	4.3	3.7	3.8
c. Retained profits of state and cooperative enterprises	7.0	8.3	3.5	10.8
d. Total	11.0	12.6	9.2	18.6
2. Charges to economic enterprises for special funds				
a. For social insurance budget	6.6	8.5	9.0	16.2
b. For special funds for workers' training and education[c]	2.2	2.7	1.8	3.1
c. Total	8.8	11.2	10.8	19.3
3. Indirect taxes; other payments out of incomes by economic enterprises to government budget				
a. Taxes on incomes of collective farms	.5	.8	1.0	2.0
b. Payments from profits of state enterprises to the government budget	9.3	21.7	21.4	26.5
c. Taxes on incomes of cooperative organizations	.8	1.8	1.5	2.0
d. Turnover tax	75.9	105.9	94.9	247.5
e. Miscellaneous	2.7	5.5	11.4	17.3
f. Total	89.2	135.7	130.2	295.3
4. Custom duties	1.3	2.9 }	24.0	6.0
5. Government receipts from sale of Lend-Lease; reparations	...	... }		10.5
6. Allowance for subsidized losses	(—)8.0	(—)14.0	(—)16.0	(—)53.0
7. Consolidated total charges against current product, net of depreciation	102.3	148.4	158.2	296.7

8. Depreciation	5.8	13.0	11.0	14.0
9. Consolidated total charges against current product	108.1	161.4	169.2	310.7
10. Transfer receipts				
a. Net savings of households	5.4	8.4	45.6	23.1
b. Direct taxes	4.0	10.8	48.8	37.5
c. Total	9.4	19.2	94.4	60.6
11. Consolidated total income	117.5	180.6	263.6	371.3
B. OUTLAYS				
1. Communal services				
a. Health care	8.9	11.1	10.2	23.1
b. Education	17.5	23.8	19.7	60.0
c. Other	1.0	1.5	1.0	2.0
d. Total	27.4	36.4	30.9	85.1
2. Government administration	4.4	6.8	7.4	13.1
3. NKVD (MVD and MGB)	3.0	7.1	6.6	25.8
4. Defense (as recorded in budget)	17.5	56.7	137.7	66.3
5. Gross investment, including investments in fixed capital, inventory accumulations, additions to stockpiles, etc.	56.1	62.7	55.9	150.1
6. Consolidated total value of goods and services disposed of, exclusive of sales to households	108.3	169.7	238.5	340.4
7. Transfer outlays				
a. Pensions and allowances	6.1	7.1	19.7	26.1
b. Stipends and scholarships	2.2	2.4	2.1	3.0
c. Interest payments to households	.9	1.4	3.3	1.8
d. Total	9.2	10.9	25.1	30.9
8. Consolidated total outlay, net of sales to households	117.5	180.6	263.6	371.3

a Data for 1937 are from *Soviet National Income*, p. 20. Minor discrepancies in these data between calculated sums of items and indicated totals are due to rounding. Sources and methods for the figures for 1940, 1944, and 1948 are set forth in Appendix B.

b ... = not applicable or negligible.

c Includes allocations to trade unions in 1937 and 1940. Apparently no such allocations were made in later years.

TABLE 5

GROSS NATIONAL PRODUCT ACCOUNT, USSR, 1937, 1940, 1944, AND 1948[a]

(Billions of rubles)

	1937	1940	1944	1948
A. INCOMES				
1. Total income of households currently earned (Table 3)	183.8	296.6	318.2	500.5
2. Consolidated charges of government, social, and economic organizations against current product, net of depreciation (Table 4)	102.3	148.4	158.2	296.7
3. Net national product	286.0	445.0	476.4	797.2
4. Depreciation (Table 4)	5.8	13.0	11.0	14.0
5. Gross national product	291.8	458.0	487.4	811.2
B. OUTLAYS				
1. Total outlays of households on goods and services (Table 3)	183.5	288.3	248.9	470.8
2. Consolidated total value of goods and services disposed of by government, social, and economic organizations, exclusive of sales to households (Table 4)	108.3	169.7	238.5	340.4
3. Gross national product	291.8	458.0	487.4	811.2

[a] For the year 1937, minor discrepancies between calculated sums of items and indicated totals are due to rounding.

TABLE 6

GROSS NATIONAL PRODUCT BY USE IN ESTABLISHED PRICES, USSR, 1937, 1940, 1944, AND 1948[a]

(Billions of rubles)

ITEM	1937		1940		1944		1948	
	BILLION RUBLES	PERCENT	BILLION RUBLES	PERCENT	BILLION RUBLES	PERCENT	BILLION RUBLES	PERCENT
1. Consumption of households								
a. Civilian[b]	181.0	62.0	280.3	61.2	217.9	44.7	451.8	55.7
b. Military subsistence	2.5	.9	8.0	1.8	31.0	6.4	19.0	2.3
c. Total	183.5	62.9	288.3	63.0	248.9	51.1	470.8	58.0
2. Communal services	27.4	9.4	36.4	8.0	30.9	6.3	85.1	10.5
3. Government administration	4.4	1.5	6.8	1.5	7.4	1.5	13.1	1.6
4. NKVD (MVD and MGB)	3.0	1.0	7.1	1.5	6.6	1.4	25.8	3.2
5. Defense (as recorded in budget)	17.5	6.0	56.7	12.4	137.7	28.3	66.3	8.2
6. Gross investment	56.1	19.2	62.7	13.7	55.9	11.5	150.1	18.5
7. Gross national product	291.8	100.0	458.0	100.0	487.4	100.0	811.2	100.0

[a] Minor discrepancies between calculated sums of items and indicated totals are due to rounding. Data are from Tables 3, 4, and 5.

[b] Including expenditures of military money income.

TABLE 7

THE GOVERNMENT BUDGET OF THE USSR, 1937, 1940, 1944, AND 1948[a]

(Billions of rubles)

A. REVENUES	1937	1940	1944	1948
1. Direct taxes	4.0	10.8	48.8[b]	37.5
2. Net borrowing				
a. From households	2.9	7.7	26.2	20.6
b. From economic organizations and financial system	(−) .7	2.1	6.4	1.5
c. Total	2.2	9.8	32.6	22.1
3. Statistical discrepancy between budget data on current loan transactions and other data on outstanding debt	1.3	...[c]	...	...
4. Revenues of social insurance budget	6.6	8.5	9.0	16.2
5. Indirect taxes and other payments out of incomes by economic enterprises to government budget				
a. Taxes on incomes of collective farms	.5	.8	1.0	2.0
b. Payments from profits of state enterprises to government budget	9.3	21.7	21.4	26.5
c. Taxes on incomes of cooperative organizations	.8	1.8	1.5	2.0
d. Turnover tax	75.9	105.9	94.9	247.5
e. Miscellaneous	2.7	5.5	11.4	17.3
f. Total	89.2	135.7	130.2	295.3
6. Custom duties	1.3	2.9		6.0
7. Government receipts from sale of Lend-Lease; reparations	...	...	24.0	10.5
8. Other revenues	2.3	8.1	22.1	17.1
9. Total revenues	107.0	175.8	266.7	404.7

B. EXPENDITURES

Item				
1. Interest charges on debt				
a. To households	.8	1.2	2.8	1.4
b. To savings banks and other organizations	.4	.2	.4	.3
c. Total	1.1	1.4	3.2	1.7
2. Pensions and allowances, including those paid by the social insurance system	6.1	7.1	19.7	26.1
3. Communal services				
a. Health care, including capital construction	6.9	9.0	10.2	19.6
b. Education, including students' stipends and capital construction	16.5	22.5	20.7	55.1
c. Total	23.4	31.5	30.9	74.7
4. Government administration	4.4	6.8	7.4	13.1
5. NKVD (MVD and MGB)	3.0	7.1	6.6	25.8
6. Defense	17.5	56.7	137.7	66.3
7. Financing the national economy				
a. Budget subsidies, including net appropriations for operating expenses of MTS	8.0	13.0	15.0	52.0
b. Other	35.4	43.3	37.9	93.6
c. Total	43.4	56.3	52.9	145.6
8. Other expenditures	5.0	3.1	2.6	11.8
9. Indicated budget surplus	3.1	5.8	5.7	39.6
10. Total expenditures	107.0	175.8	266.7	404.7

[a] Data for 1937 are from *Soviet National Income*, p. 40. For these data, minor discrepancies between calculated sums of items and indicated totals are due to rounding. Sources and methods for the figures for 1940, 1944, and 1948 are set forth in Appendix C.

[b] Includes net lottery subscriptions amounting to 4.6 billion rubles, and cash donations to patriotic funds amounting to 3.3 billion rubles.

[c] . . . = not applicable or negligible.

that the values created through the levying of taxes on imports become a form of "national product domestically produced" in the importing country. For this reason, the procedure occasionally has been questioned and no doubt rightly so. The procedure seems the more dubious when extended to Lend-Lease and reparations; insofar as these goods and the revenues realized from them are included at all in the national economic accounts, the end product clearly is more in the nature of "disposable national product" rather than, as is usually assumed, "national product domestically produced." The imports in effect are assigned a zero value at the border and their entire value in the accounts (i.e., the taxes levied on them) becomes a part of the national product of the recipient country, as calculated. This should be borne in mind in interpreting our accounts for war and postwar years.

Military subsistence. Along with defense expenditures generally, military subsistence is a notably large item in one of the years studied, 1944. In accord with the Department of Commerce practice, this item is shown twice in the outlay side of our accounts: once under defense expenditures (Table 4) as a part of the value of the services of military personnel and once under household consumption (Table 3) as an element in the total consumption of the population. The result of this practice is the same as would be realized if military personnel were paid entirely in monetary terms and not at all in kind. The monetary pay, then, would be recorded once under defense outlays and again, when it was spent, under retail sales.

Farm income in kind. In *Soviet National Income* use was made of the conventional procedure of valuing farm income in kind at the average of realized farm prices. In the case of the USSR, this means the average of the various prices paid by the government for obligatory and other deliveries made to it and of the relatively high prices prevailing on sales in the collective farm markets.[2] The use of realized farm prices to value income in kind is often questioned, and it was acknowledged in *Soviet National Income* that in the case of the USSR the procedure might be especially dubious. But it was contended that once the national economic accounts generally are revalued to allow

[2] *Soviet National Income*, p. 26. The realized prices are construed as net of sales taxes on farm produce and also gross of subsidies allowed to agricultural enterprises, including the MTS.

for special features of the ruble price system, this valuation of farm income in kind probably becomes more meaningful than it might be otherwise.

In the present study, we follow this same procedure for the years 1940 and 1948. In the case of calculations for 1944, however, farm income in kind is valued at the average realized farm prices of 1940 rather than of 1944. During the war collective farm market prices rose to extreme levels, while the government apparently held the line on the prices of its agricultural procurements. An average of realized farm prices in 1944, then, would be an average of these artificial and totally-disparate levels. For the sake of consistency there still might be something to say for valuation on this basis for 1944, but it was felt that on the whole the accounts might be easier to interpret if the pre-war valuation were used. In the last analysis the question at issue is the valuation of farm services. This subject is discussed subsequently (pp. 58 ff.). As will appear, the valuation of income in kind for 1944 at 1940 farm prices yields a more satisfactory value for farm services than would the alternative valuation.

As is shown in Tables 3 and 4, 1944 farm income in kind, including investments, comes to 33 billion rubles at 1940 farm prices. If the valuation is in terms of 1944 farm prices, farm income in kind comes to some 83 billion rubles.

We have already described the changes in Soviet boundaries that occurred in the period under study. These were mainly important in the years 1939 and 1940 (see Table 1, p. 6). To what extent do our national economic accounts for 1940 cover the newly incorporated areas? Soviet sources are rarely explicit regarding the territorial coverage of the statistical data underlying our accounts for 1940. The accounts are believed to be more or less comprehensive not only for the territories added in 1939 but also for those added in 1940. Possibly the territories added in later years are also included, though these changes in any case were negligible statistically. All the indications are that the Soviet statisticians lagged little behind the Red Army in attaching the new territories to the USSR. Furthermore, the raw data used to compile our accounts for 1940 are taken largely from postwar sources. A comparison of statistical data for 1940 in postwar sources with data for the same year in prewar sources indicates many minor revisions, which probably were made to complete the incorporation of new territories.

There may still be some question as to the comprehensiveness of the 1940 data used here, and in any case one wonders how reliable the statistics on the incorporated areas available to the Russians may have been. But in general we consider our accounts for 1940 as referring to the enlarged territories. In any event, we believe that differences in territorial coverage could not give rise to any appreciable divergencies in structure between the 1940 accounts and those for later years.

Of course, the coverage for 1940 as well as for later years differs significantly from that for 1937. This will have to be kept in mind in interpreting changes in structure shown by the accounts.

A more detailed statement on the territorial coverage of the national economic accounts for 1940 is made in Appendix E.

As has been mentioned, the Red Army by the beginning of 1944 had liberated a major part of the areas occupied by the Germans at one time or another during the war. By the end of the year the Russians controlled all their present territory except for some areas of the Latvian and Lithuanian republics. Soviet sources have been no more explicit concerning the territorial coverage of wartime statistics than on the coverage of prewar data, but it seems clear our accounts for 1944 are to be viewed as referring more or less to the territory under Soviet control on the average in the course of the year. Furthermore, economic activity in the remainder of the present Soviet territory was at an extremely low level, so the 1944 accounts for all practical purposes refer also to the entire USSR within the present boundaries.

So much for methodology and territorial coverage. The balance of this chapter is given over to brief comment on the income and outlay categories tabulated in the different accounts. These comments are intended, insofar as the captions are not adequate for the purpose, to indicate the nature and scope of the different categories. Our concern is also to provide a general impression of the nature and limitations of the calculations. Details on the sources used as well as on various independent estimates made will be found in Appendices A through C.

We comment first on the household account and then on the consolidated account for organizations. Following this we consider the government budget. The various income and outlay categories in the remaining two tabulations compiled, i.e., the gross national product account and the tabulation of the gross national product by use, are taken directly from other accounts and need no separate explanation.

THE HOUSEHOLD ACCOUNT (TABLE 3)

Wages of farm labor (on state farms, MTS, etc.). These consist almost entirely of wages paid to employees of state-owned and operated agricultural enterprises, particularly the state farms and machine-tractor stations. But the total also includes wages paid to a limited number of nonmember employees hired by collective farms. The total wages paid to agricultural workers of both types in 1940 is estimated mainly on the basis of goals for agricultural employment and wages in the Third Five Year Plan (1937–42) and on information on the probable degree of their fulfillment. For 1944 and 1948 the wages of agricultural employees are calculated from estimates of the total wage bill for the whole economy (see below) and from the prewar ratio of the wages paid agricultural employees to the total wage bill. It is supposed, however, that the ratio had declined in 1944 in view of the sharp wartime reduction in MTS activities.

Money payments to collective farmers on labor-day basis; salaries of collective farm executives; premiums. For purposes of estimating these incomes, it was necessary first to know the total money earnings of collective farms. For 1940 this is given in a Soviet source. For 1944 it was calculated from a Soviet figure on the average money income per collective farm and the number of collective farms as indicated by other Soviet data. For 1948 a rough estimate of collective farm money income was derived mainly from information on the absolute amount and probable share in collective farm money income of contributions to the "indivisible fund," i.e., broadly speaking, the invested capital of the collective farm.

Given total collective farm money income, the amount paid to collective farmers on a labor-day basis, etc., is calculated from the relation of such payments to total collective farm money income prevailing in

1937 and 1938. A rule-of-thumb allowance is made for probable trends in this relation in the period studied.

Net money income from sale of farm products. This is intended to include revenues derived by collective and other farm households (as distinct from collective farms) from sales to government procurement agencies as well as on the collective farm market. The amounts of these sales are determined from a rather involved calculation and one which probably is subject to a sizable margin of error. Among other things, it was necessary to extrapolate from the 1937 experience regarding the sources of collective farm money income, particularly the shares of sales to government procurement agencies and on the collective farm market, and also regarding the relation between sales to government procurement agencies by collective farm households and such sales by collective farms. Furthermore, use is made of data derived subsequently on total sales on the collective farm market by collective farm households and collective farms taken together. As will appear, our figure on such sales for 1944 is something of a guess, while that for 1948 may also err appreciably.

"Net money income from sale of farm products" represents the total household revenues from sales to government procurement agencies and on the collective farm market, *less* an allowance for the money expenses incurred by the farm household in farm operations. The allowance is a rule-of-thumb estimate which takes into account the 1937 experience.

Net farm income in kind. This is intended to represent the amount of produce that is left at the disposal of the collective and other farm households (including workers' households with garden plots) after sales are made and production expenses are covered and that, accordingly, is available for investment in the expansion of farm operations or for consumption. The income is valued at average realized farm prices current in the year concerned except for 1944, where the valuation is at 1940 farm prices.

For all years the magnitude of farm income in kind is calculated as a residual and may err markedly. To refer only to the outstanding features, the calculation involves reference to data on farm marketings derived above in connection with the computation of household revenues from sales of farm products. For the years 1940 and 1948 we rely also on the 1937 experience concerning the relation of these marketings and that of production expenses to total output, and on scattered information on the probable trends in these relations. From this information we calculate both the total output and its disposition, including the share remaining for farm consumption and investment. For 1944 total output in 1940 prices is estimated from various indicators of agricultural activity, particularly crops, and the disposition of this output is appraised on several bases, including the data on marketings in current rubles previously derived and information on the probable magnitude of wartime price changes.

Wages and salaries, nonfarm. For prewar years the Russians have published a statistical series on the wage bill compiled by TSUNKHU, the leading Soviet statistical agency.[3] This is believed to represent the total wages and salaries paid out in the USSR with a number of exceptions, such as certain premium payments and wages paid workers in some local industries and secondary lines of activity (factory restaurants, etc.).

The figure cited in Table 3 on wages recorded in current statistical reports in 1940 is taken from this TSUNKHU series after the deduction of the wages paid agricultural employees. We have already recorded the latter elsewhere in the table (item 1a).

For various years, including 1940, the Russians have also published data on the wage bill which are believed to be comprehensive. These data cover, in addition to the TSUNKHU wage bill, the various items omitted from the TSUNKHU series that were just referred to. Also, the TSUNKHU figures refer only to free workers, whereas the comprehensive data probably include wages paid to penal labor.[4] Finally, the comprehensive wage bill includes military pay and also the earnings of cooperative artisans. The figure cited in Table 3 on the total

[3] The full title is *Tsentral'noe Upravlenie Narodno-khoziaistvennogo Ucheta* (Central Administration of National Economic Accounting). In 1939 this agency was renamed TSU, which stands for *Tsentral'noe Statisticheskoe Upravlenie* (Central Statistical Administration). It has been reorganized on several occasions in the period of interest here.

[4] On the question of the rates of pay and numbers of penal workers, see *Soviet National Income*, pp. 122 ff.; also N. Jasny, "Labor and Output in Soviet Concentration Camps," *Journal of Political Economy*, October, 1951; A. D. Redding, "Reliability of Estimates of Unfree Labor in the U.S.S.R.," *Journal of Political Economy*, August, 1952.

wages and salaries paid in 1940 is obtained by deducting from the Soviet figure on the comprehensive wage bill for that year several items which we show elsewhere in the table: farm wages, military pay, and cooperative earnings. The figure cited for "Other" wages in Table 3 is obtained as a residual.

The total wages paid nonfarm workers in 1944 were estimated from Soviet information on the wartime changes in the labor force and average wages. For 1948 the total wages paid nonfarm workers had to be estimated from a figure given in the annual plan for 1947 on the goal for that year for the comprehensive wage bill, but the result is broadly substantiated by various other evidence on the relation of the 1948 wage bill to that of 1940.

Incomes of artisans; other money income currently earned. This comprises the earnings of both cooperative and independent artisans (shoemakers, tailors, etc.) and also incomes from various other personal services, including domestic service, draying, etc. The figures cited may also cover rents from privately owned housing. The earnings of cooperative artisans are extrapolated from Soviet data for the period 1934-38. The extrapolation takes into account scattered information on the volume of activity of the cooperatives and probable trends in average earnings. The earnings of independent artisans and other money incomes currently earned had to be extrapolated from the 1937 figure for this category on the basis of trends in the total wage bill of nonfarm workers. An allowance was made for a probable relative decline in the earnings of independent artisans, etc., in 1944.

Imputed net rent of owner-occupied dwellings. Information in Soviet sources provides the basis for rough estimates of the amount of privately owned housing available in the years studied. While this housing is located mainly in rural areas, we arbitrarily value the services it yields at the rental rates fixed by the government for state-owned apartments in the city. Generally, of course, this sort of calculation should measure gross rather than net imputed rent, but in view of the very low level of the government rental rates our results may just as well stand for the latter.[5]

---

[5] In Appendix A, our figures on imputed net rent were derived from a Soviet formula for rental rates. Too late for consideration in our calculations, we have become aware

Incomes of armed forces. On the basis of diverse information, we take the Soviet armed forces as numbering in 1940, 3.5 million men; in 1944, 12 million; and in 1948, 4 million. Total military pay is estimated on the basis of scattered Soviet and other information on average rates for different personnel. In the calculations for 1937, military subsistence was taken at 1,500 rubles per man at the prices paid for such goods by the military establishment. We assume that in "real" terms the amount of subsistence per man remains unchanged throughout the period studied. In order to obtain the value of subsistence in current prices, a crude allowance is made for price changes over the intervals considered.

As it turns out, the military pay and subsistence as estimated here total 33 billion rubles in 1948. This is almost half the total defense outlays recorded in the Soviet government budget for that year. The corresponding ratios for the previous years studied are all smaller, running from about one-third to one-fourth of the defense outlays. While our 1948 estimate may well be in error, a relatively high ratio of military personnel costs to total defense costs for that year seems entirely consistent with what is known of the changes in relative prices. In the immediate postwar years prices of consumers' goods as well as military pay rates increased substantially, whereas prices of producers' goods, including presumably munitions, were kept more or less unchanged.[6] Beyond this, in "real" terms, one would expect military pay and subsistence to claim a relatively large slice of the defense budget in a period such as 1948. This year, according to Soviet statements, marked the completion of Russia's postwar demobilization, but the number of men under arms remained inordinately high by peacetime standards, while the extent of munitions procurement was no doubt relatively limited compared with the prewar mobilization years or with the years of actual conflict.

Statistical discrepancy. This represents the difference between the sum of accounted for incomes and the sum of accounted for outlays.

---

that this derivation erroneously neglects a Soviet official ceiling on rental rates of 1.32 rubles per square meter. If account is taken of this ceiling, the imputed net rent for 1944 is reduced to 6.8 billion rubles and that for 1948 is reduced to 7.4 billion rubles.

[6] We are guided here mainly by a number of unpublished RAND studies, which it is hoped will be made generally available in due course.

The difference, it is believed, is more likely to affect the "Total income currently earned" (Table 3–A, item 7) than the "Total transfer receipts" (Table 3–A, item 11), and has been classified accordingly in the table. The statistical discrepancy may be viewed as a partial check on the reliability of our household account generally. As will appear, however, collective farm market sales for 1944 had to be estimated more or less as a residual in the household account, so for this year the statistical discrepancy can have no import regarding reliability one way or another. Furthermore, the possible magnitude of the discrepancy almost inevitably influenced our calculations for other years as well.

Pensions and allowances. This includes not only pensions and allowances received under social insurance arrangements but also military pensions, payments to mothers of many children, etc. The amounts of the different kinds of pensions in some instances are taken directly from Soviet sources. In other instances we calculate the pensions from budgetary outlays on social insurance and the like. In addition to pensions, the budgetary outlays also include various other expenditures, e.g., maintenance of rest homes and sanatoriums. The share going to pensions is estimated on the basis of diverse Soviet information.

Stipends and scholarships. This comprises the living allowances and tuition scholarships paid students in all educational institutions. Tuition generally was free in the USSR prior to October 2, 1940, but charges were made after that date for secondary and higher education. The cited figures on stipends and scholarships are very rough estimates which take account of various sources of information, including Soviet data on stipends for the years 1934–38, the official tuition scale, tuition revenues in the budget, information on enrollment trends, and the like.

Interest receipts. The total interest paid households on government bonds, including net winnings on lottery bonds, is given in Soviet sources. In addition to such receipts, we include here interest on savings deposits. This is calculated as the product of an average rate of 3.25 percent and the outstanding savings deposits as indicated by Soviet sources. The actual rates allowed are 3 percent on deposits payable on demand and 5 percent on deposits left for six months or longer. For 1944 we include not only ordinary savings deposits such as these but also special accounts opened for employees in compensation for accumulated wartime leave. It is not clear whether the Soviet data used cover deposits of unknown magnitude in the "field banks" opened for military personnel during the war.

Retail sales to households. a. In government and cooperative shops and restaurants. The sales by these organizations to households are obtained as the difference between their total sales and their sales to institutions. The figure on total sales for 1940 is given in a Soviet source. For 1944 the figure on total sales is calculated from Soviet data on the percentage change of different elements of these sales in wartime, taken together with corresponding absolute figures for 1940. The total sales figure for 1948 is calculated from a variety of Soviet information, including data indicating the volume of sales in 1947 and various indicators of the change from that year to 1948. The calculation relied on, it is believed, resolves satisfactorily a conflict encountered in the underlying Soviet data, but an alternative calculation yielding a sales volume about 5 percent greater is not excluded.

Sales to institutions are estimated very roughly as a percentage of total sales on the basis of the 1937 experience and of diverse information on the probable trends since then.

Retail sales to households. b. In collective farm markets. This item is obtained by deducting from total sales in collective farm markets the sales made to institutions. The figure on total sales in collective farm markets in 1940 is a Soviet official one. For 1944 total sales had to be calculated more or less as a residual in the household account. Collective farm sales are largely balanced in the account for all households by the incomes they yield, but the sales are made primarily to the urban population, whereas the incomes are received by the farmers. Accordingly, the calculation was made separately for urban and rural households, and it involved an attempt to determine collective farm sales in the light of unaccounted for differences between all other outlays and incomes for urban households on the one hand and rural households on the other.[7] Almost inevitably the calculation is subject to a sizable margin of error. For example, a plausible alternative

---

[7] This calculation was suggested by a comment of Gregory Grossman on an earlier privately circulated version of our 1944 accounts.

assumption to the one used on the distribution of collective farm market sales between city and country leads to a figure some 10 billion rubles less for total sales. The total sales figure for 1948 is estimated from Soviet information on the share of these sales in the retail turnover.

For all years the deductions for sales to institutions are rule-of-thumb estimates. Account is taken of the 1937 experience and of various sources of information on the trends since then.

Housing (including imputed net rent of owner-occupied dwellings); services. In addition to the imputed net rent of owner-occupied dwellings as previously calculated, this includes the following: (i) rents paid for government-owned housing, as calculated from the official rental scale and the estimated amount of government-owned housing; (ii) tuition payments previously derived; (iii) outlays for utilities, transportation, entertainment, and probably personal services. These last outlays are calculated rather arbitrarily on the basis of assumed trends in their relation to retail sales since 1937.[8]

Trade-union and other dues. Trade-union, Communist Party, and other dues are taken to be one percent of the wage bill throughout. According to Soviet data, this was the prewar relationship and it is believed to be still in effect.

Consumption of farm income in kind; army subsistence. We record here the full amount of farm income in kind, without allowing for the amount invested.

Net savings. The net bond purchases are calculated from budgetary data on gross purchases and various information on debt retirement. The increment in savings deposits is calculated from Soviet data on the amounts of deposits held at the beginning and end of the year. Such Soviet data are believed to refer to ordinary deposits, and for 1944 we include in addition the amount indicated in a Soviet source as being placed in special deposits opened to compensate workers for accumulated wartime leave. It is not known whether the total increment as

---

[8] It is not clear whether the figure on outlays for utilities, etc., in 1937 also includes expenditures for housing repairs. The figures on imputed net rent of owner-occupied dwellings considered here are the same as those included in the tabulation of household incomes. Logically, the figures on the income and outlay sides should differ by the amount of maintenance, depreciation, and other expenses.

calculated includes deposits in the "field banks" that serviced military personnel during the war.

We assume more or less arbitrarily that there was no change in cash holdings in 1940. A Soviet source indicates that in fact these decreased. For 1944 we allow a sizable increase in cash holdings mainly on the basis of a Soviet statement about the increase in cash holdings in previous war years. For 1948 we again assume arbitrarily that there was no change.

On the question of the change in cash holdings for all years studied, and especially for the year 1948, consideration was given to the size of the government budget surplus. We comment subsequently (pp. 50 ff.) on the relation of this surplus to cash holdings by the population. While there is still room for a sizable margin of error in our assumptions on cash holdings, especially for 1944, it is believed that the order of magnitude of net savings generally might not be greatly affected.

In addition to the increment in cash holdings, "other" savings include a small amount of savings in the form of life insurance premiums and the like.

The total net savings as computed are understated insofar as they do not include: (i) Investments by farm households out of their income in kind, which have been classified in Table 3 as consumption. These investments probably were negligible in 1940 and quite small in 1944. At realized farm prices they may have amounted to a few billion rubles in 1948. (ii) Investments in housing by both the farm and nonfarm population. These investments must have been quite small in 1940 and probably also in 1944. In 1948 they may have been of the order of several billion rubles.

Direct taxes. This includes revenues from: (i) The "income tax," so-called, levied mainly on wages, salaries, honoraria, and incomes of artisans. (ii) "The cultural and housing construction tax," for all practical purposes another income tax but applying to farm as well as to nonfarm population. This tax was levied in 1937 and 1940 but not in the later years studied. (iii) The "agricultural tax," levied on the farm population and since 1939 broadly based on income. (iv) The special taxes introduced during the war on the incomes of unmarried persons and persons of small families. (v) The "war tax," representing still another income tax, which applies only to 1944 among the years studied.

The foregoing exhaust the Soviet budget category "taxes and levies on the population," which is often taken to represent the sum of direct taxes on the Soviet population. For present purposes it has seemed in order to include here also: (vi) Miscellaneous governmental charges on the population, e.g., notarial fees, property taxes, etc., which generally are classified under other Soviet budget headings. (vii) For the year 1944 only, net subscriptions to the state lottery of that year. (viii) For the year 1944 only, contributions to wartime patriotic funds, e.g., the "Red Army" fund.

The amount of revenues in the budget category "taxes and levies on the population" is given in Soviet budgetary sources. The miscellaneous governmental charges on the population were determined through a rule-of-thumb breakdown of the budget headings that include them. The net lottery subscriptions were estimated from Soviet information on the gross subscriptions and winnings. The donations to patriotic funds represent the total donations as given in a Soviet source to two funds, the "Red Army" fund and the fund for "defense." In Soviet sources reference has been found to still another patriotic fund, namely, that for "the reconstruction of areas liberated from the German occupation." We assume here, with some reservations, that only the first two were the object of donations on any scale by households as distinct from economic organizations, e.g., collective farms. According to the Soviet budget forecast for 1944, the total donations to all funds were to amount to 17.8 billion rubles in that year. The actual donations to the "Red Army" and "defense" funds alone amounted to 3.3 billion rubles.[9]

[9] This latter figure, which is recorded among the direct taxes in Table 3, probably includes in addition to cash donations various gifts of property, such as government bonds, precious metals, and ordinary commodities. Strictly speaking, however, only the cash donations ought to be shown at this point. The other payments represent either capital transactions which have no place in our accounts or offsets to household consumption. The donations by economic institutions were also partly and perhaps mainly in kind, e.g., in the form of livestock and agricultural machinery, and might have fallen heavily on the collective farm as distinct from the collective farm household. As is explain in Appendix A, p. 163, the figure of 17.8 billion rubles may not include all

THE CONSOLIDATED INCOME AND OUTLAY ACCOUNT OF GOVERNMENT,
SOCIAL, AND ECONOMIC ORGANIZATIONS (TABLE 4)

Retained income in kind of collective farms. The cited figures are
guesses as to the amount of farm income in kind invested by collective farms (as distinct from member households) in livestock herds,
seed and fodder funds, and other capital. The farm income in kind
shown previously in the household account is net of the amount retained by collective farms.

Retained money income of collective farms. This consists mainly of
money incomes allocated to the "indivisible fund," for capital investment and debt repayment. The amount so allocated in 1940 is calculated from a Soviet figure on the average allocation per collective farm;
the allocations for 1944 and 1948 are given in Soviet sources.

Retained profits of state and cooperative enterprises. This represents
the amount of profits earned by all Soviet economic organizations less
the amounts transferred to the government budget in the form of
"payments out of profits" (*otchisleniia ot pribylei*) in the case of state
enterprises, and in the form of the "income tax" (*podokhodnyi nalog*)
in the case of cooperative enterprises. Data on the aggregative profits
and the payments into the budget are for the most part either taken
from Soviet budgetary releases or calculated directly from other data
given in such sources. The figures on aggregate profits given in Soviet
budgetary sources might easily be construed as true net-profits figures,
but it is clear that this is not the case. Rather, the figures represent the
total profits before the deduction of certain losses, particularly losses of
khozraschet organizations covered by subsidies from the government
budget, losses of the MTS and such other economic organizations as
are attached directly to the government budget, and possibly also some
losses covered through bank-credit creation. Accordingly, an attempt
is made elsewhere in Table 4 to allow for these losses.

*Charges to economic enterprises for special funds. a. For social in-
surance budget.* This is the total amount, as indicated by Soviet budgetary sources, of premiums collected from economic organizations for
the financing of the government social insurance program. The entire

---

donations to patriotic funds. On the other hand, it may include some budgetary revenues
other than donations.

amount of the premium is an expense of the economic organization; the insured, nominally, does not bear any part of the cost.

Charges to economic enterprises for special funds. b. For special funds for workers' training and education. The Soviet employing establishment is required by law to maintain, by charges against income before profits, certain funds for the support of training and educational activities among the workers, including factory apprentice schools, advanced technical courses, stipends for workers on leave for study at outside educational institutions, and so on. At least this was the law before the war, and in the absence of contrary information we assume these arrangements continued in operation throughout the period studied. The figures cited in Table 4 are rough estimates of the sum of these charges and, in the year 1940, certain other items, namely, contributions which the employing establishment had to make for the support of trade unions. These contributions were once an important source of trade-union income, but they were discontinued after 1940.

Taxes on incomes of collective farms. The amount of income taxes paid by collective farms (as distinct from collective farm households) in 1940 is given in a Soviet budgetary source. The corresponding figures for 1944 and 1948 had to be estimated from diverse information.

Payments from profits of state enterprises to the government budget. See the comments on retained profits made above.

Taxes on incomes of cooperative organizations. See the comments on retained profits made above.

Turnover tax. On this important tax, levied in relation to sales at diverse stages, especially agricultural procurements and manufacturing, we cite here Soviet budgetary data.

Miscellaneous. The cited figures are estimates of the total of a variety of indirect taxes and other budgetary levies falling on economic organizations, including among other things the tax "on noncommodity operations" levied on the sales of organizations engaged in custom tailoring, repair work, etc.; certain stumpage fees levied on organizations using the state forests; a variety of local taxes and fees, including ground rents and real estate taxes (there are such in the USSR); and notarial and similar charges, insofar as they were paid by economic organizations. Because of differences in methods of calculation, the figures for 1940 and later years are not entirely comparable with those for 1937.

Custom duties. Government receipts from sale of Lend-Lease; reparations. For the year 1940, of course, this item refers only to custom duties. The amount of such duties is given in a Soviet budgetary source. For the year 1944 we cite a budget forecast of "custom receipts." In view of the large magnitude of this item we assume that it includes not only duties on ordinary imports but such revenues as may have been realized on the transfer of Lend-Lease imports to economic organizations. The government, it is believed, transferred Lend-Lease goods at a price above the amount of the regular duty, but in any event the aggregate revenues realized appear to have been included in the budget forecast for custom receipts. On the other hand, insofar as this is not the case the cited figure represents a corresponding understatement. For 1948, for both custom duties and government receipts from the sale of reparations taken together, we accept a budget forecast on the sum of "custom receipts" and the "income from the sale of goods ceded as compensation to the Soviet Union for losses caused by war action and by occupation of Soviet territory." The breakdown of this sum as between the two types of charges is based on budgetary data for 1947.

Allowance for subsidized losses. This is an allowance for various losses which, as was explained previously, are not deducted in the computation of aggregative Soviet profits figures: losses of *khozraschet* organizations covered by subsidies from the government budget; losses of the MTS and other economic organizations attached fully to the government budget;[10] and the losses of *khozraschet* organizations covered by bank-credit creation.

Among these different types of losses the main one throughout the period studied was that comprising the losses of *khozraschet* organizations covered by subsidies from the government budget. The Russians are notably secretive on this matter, and the magnitudes had to be estimated from indirect evidence. The estimates are believed, however,

[10] The MTS were not attached fully to the government budget until 1938, but the subsidies granted them from the budget previously are included in the "Allowance for subsidized losses" for 1937, so the comparability of the figure cited for that year with those cited for later years is unaffected.

to be broadly reliable. This includes the estimate for 1948, 44 billion rubles, which may strike the reader as strangely large. According to Soviet budgetary practice, subsidies are included along with a variety of other outlays, e.g., grants to enterprises for fixed- and working-capital investments, in a broad expenditure category, "Financing the National Economy." Essentially, the estimates for subsidies were obtained through an attempt, on the basis of published data, to break down the item "Financing the National Economy" into its various components.

During the period studied the MTS are believed to have been the only economic organizations of any consequence attached fully to the government budget. The losses of these organizations have something of a bookkeeping character insofar as they arise from the valuation of the MTS income in kind at the low government procurement prices for agricultural produce, but they must be taken into account here, nevertheless. The losses were estimated mainly from budgetary data. We rather arbitrarily take the losses of *khozraschet* organizations financed by bank-credit creation as 1.0 billion rubles for all the years studied.

Depreciation. Under the *khozraschet* system, economic enterprises in the USSR, like their counterparts in Western countries, include among their expenses a charge for depreciation on capital. The amount is calculated according to rates fixed by law. The *khozraschet* system, however, does not extend to the MTS and collective farms. While in the case of the MTS there apparently is some sort of depreciation accounting, nevertheless none is practiced in the case of the collective farms. The figures cited on depreciation in Table 4 are intended to represent the aggregative charge for depreciation recorded on the books of *khozraschet* organizations, together with an allowance, according to *khozraschet* standards, for depreciation on the capital of the MTS and collective farms. Also, we include an allowance for depreciation on privately owned housing. The magnitudes had to be estimated from diverse Soviet information and in the case of those for 1944 and 1948 may be appreciably in error.

It was said that our depreciation figures cover the depreciation on the capital of *khozraschet* organizations, MTS, and collective farms, and also that on privately owned housing. This is true for the figures calculated here for 1940, 1944, and 1948. The figure for 1937 cited from *Soviet National Income* probably represents only the depreciation of *khozraschet* organizations. For this reason, it is not comparable with the figures calculated here for later years.

Transfer receipts. See the comments on the transfer outlays of households given above (pp. 38 ff.).

Communal services. These consist mainly of the amount, as indicated in Soviet budgetary releases, of government budget outlays for "health care" and "education." On the basis of various information we deduct from the pertinent budget figures outlays on capital construction which are recorded subsequently under investment; we also deduct transfer payments, i.e., stipends and tuition payments. In addition to the government outlays for education and health care that are so recorded in the budget, an attempt has been made to allow for expenditures on rest homes, sanatoriums, etc., supported out of government budget appropriations for "social insurance." Also, allowance is made for other nonbudget expenditures such as those made by the state factories for workers' training and education. This last allowance is rather arbitrary.

As calculated, the outlays for education and health care include a variety of items. The government budget outlays for education, for example, comprise expenditures not only for schools, libraries, and the like, but also for scientific research, the press, and the theater. In 1948 this category may have included research on atomic energy.

The figures cited for "other" communal services are arbitrary allowances for outlays made for such activities as physical culture, social insurance administration, etc.[11]

Government administration. On the basis of Soviet data, we record here the government budget appropriations for "government administration." These appropriations are for the upkeep of all higher and local organs of government, except the ministries concerned with internal security and the armed forces.[12]

---

[11] In the absence of any data, this account might be assumed to allow also for the excess, if any, of the administrative costs of trade-union, party, and other social organizations over and above the aggregate receipts from membership dues. According to strict logic, an allowance should be made for this sum somewhere on the outlay side of Table 4.

[12] For a discussion of the scope of "government," including the line of demarcation between government organs and the government sectors of the economy, see Appendix B, pp. 197 ff., and *Soviet National Income*, pp. 14, 23 ff.

NKVD (MVD and MGB). The figures cited represent the government budget appropriations, as given or implied in Soviet budgetary sources, to the following government agencies: in 1940, to the NKVD (the People's Commissariat of Internal Affairs); in 1944 and 1948, to its successors—the MVD (the Ministry of Internal Affairs) and the MGB (the Ministry of State Security).[13] The precise scope of these appropriations is not clear. In addition to internal security, the NKVD (MVD and MGB) performs a variety of other civil-control activities, such as the operation of penal institutions, fire protection, civil registration, forest guards, automobile inspection, etc. For the most part, these activities are financed out of the general budget appropriation to the NKVD. Furthermore, as part of its internal securities activities, the NKVD maintains sizable military formations of various kinds, including frontier guards, military police, troops to combat "counter-revolution," etc. Insofar as these activities too are financed out of the NKVD appropriation, they must be considered as supplementing the defense expenditures referred to below.

Defense (as recorded in the budget). We cite here Soviet budgetary data on expenditures for "defense" (*oborona*). These data represent the appropriations to the military establishment, i.e., in 1940 and 1944, to the People's Commissariats of Defense and Navy, and in 1948, to the Ministry of the Armed Forces. According to a long-standing Soviet administrative practice, munitions production is the responsibility not of the ministries charged with actual military operations but of ministries specialized to this end. Accordingly, the budget defense appropriation (as in the United States) covers munitions costs only at the procurement stage. There is no evidence that munitions are stockpiled in any quantity outside the military establishment; if so, however, such outlays would be excluded from the budget defense appropriation. While some outlays for the construction of military facilities, e.g., camps, fortifications, etc., apparently are included in the defense ap-

---

[13] The NKVD was established as an all-union commissariat in 1935. In 1941 its most important chief administration was made into a separate but closely related People's Commissariat of State Security (NKGB). The Soviet commissariats generally were renamed as ministries on March 21, 1946. The two ministries were recently recombined into a single Ministry of Internal Affairs (MVD) in connection with the government reorganization of March 6, 1953.

propriation, investments in defense plant construction generally are excluded. These remarks apply not only to munitions in general but also to atomic weapons. Presumably research, development, and production of nuclear weapons are not functions of the Soviet military establishment, and outlays for these activities are not included in the budget defense allocation. The budget appropriation for defense may also omit stockpiles of these weapons. These, however, presumably were not a factor until after 1948, the last year studied here.

It is not known how the Russians have accounted in their budget for requisitions and occupation charges levied since the war in Eastern Europe and Germany. No doubt many of these charges do not show up in the budget at all. Accordingly, they too are not reflected in the budget defense appropriations. The budget expenditures do not cover the premilitary training, which to some extent is given in ordinary schools, or paramilitary training provided by various voluntary societies auxiliary to the armed forces. Also excluded are military pensions.[14]

Gross investment, including inventory accumulations, etc. This item is calculated here as a residual, i.e., as the difference between the sum of all recorded charges in Table 4 and the sum of all outlays other than investment. Available information on the different investment components, i.e., fixed capital, working capital, etc., is very incomplete for

[14] Some scattered information at hand on the magnitude of the different omissions from the budget defense outlays may be of interest:

(i) According to *Shestaia sessiia Verkhovnogo Soveta SSSR . . . 1940 g.,* pp. 433–34, a total of 8.2 billion rubles, or about one-seventh of the budget defense outlays, was appropriated to the Commissariats of Ammunition, Armaments, Shipbuilding, and the Aircraft Industry, and to the Chief Administration for War Construction for the year 1940. The appropriations were made under the budget heading of "Financing the National Economy" and probably represent mainly grants for plant construction.

(ii) Under the heading of education, the budget forecast for 1949 called for the expenditure of 6.6 billion rubles for "scientific research organizations and measures." (See A. G. Zverev, "Gosudarstvennyi biudzhet chetvertogo goda poslevoennoi stalinskoi piatiletki," *Planovoe khoziaistvo,* No. 2, 1949, p. 49.) Expenditures by industrial enterprises for the same purpose were to amount to another 2.5 billion rubles. Both these sums may include some outlays for military research and development. The indicated outlays for scientific research may be compared with the expenditures of the defense department recorded in the budget for 1948: 66.3 billion rubles.

(iii) The Russians in 1948 were quartering outside their borders probably substantially less than a million of their troops. At the values at which military subsistence is recorded in our accounts, the total cost of feeding these soldiers may have amounted to several billion rubles. This again may be compared with the 66.3 billion rubles of defense department outlays recorded in the 1948 budget.

the years studied. An independent calculation of total investment on this basis, however, indicates that we may be understating this magnitude in 1940, but probably only to a rather limited extent. There is no basis to think that the 1944 figure errs significantly one way or another. The data on investment components for 1948 are especially inadequate, but as such seem broadly consistent with our calculation of investment as a residual.

Insofar as defense plant construction is not included under "defense," above, it necessarily is included in gross investment calculated as a residual. Presumably also included here are gold production and the net foreign balance. According to an established practice, the Soviet government supports out of its budget a variety of quasi-investment activities, including prospecting, resettlement, conservation, antipest measures in agriculture, etc. Expenditures for these activities should find their way, too, into our residual category.

Transfer outlays. See the comments on the transfer receipts of households given above (pp. 36 ff.).

THE GOVERNMENT BUDGET (TABLE 7)

The budget referred to in Table 7 is the "State Budget of the USSR," a consolidated budget of the all-union, republic, and local governments. For purposes of clarifying the relation of this account to others presented in this study, we have taken the liberty of revising the classification and, on the basis of diverse information, of elaborating certain of the categories that appear in the usual Soviet version of this budget. The nature of the revisions can be ascertained at once by comparing Table 7 with the budget shown in the Soviet sources cited in Appendix C.

There is no statistical discrepancy between budgetary and other data on loan transactions after 1937, because the calculations for later years had to be based solely on the budgetary data. As far as their nature is known, the "Other revenues" in Table 7 are rather diverse, but it is believed that with minor exceptions they may be viewed as revenues on capital account. Accordingly, in contrast to indirect taxes, they are not among the charges against the current income of economic organizations that are listed in Table 4. Thus, for 1940 "Other revenues" include among other things certain unexpended budget balances retained from the previous year, and certain payments of enterprises into the budget connected with the financing of additional inventories by bank credit. Probably the latter item refers to the substitution of bank credit for government grants to finance working-capital investments. For 1944 the principal item is donations to wartime patriotic funds. Of the 17.8 billion rubles expected to be donated to these funds in 1944, we have assumed previously that 3.3 billion were donated by households. The balance, therefore, was donated by economic organizations. Probably these donations were made in good part by collective farms and consisted of cattle and other property, but in any event they presumably were not recorded as charges against the current income of the economic organizations. For this reason they were not included among the charges in Table 4. In 1948 a major item is revenues, derived from an inventory revaluation, the precise nature of which is not clear. For all years the total of "Other revenues" represents in addition to revenues such as the foregoing, which are separately itemized in Soviet budgetary releases, certain more or less arbitrarily determined shares of other broad budget headings that were believed to include some revenues of the general type now under consideration.

As is indicated in Table 7, "Financing the National Economy" includes subsidies to economic organizations and the appropriations for the operating losses of the MTS. It also includes various other items. Among these the chief are funds transferred to the banking system to finance the fixed- and working-capital investments made in the economy. The investments ultimately take the form, in the case of both fixed and working capital, of interest-free grants. In the case of working capital, the government funds are used to finance minimum as distinct from seasonal peak needs, the latter requirements being met through bank-credit creation. "Financing the National Economy" also includes government appropriations for commodity stockpiling and "operational expenditures." The latter are the various quasi-investment activities referred to previously: prospecting, resettlement, conservation, antipest measures in agriculture, etc.[15]

The residual expenditure item is a catchall, and includes among

[15] See above, p. 48.

other things various budgetary outlays on "social-cultural measures" other than education and health care, i.e., administrative expenses of the social insurance system, physical culture, etc. A small part of "Other expenditures" is taken to be analogous to the transactions on capital account that are included under "Other revenues" on the income side.

The budget surplus has to be viewed in the light of the inclusion in the budget of such transactions on capital account. If allowance is made for these items, it may be calculated that instead of a surplus in 1940 there was a deficit of 1.5 billion rubles. Similarly in 1944 there was a deficit of 14.5 billion rubles. On the other hand, in 1948 there was still a surplus of 27.2 billion rubles.

As recalculated in this way, the budget surplus represents the difference between government revenues and expenditures of a sort that are recorded in our consolidated national economic account for government, economic organizations, etc., i.e., in Table 4. For reasons elaborated upon in Appendix C, but which may readily be surmised, such a surplus means one or another or all of several things, including chiefly: (i) bank-financed investments in working capital; (ii) a decrease in the bank balances of economic organizations; and (iii) a decline in cash balances of the population.

It was indicated previously (p. 39) that the government surplus was among the evidences considered in appraising the changes in cash holdings. This was done with the foregoing relations in mind. Taking into account available information on bank-financed investments in working capital and the bank balances of economic organizations, the calculated surpluses seem broadly consistent with our assumption that there was no significant change in the cash holdings of households in 1940, and that there was an increase in such holdings of 14.6 billion rubles in 1944. The almost exact correspondence of this latter magnitude with the recalculated budget deficit, 14.5 billion rubles, is of course a coincidence, but the bank-financed investments in working capital probably were quite small in 1944, so the two magnitudes should be quite close.

The notably large budget surplus for 1948 is believed to have been associated mainly with a large volume of bank-financed working-capital investment, but there may be here, nevertheless, a conflict with our assumption that no significant change occurred in household cash holdings. There may have been an appreciable reduction of the latter.

There has been a notably large budget surplus in the USSR not only for 1948 but also for other postwar years. It sometimes is suggested that such surpluses are not bona fide but instead represent concealed outlays, possibly on military activities. This may be so, but the writers see little basis for this belief. On the one hand, in view of the limited budgetary detail the Russians release, there are opportunities enough for concealment without the introduction of a fictitious budget surplus. For example, the government might, if it wishes, conceal all sorts of expenditures under "Financing the National Economy." On the other hand, the surpluses seem more readily understood in terms already indicated, namely, as the counterpart of bank-financed working capital and of reductions in cash balances of economic organizations and households. This relation has an economic as well as accounting character. In effect the surplus is a fiscal device to absorb excess purchasing power released through credit creation and reduction in cash holdings. According to a Soviet source, the surpluses "serve as a principal source for extending short term credit to the national economy," and thus promote monetary stability.[16] Seemingly, this Soviet explanation comes to the same thing as the one the writers have just suggested; understood in this way there is not much basis to question it.

[16] *Pravda,* May 18, 1949, p. 2.

III. NATIONAL INCOME
AT ADJUSTED FACTOR COST

INTRODUCTION

The Adjusted Factor Cost Standard of national income valuation, broadly speaking, has the following properties: (i) All commodity prices resolve fully into charges for primary factors, particularly capital, land, and labor. (ii) For capital, there is a net charge, "interest," corresponding to the average internal return on this factor in the economy generally. Also, there is an allowance for depreciation consistent with conventional accounting principles. (iii) The charge for land, "rent," corresponds on the average to the differential return to superior land. (iv) "Wages" are at a uniform rate for any occupation; as between occupations, they differ in accord with differences in productivity and Disutility. (v) Similar principles apply in the case of the relation of wages to farm income. (vi) Commodity prices are uniform in any given market area.

Adjusted Factor Cost is intended as a standard of national income valuation where the concern is to appraise "real" as distinct from purely "monetary" phenomena. Depending in part on whether reference is to *current* Adjusted Factor Cost or to an Adjusted Factor Cost that refers to some one year taken as base, the "real" phenomena are of diverse types. In the former case the "real" phenomena are structural in nature. By valuing the national product at *current* Adjusted Factor Cost, one in effect measures it in terms of resource cost or input, and with this there is a basis to appraise different aspects of resource allocation, e.g., the disposition of resources between consumption, investment, etc. Insofar as valuation is at the Adjusted Factor Cost relating to some one year taken as a base, there is a basis to appraise changes over time in the "real" national product and its components.

This briefest possible explanation of the rationale of Adjusted Factor Cost is, we fear, also quite an oversimplification. But, for a detailed discussion of this question and also of various theoretic limitations to which the Adjusted Factor Cost Standard is subject, the reader may be referred to *Soviet National Income* (Chapter 3). We propose here to turn at once to the twofold task that has been assigned to the present chapter: to survey briefly the relation of ruble prices to Adjusted Factor Cost in the years studied; and to appraise, and insofar as is feasible to correct for, the effects of divergencies on our national economic accounts. As was explained at the outset, our concern under both headings is exculsively with *current* Adjusted Factor Cost rather than with Adjusted Factor Cost for some one year taken as a base.

RUBLE PRICES VERSUS ADJUSTED FACTOR COST

To proceed first with the survey of the relation of ruble prices and Adjusted Factor Cost, we refer in turn to the more important features of the ruble price system in the years studied and ask in each case how this affects the relation of ruble prices to Adjusted Factor Cost.

Turnover tax. There appears to be no place in Adjusted Factor Cost for the famous turnover tax of the USSR. The tax is probably a more complex fiscal device than is generally supposed and among other things is calculated in very diverse ways, i.e., as a percentage of sales, as a fixed absolute charge per unit, as a residual charge to the distributor after allowance for a standard trade margin, etc.[1] But in all its manifestations the tax for all practical purposes comes to the same thing as a sales tax, this being understood as a charge against sales revenue based on the volume of sales and yielding a corresponding revenue to the government budget. As such, the tax represents a charge over and above the charges to factors. Accordingly, for all the years studied it must be reckoned as an initial source of divergence between ruble prices and Adjusted Factor Cost.

Such a divergence is of concern here of course only to the extent that it varies between different elements in our accounts, e.g., consumption and investment. Even a uniform sales tax would have this

---

[1] On the turnover tax, see *Soviet National Income*, pp. 56–57; also Appendix D, Section A, of the present study.

result, however, insofar as the tax would tend to pyramid in the process of the conversion of raw materials into finished goods. But in any case an outstanding feature of the turnover tax is the wide variation in rates. Throughout the period studied the rates have been practically nominal on basic industrial goods and notably high though still diverse on agricultural produce and consumers' goods. The rates in effect in the year 1940 are believed to be broadly illustrative of all the years considered. The tax was levied in 1940 at the rate of 1.0 percent on machinery and chemicals and .5 percent on coal, peat, and metal products. For men's leather shoes the rate was 10 to 40 percent; for salt, 70 to 80 percent; and for aluminum kitchenware, 50 to 60 percent.[2] Unlike practically all basic industrial goods, petroleum products were subject to a relatively high tax, e.g., in the case of fuel and motor oil, 60.5 percent; in the case of kerosene, 71.7 percent.[3] Under the circumstances, it turns out that the turnover tax is not only a cause of divergence between ruble prices and Adjusted Factor Cost but the most important one with which we have to deal.

Subsidies. Of a piece with a sales tax, though with opposite effects on the relation of prices to Adjusted Factor Cost, is a subsidy which permits operation at a price less than that corresponding to the charges for productive services. As is already clear, this is also a feature in the USSR, though one of varying importance in the different years studied.[4] Under a price reform of April, 1936, the government limited the previously extensive practice of granting subsidies to state enterprises, but such payments continued thereafter on some scale, and according to very rough calculations, which we have previously summarized in Table 4 (pp. 22 ff.), had again increased by 1940. During the war the government apparently was able to limit the total amount of subsidies to something like the 1940 level, but there was still another and notably large increase in the mid-forties. In 1948 subsidies had reached the impressive sum of over 50 billion rubles, or about 6.5 percent of

[2] See the sources cited in Appendix D, Section A. For machinery, chemicals, coal, peat, metal products, and salt the rates refer to the wholesale price gross of the tax. For leather shoes the rates refer to the retail price, and for aluminum kitchenware they refer to the retail price less an allowance for retail distribution costs.

[3] The rates refer to the wholesale price gross of the tax.

[4] On Soviet subsidies, see *Soviet National Income,* pp. 57–58, 114 ff., 128 ff., 139 ff.; also the present study, Appendix B, pp. 175 ff., Appendix D, Section B.

the gross national product. The government again curtailed subsidy payments, however, under a second major price reform of January, 1949.

As with the turnover tax, so with subsidies: what concerns us here is the relative incidence in different economic sectors. A major recipient of subsidies throughout was industry, especially the basic industrial branches. As subsidies mounted after the war this sector was by far the principal beneficiary. Because of the undervaluation of the income in kind of the MTS, however, this sector also had to be granted sizable subsidies, and at the low procurement prices paid state farms for their produce probably these too had to be subsidized continually. Varying sums were paid at different times to transport and other sectors.

To just what extent subsidies caused a relative divergence of ruble prices from Adjusted Factor Cost for different elements in our accounts is a matter for subsequent inquiry; but enough has been said to make clear that such an inquiry is much in order.

Interest and profits; depreciation. Under the *khozraschet* system, the Soviet enterprise obtains most of its capital without payment of interest. Interest is charged on short-term loans obtained from the State Bank for seasonal and other working-capital needs, and also on some long-term loans to agriculture and cooperatives; but for the rest capital is provided to the enterprise in the form of interest-free grants. On the other hand, except in the case of subsidized enterprises, prices generally are fixed to allow the enterprise a profit for operating in accord with the plan. At the same time, there necessarily are unplanned profits due to deviations from the plan.

Following the procedure of *Soviet National Income,*[5] we assume provisionally that planned profits are a more or less arbitrary category in Soviet accounts, and in any case not a bona fide charge for capital. Soviet sources have little to say about the determination of planned profits, and without a more detailed inquiry into the *khozraschet* system than can be undertaken here, we cannot exclude the possibility that the planned profits represent an indirect interest charge, but it is believed that the final upshot of our study is hardly affected by our assumption to the contrary. As to the extraplan profits, for present

[5] Pages 58–59.

purposes these must be considered as wages of management, insofar as they represent superior administrative ability or alternatively as a windfall gain of the type familiar under capitalism.

At this point, then, it is necessary to reckon with two divergencies between ruble prices and Adjusted Factor Cost: on the one hand, the omission of a systematic charge for interest in the case of most capital; on the other, the inclusion of a category "profits" which only in part represents a productive service rendered.[6]

Under the Soviet *khozraschet* system, ruble costs generally include a charge for depreciation, made at rates established by law. There are reasons to believe, however, that this charge is inadequate for purposes of this study. In the first place, it often is suggested that the charge, made at rates regulated by law, tends to overestimate the service life of fixed assets under the conditions of the five year plans. Whether and to what extent this is so in general must be left to a separate inquiry, but there clearly was such an overestimation, at least under wartime conditions of extreme use. Furthermore, depreciation is calculated in the USSR on the basis of original cost. In view of the price inflation under the five year plans, the corresponding allowance in terms of replacement cost undoubtedly would be much higher.

Beyond this, the *khozraschet* system does not apply to all branches of the economy; in particular it does not extend to the MTS or collective farms.[7] As will appear, the question of the relation of ruble prices to Adjusted Factor Cost for agricultural products revolves largely around the highly conjectural problem concerning the valuation of agricultural labor services; but in any wholly complete analysis one may also wish to take into account the omission from agricultural accounts of any systematic charge for depreciation.

Agricultural rent. In the USSR, there is no explicit charge for agricultural land comparable to the "rent" included in Adjusted Factor Cost. A concealed charge is made for this factor, however, under the

---

[6] Even in the case of short-term capital obtained in the form of loans from the State Bank a question is still in order as to whether the rate of interest charged is in accord with Adjusted Factor Cost. Furthermore, it will be evident that even unplanned profits cause a divergence from Adjusted Factor Cost insofar as they represent windfall gains rather than wages of management.

[7] In the case of the MTS, some type of depreciation charge is probably recorded in income accounts that are drawn up for individual stations. But no allowance is included

complex agricultural procurement system. More particularly, the obligatory deliveries at nominal prices tend to vary in accordance with differences in the quality and possibly also in the location of the land. At the same time, differences in procurement prices between obligatory and other deliveries are largely offset by differential turnover taxes. As a result, the farmers with better land are indirectly charged a higher tax than their fellows. Insofar as the turnover tax becomes in this way a form of agricultural rent, there is in effect an exception to the view expressed previously that the tax is a source of divergence between ruble prices and Adjusted Factor Cost.[8]

Wage differentials; collective farm incomes; military pay. According to *Soviet National Income*,[9] there probably was a very broad correspondence around the period considered, i.e., 1937, between wage differentials and productivity and possibly also between wage differentials and Disutility. This view was based on a variety of considerations, including chiefly the prevalence of the *khozraschet* system according to which state enterprises tended to economize money costs and consequently to limit their employment of different kinds of labor in the light of the relation of wages and productivity; the system of wage administration whereby wages tended to be differentiated on much the same basis as under capitalism; and the extensive reliance on an open market to recruit labor in accordance with the requirements of the plan.

The *khozraschet* system has continued to operate in the USSR in the period now studied, and in the light of the progress of Soviet planning as a whole the concern about money cost economy may well have grown in the course of time. The government similarly has continued to administer wages along the general lines marked out in the

---

in the comprehensive financial accounts that are used in the preparation of the government budget. See the comments on depreciation in Appendix B, pp. 189 ff.

[8] See *Soviet National Income*, pp. 59 ff. As was explained in the cited pages, there may be other instances of this sort where the turnover tax is a concealed factor charge. Also, in the case of subsidies, it is necessary to reckon with the analogous possibility that these are sometimes an offset to an excessive factor charge. For reasons that will become sufficiently clear, however, the end result of this study will be little affected if for the most part we pass by these special cases and proceed on the assumption made previously that the turnover tax and subsidies both represent to their full extent divergencies between ruble prices and Adjusted Factor Cost.

[9] *Ibid.*, pp. 63 ff.

thirties, though just how differentials have varied in the course of time has yet to be adequately explored.[10] On the other hand, as already has been explained,[11] the Russians, since 1940, have been relying to a significant extent on direct controls in recruiting labor. The change dates mainly from 1940, and in accordance with familiar economic reasoning this development, while perhaps not affecting the relation of wage differentials and productivity, would tend to impair the relation between wages and Disutility in the years of concern here. This relation has no doubt also been affected by the developments in the retail market in the years studied, including the growing deficiencies and the appearance of a spread in state and collective farm market prices before the war, the application of rationing after the outbreak of the war and until December, 1947, and the extremely high prices in the wartime collective farm market and "commercial shops." Under the circumstances, money wage differentials must have tended to lose significance to the Soviet worker, and the relation between wages and Disutility could only have been further impaired.

The precise relation between farm and city incomes that ought to prevail under Adjusted Factor Cost is conjectural, but it may be of interest here that the collective farmer's "real" income in 1937 probably was not much below that of the industrial worker. The average income of the Soviet collective farmer in 1937 was 1,760 rubles per full-time man-year.[12] This represents the sum of money earnings together with income in kind valued at realized farm prices. If allowance were made for the relative undervaluation of income in kind, the figure would be a good deal higher, and might approach the 3,005-ruble wage earned by the average industrial worker in the same year.

Because of gaps in information, trends in the relation of collective farm and industrial earnings over the years now studied have to be appraised from the following data (in percent of 1937), based in part on rule-of-thumb calculations:[13]

[10] See Schwartz, *Russia's Soviet Economy*, pp. 463 ff.

[11] See above, p. 14.

[12] *Soviet National Income*, pp. 68 ff.

[13] The figures on farm incomes are calculated from the data in Table 3, p. 20, on the total income of households from agriculture, and the following guesses as to the farm labor force: 1937, 35 million; 1940, 40 million; 1944, 30 million; 1948, 40 million. In contrast to the calculation of the 1937 study, the average farm income as now computed

YEAR	AVERAGE FARM INCOME	AVERAGE WAGE OF HIRED WORKERS	RELATIVE EARNINGS OF COLLECTIVE FARMERS AND HIRED WORKERS
1937	100	100	100
1940	159	134	119
1944	179	190	94
1948	194	234	83

Farm income in this tabulation represents farm income as it is recorded in our accounts, and changes in the relation of this to money wages do not necessarily measure changes in relative "real" income. Among other things, relative incomes as calculated might differ from relative "real" incomes because of the arbitrary valuation of farm income in kind in 1944 at 1940 farm prices. The wartime rationing obviously is a further source of divergence.

It is open to question, however, whether valuation at Adjusted Factor Cost necessarily involves valuing farm and nonfarm services in accordance with year-to-year changes in the relative "real" incomes accruing to them. What, for example, if the changes are only of a "windfall" character, due, say, to an abrupt shift in demand? In any event, we propose to adopt here an extremely simplified expedient: for purposes of appraising the relation of ruble prices to Adjusted Factor Cost, we arbitrarily take the relative values of farm and nonfarm services recorded in our accounts for 1937 as a norm, and we inquire as to the extent to which there have been divergencies in relative values from this norm in subsequent years. From this standpoint, then, the tabulation just set forth suggests a possible overvaluation of farm services in 1940 and an undervaluation of these services in 1948.[14]

relates to all farm workers and not merely to collective farmers. Also, the 1937 study took account of off-the-farm earnings together with off-the-farm working time, while in the present calculation we pass by both these aspects. For present purposes it will be evident that these divergencies in method are immaterial. In the case of the earnings of hired labor we start with a figure of 3,038 rubles representing the average earnings of all such workers in 1937. See Gosplan, *Tretii piatiletnii plan razvitiia narodnogo khoziaistva Soiuza SSR (1938–42 gg.) (proekt)*, p. 228. The figure of 3,005 rubles cited in the 1937 study refers to industrial workers alone. For the years 1940, 1944, and 1948 reference is made to the data on wages compiled in Appendix A, pp. 127 ff. These data again refer to the earnings of all hired labor.

[14] To come back to the valuation of income in kind in 1944, our national economic accounts and the tabulation given above, are based on valuation in terms of average realized farm prices of 1940, with the resultant magnitude of 33 billion rubles. If the

Military pay becomes an especially important item in one of the years studied; for this reason separate reference to this item is in order. In our accounts, we have sought to value military services at the prevailing military pay rates (for the remuneration in money) and at the costs of food and clothing to the government (for the remuneration in kind). The resulting earnings of military personnel averaged 2,286 rubles per man in 1937, 3,457 rubles in 1940, 3,767 rubles in 1944, and 8,250 rubles in 1948.[15] We tabulate, below, data on the relation of these earnings to the pay of hired civilian workers in the corresponding years:

YEAR	AVERAGE MILITARY EARNINGS AS PERCENT OF AVERAGE EARNINGS OF HIRED CIVILIAN WORKERS	RELATION OF AVERAGE MILITARY EARNINGS TO AVERAGE EARNINGS OF HIRED CIVILIAN WORKERS (1937 = 100)
1937	75	100
1940	85	113
1944	65	87
1948	116	154

As with collective farm services, so with the services of military personnel: the precise valuation called for by the Adjusted Factor Cost standard is open to diverse interpretations. If, as might be suggested, civilian earnings are taken as a norm, military services in our accounts are overvalued in 1948 and undervalued in all other years, especially 1944. On the other hand, we might instead adopt the expedient intro-

---

valuation had been made instead at the average realized farm prices of 1944, income in kind in that year would have come to some 83 billion rubles. With this revision, the average farm income in 1944 would be raised from 179 to 286 percent of that of 1937. The index of the relative earnings of collective farmers and hired wage earners (1937 = 100 percent) would be increased correspondingly from 94 to 150. In suggesting previously (p. 28) that valuation of 1944 income in kind at 1940 prices resulted in a more plausible figure for the value of farm services than did valuation at 1944 prices, we had in mind the foregoing relationships.

Regarding the problem of the valuation of farm services generally, evidently what is in question for present purposes is the relation to industrial wages of farm incomes qua returns to labor as distinct from land or capital. As is explained in *Soviet National Income*, p. 62, the farm earnings recorded in our accounts probably include elements of both rent to land and interest on capital in addition to the return to labor. In the context, however, any attempt to reckon with this aspect surely would represent an undue refinement.

[15] See Appendix A, pp. 136 ff.

duced with regard to agricultural services, i.e., take the 1937 relation to the earnings of civilian workers as a norm. In this case there is a limited overvaluation of military services in 1940, a comparable undervaluation in 1944, and a sizable overvaluation in 1948. In the subsequent attempt to appraise the effects on our accounts of divergencies between ruble prices and Adjusted Factor Cost, we shall be guided by the second of these two approaches to the valuation of military services.

Multiple prices. An outstanding case of multiple prices in the USSR has already been referred to. This is the case of agricultural procurement prices. But reference here is only to agricultural raw materials at the procurement stage. As a result of the imposition of turnover taxes, the prices charged to the processors of these materials are made more or less uniform. Accordingly, so far as the prices of processed goods are concerned, there is no major divergence of prices and Adjusted Factor Cost on this account.

But the use of taxes to equalize the prices of agricultural products, while the general rule, is not universal. For purposes of stockpiling and export, grain and possibly other unprocessed agricultural goods are turned over to the agencies concerned at the same low prices the government pays farmers for obligatory deliveries. At least this was the practice before the war and very likely it has continued.[16] To this extent, then, there is a divergence between prices and Adjusted Factor Cost which affects our accounts.

It was mentioned earlier that developments in the retail market in the period studied, particularly shortages, rationing, and multiple prices, would have tended to undermine the relation of money wages to Disutility and in this way cause a divergence of ruble prices from Adjusted Factor Cost. But insofar as there are multiple prices, this in itself constitutes a divergence from Adjusted Factor Cost, and one that was especially notable in the period considered. On the basis of diverse information, we think in terms of an average differential of 50 percent between collective farm market prices and state shop prices in 1940.[17] In 1944 collective farm market prices may have been of the order of eight times as high as state shop ration prices, while the differential

[16] *Soviet National Income,* p. 63.
[17] See Appendix D, Section C.

between the wartime "commercial shop" prices and the ration prices must have been similar. In 1948, after the abandonment of rationing, prices in the collective farm market probably were not substantially above the state shop level.

It is sometimes suggested that the ruble price system tends to "favor" the armed forces in the sense that prices are systematically differentiated so as to reduce the procurement costs to the military. Evidently, the prices of munitions "benefit" in at least the same manner as other nonconsumption goods from the uneven impact on different commodities of turnover taxes on the one hand and subsidies on the other. But the question that is raised here concerns the possibility that, over and above this, the armed forces and defense industries might be in a position to procure goods on uniquely favorable terms compared with other purchasers as a result of the extension to them of special exemptions from, or special low rates of, the turnover tax, of special subsidies, or of other discriminatory accounting arrangements. No evidence has been found in Soviet sources to support the suggestion that ruble prices are differentiated in this way. In fact, available information, including a price handbook issued by the Soviet air force procurement division, indicates important instances to the contrary. More particularly, in the case of grain, various other foods, and oil products, the armed forces apparently pay the same prices, inclusive of the turnover tax, as wholesale consumers generally.[18] The evidence on this matter is clearly insufficient to permit a definite conclusion, but in the absence of any

[18] According to A. K. Suchkov, *Gosudarstvennye dokhody, SSSR*, p. 81, the state grain procurement agency sells its grain at the same price, inclusive of the tax, to the military establishment as to other wholesale consumers. Elsewhere (p. 107) Suchkov informs us that the turnover tax is levied on aviation gasoline and lubricants; there is no suggestion that the armed forces are exempted from the tax. A 1944 compilation of turnover tax rates and regulations shows that various food products are sold to the military establishment at the same prices, inclusive of turnover tax, as are charged other consumers. See Narkomfin, SSSR, Upravlenie Gosdokhodov, *Spravochnik po stavkam naloga s oborota i biudzhetnoi raznitse po prodovol'stvennym tovaram*, 1944, e.g., pp. 21, 22, 25, 33, 44, 49, 53, 56, 60. The Soviet air force price handbook referred to is RKKA, Upravlenie Voennykh Vozdushnykh Sil, *Tsennik-spravochnik po material'noi chasti VVS RKKA, Chast' III*, pp. 69–71. A comparison of the petroleum prices quoted in this source with those cited in other price handbooks reveals that they are the prices which were established by a decree of the Economic Council under the Council of Commissars (No. 1,432 of August 19, 1940). These prices are inclusive of the turnover tax and evidently apply to all wholesale consumers.

positive indications we assume that special pricing arrangements of the sort mentioned do not constitute an important source of divergence between ruble prices and Adjusted Factor Cost.

During 1944 the Russians received about 3.5 billion dollars worth of imports on Lend-Lease account.[19] The Soviet government is believed to have transferred these imports to Soviet economic and military organizations for some 24 billion rubles, or at a ratio of about 7 rubles to a dollar.[20] If one adheres strictly to the view which has been the guiding one in this study, that customs and similar charges represent a form of national product domestically produced, there appears to be little basis to question this or any other valuation that the Soviet government might have placed on Lend-Lease goods. On the other hand, if these charges are included on the understanding that the end result is to be disposable national product, one might wish to value Lend-Lease imports more or less in accordance with ruble prices of similar domestic goods. Whether and to what extent the Soviet government's valuation approaches this result, however, must be left conjectural here. In terms of retail prices, a parity of 7 to 1 certainly overvalues the ruble, but it is not clear whether and to what extent this was also true of wartime wholesale prices. The fact that the arbitrary Soviet official exchange rate was 5.3 to 1 at the time considered is, of course, not especially pertinent to the appropriate valuation of the Lend-Lease goods.[21]

NATIONAL INCOME REVALUED

Our concern so far has been to survey the relation of ruble prices to Adjusted Factor Cost in the years studied; it remains to appraise, and

[19] Lend-Lease shipments from the United States alone amounted to 3.4 billion dollars. See United States Department of Commerce, *International Reference Service,* December, 1945, p. 3. In addition, a small amount of goods was shipped from Canada and the United Kingdom.

[20] See above, p. 43.

[21] In addition to the cases of multiple prices cited in the text, there have been various others in the USSR in the years studied, but it is believed that these are of relatively limited consequence for present purposes. Among the remaining cases, mention may be made of the limited premium above state shop prices which cooperatives were permitted to charge around 1948 on sales of goods procured locally as distinct from sales of goods obtained from central sources. See on this J. Chapman, *Retail Prices in the USSR, 1937–48,* pp. 42 ff.

where possible to correct for, the effects of divergencies on our national economic accounts. In this connection we propose to focus on only one of the various income tabulations compiled, namely, that of the national product by use. This tabulation seems by far the most interesting one to consider from the present standpoint.

Incidence of turnover tax. To refer first to the divergence between ruble prices and Adjusted Factor Cost that is due to the turnover tax, Table 8 shows the results of an attempt to calculate the extent of this divergence for different categories of national product use. The figures are intended to show the total amount of the tax, paid either directly or indirectly; e.g., under consumption are included not only taxes on retail sales but also taxes on agricultural procurements, insofar as these go ultimately to consumption. To the extent that these data show the incidence of the tax, evidently they also provide a basis on which to correct our figures on the national product by use in terms of current rubles for the divergence due to the turnover tax.

The calculations on which Table 8 is based are only broadly reliable. The first step was to obtain a detailed breakdown of the national product by use. To this end, rule-of-thumb estimates were made of the breakdown of government expenditures between commodities and services; of the breakdown of gross investment between fixed capital, working capital, and stockpiles; and so on. It is known that certain use categories, most importantly services, are entirely free of the turn-over tax. For the use categories subject to the tax, we calculated for each year the average effective rate of the tax as the ratio between the total tax revenue and the total value of product subject to the tax. The average effective rate comes to 32.7 percent in 1940, 29.2 percent in 1944, and 42.1 percent in 1948. For purposes of calculating the incidence of the tax by use category, we arbitrarily assume that the average effec-tive rate itself applies to a number of use categories, including com-modities used in the provision of the communal services, government administration, and the NKVD. It also applies to working-capital investment. Except for the taxes on retail sales which are calculated as a residual, the taxes on other use categories are estimated from diverse information, especially the official schedules of turnover tax rates by commodities. The schedules applicable in 1940 and in 1944

TABLE 8

INCIDENCE OF THE TURNOVER TAX BY NATIONAL PRODUCT USE CATEGORY, USSR, 1937, 1940, 1944, AND 1948[a]

ITEM	1937		1940		1944		1948	
	BILLION RUBLES	PERCENT	BILLION RUBLES	PERCENT	BILLION RUBLES	PERCENT	BILLION RUBLES	PERCENT
1. Consumption of households								
a. Civilian	60.2	79.3	85.4	80.6	67.8	71.4	191.1	77.2
b. Military subsistence	.9	1.2	2.6	2.5	9.1	9.6	8.0	3.2
c. Total	61.1	80.5	88.0	83.1	76.9	81.0	199.1	80.4
2. Communal services	4.8	6.3	6.0	5.7	3.2	3.4	17.9	7.3
3. Government administration, including NKVD (MVD and MGB)	.5	.7	1.0	.9	.4	.4	3.3	1.3
4. Defense (as recorded in budget)	1.0	1.3	3.3	3.1	6.9	7.3	2.5	1.0
5. Gross investment	8.5	11.2	7.6	7.2	7.5	7.9	24.7	10.0
6. Gross national product	75.9	100.0	105.9	100.0	94.9	100.0	247.5	100.0

[a] See Appendix D. Minor discrepancies between calculated sums of items and indicated totals are due to rounding.

TABLE 9

INCIDENCE OF SUBSIDIES BY NATIONAL PRODUCT USE CATEGORY, USSR, 1937, 1940, 1944, AND 1948[a]

ITEM	1937 BILLION RUBLES	1937 PERCENT	1940 BILLION RUBLES	1940 PERCENT	1944 BILLION RUBLES	1944 PERCENT	1948 BILLION RUBLES	1948 PERCENT
1. Consumption of households								
a. Civilian	4.1	51.2	6.4	45.8	4.8	30.0	13.5	25.5
b. Military subsistence	.1	1.3	.3	2.1	1.3	8.1	.8	1.5
c. Total	4.2	52.5	6.7	47.9	6.1	38.1	14.3	27.0
2. Communal services	.5	6.3	.7	5.0	.5	3.1	1.9	3.6
3. Government administration, including NKVD (MVD and MGB)	...[b]	...	.1	.7	.1	.6	.3	.6
4. Defense (as recorded in budget)	.7	8.8	2.8	20.0	6.0	37.5	7.6	14.3
5. Gross investment	2.6	32.5	3.7	26.4	3.3	20.6	28.9	54.5
6. Gross national product	8.0	100.0	14.0	100.0	16.0	100.0	53.0	100.0

[a] See Appendix D. Minor discrepancies between calculated sums of items and indicated totals are due to rounding.   [b] .... = negligible.

are known; for pertinent features, it is believed there was no major change in schedules through 1948. The results of our calculations for 1940 and 1948 are in general agreement with information the Russians have published for these years on the breakdown of the tax by paying commissariat. The calculations are explained in detail in Appendix D.

Incidence of subsidies. As with the data on the turnover tax in Table 8, those on subsidies in Table 9 are intended to show total incidence, both direct and indirect. As was explained previously, subsidies as recorded in our accounts comprise the subsidized losses of *khozraschet* organizations, the losses of the MTS, and certain other losses assumed to be of a minor nature. Also, the total of subsidized losses of *khozraschet* organizations was calculated by breaking down the broad government budget category "Financing the National Economy" in which such subsidies are included along with other outlays, such as grants for fixed- and working-capital investment. From diverse information, the writers have also attempted to break down this same budgetary category between economic sectors, e.g., industry, agriculture, etc. On this basis a series of estimates has been derived of subsidies of all sorts by economic sector. The calculation of the incidence of subsidies by national product use category, the results of which are shown in Table 9, rests on this breakdown of subsidies by economic sector. Relying on broadly plausible assumptions as to the ultimate disposition by use categories of the output of different economic sectors, we more or less arbitrarily allocate by use category the subsidies paid each economic sector. Details are set forth in Appendix D.

Incidence of collective farm market prices. We have said that the data in Table 8 provide a basis to correct our national income calculations for the divergencies between ruble prices and Adjusted Factor Cost due to the turnover tax. Similarly, the data in Table 9 provide a basis to correct for divergencies due to subsidies. Such corrections, however, are in effect revaluations, and seen from this standpoint they are in principle subject to one deficiency. It happens that retail collective farm market sales are free of the turnover tax and subsidies. Under the heading of consumption, the turnover tax and subsidies fall almost exclusively on the goods sold at retail in state and cooperative shops.[22]

---

[22] Strictly speaking, we are stating here the assumptions on which Tables 8 and 9 are

Accordingly, a correction for taxes and subsidies means that the prices in state and cooperative shops are changed—on balance there is a reduction—while comparable goods sold on the collective farm market continue to be valued at their old prices. Moreover, these prices to a varying extent exceed the state and cooperative shop prices even before the reduction of the latter. Obviously logic requires that in any revaluation the retail collective farm market prices be reduced first to the level of the state and cooperative shop prices before the correction for turnover taxes and subsidies. Then they must be reduced additionally in the same proportion as state and cooperative shop prices fall as a result of the correction.

The data in Table 10 are intended in part to measure the incidence of this reduction in collective farm market prices and in part to measure the effect of an *increase* in the average level of farm procurement prices now to be explained. Since the value of farm services is a matter for separate consideration, we proceed for the moment on the assumption that these services are unaffected by the reduction in collective farm market prices. The reduction in collective farm market prices, however, means a reduction in farm incomes and hence in the value of farm services. Accordingly, we assume an increase in farm procurement prices which just offsets this reduction.

So far as the different use categories are concerned, the reduction in collective farm market prices is reflected only in consumption. The increase in farm procurement prices, however, also shows up to a limited extent in other categories. Necessarily this calculation was based on guesswork. Details are presented in Appendix D.

We have explained that in the Soviet retail market there are differentials in prices besides those prevailing between state and cooperative shops on the one hand and the collective farm market on the other. During the war there were also differentials between the prices of rationed goods in the state and cooperative shops and the prices prevailing in

---

based rather than the actuality. In fact, there is a small turnover tax on collective farm market sales (see *Soviet National Income,* p. 78, n. 37), while in the case of subsidies, those of the MTS might well be viewed as falling on collective farm market sales as well as on state shop sales. On the other hand, as will become clear, the end result of our revaluation is unaffected by our having disregarded these aspects, and for convenience the discussion proceeds here on this basis.

the open "commercial shops." These latter differentials, however, were reflected in corresponding differentials in the turnover tax, the extra income earned in the "commercial shop" being transferred to the budget in this way. Accordingly, insofar as we correct our national product use categories for the turnover tax, there is also an appropriate revaluation of the "commercial shop" sales.

TABLE 10

INCIDENCE OF REVALUATION OF COLLECTIVE FARM MARKET
SALES BY NATIONAL PRODUCT USE CATEGORY, USSR,[a]
1937, 1940, 1944, AND 1948
(*Billions of rubles*)

ITEM	1937	1940	1944	1948
1. Consumption of households				
a. Civilian	(—)2.0	(—)5.5	(—)17.4	(—)8.3
b. Military subsistence	.1	.8	7.7	1.2
c. Total	(—)1.9	(—)4.7	(—)9.7	(—)7.1
2. Communal services	.7	1.7	2.7	2.6
3. Government administration, including NKVD (MVD and MGB)	...[b]	.2	.4	.5
4. Defense (as recorded in budget)	.1	.9	3.1	.6
5. Gross investment	1.0	1.8	3.5	3.5
6. Gross national product	...	...	...	...

[a] See Appendix D. Minor discrepancies between calculated sums of items and indicated totals are due to rounding.
[b] ... = negligible.

National income in adjusted rubles. It will be of value to have a separate summary of the effect on the national product use categories of adjustments for the turnover tax, subsidies, and the revaluation of collective farm market sales as just explained. In Table 11 we show the national product data for the years now studied before and after these adjustments, along with corresponding figures for 1937. For each year we first show national product by use in terms of prevailing rubles. Then we show the corresponding data obtained after deducting turnover taxes, adding subsidies, and deducting the incidence of the reval-

TABLE 11

GROSS NATIONAL PRODUCT BY USE IN ESTABLISHED AND ADJUSTED PRICES, USSR, 1937, 1940, 1944, AND 1948[a]

A. BILLIONS OF RUBLES

ITEM	1937		1940		1944		1948	
	IN ESTABLISHED PRICES	IN ADJUSTED PRICES	IN ESTABLISHED PRICES	IN ADJUSTED PRICES	IN ESTABLISHED PRICES	IN ADJUSTED PRICES	IN ESTABLISHED PRICES	IN ADJUSTED PRICES
1. Consumption of households								
a. Civilian	181.0	122.9	280.3	195.8	217.9	137.5	451.8	265.9
b. Military subsistence	2.5	1.8	8.0	6.5	31.0	30.9	19.0	13.0
c. Total	183.5	124.7	288.3	202.3	248.9	168.4	470.8	278.9
2. Communal services	27.4	23.8	36.4	32.8	30.9	30.9	85.1	71.7
3. Government administration, including NKVD (MVD and MGB)	7.4	6.9	13.9	13.2	14.0	14.1	38.9	36.4
4. Defense (as recorded in budget)	17.5	17.3	56.7	57.1	137.7	139.9	66.3	72.0
5. Gross investment	56.1	51.2	62.7	60.6	55.9	55.2	150.1	157.8
6. Gross national product	291.8	223.9	458.0	366.1	487.4	408.5	811.2	616.7

B. IN PERCENT

ITEM	1937		1940		1944		1948	
	IN ESTAB-LISHED PRICES	IN AD-JUSTED PRICES	IN ESTAB-LISHED PRICES	IN AD-JUSTED PRICES	IN ESTAB-LISHED PRICES	IN AD-JUSTED PRICES	IN ESTAB-LISHED PRICES	IN AD-JUSTED PRICES
1. Consumption of households								
a. Civilian	62.0	54.9	61.2	53.5	44.7	33.7	55.7	43.1
b. Military subsistence	.9	.8	1.7	1.8	6.4	7.5	2.3	2.1
c. Total	62.9	55.7	62.9	55.3	51.1	41.2	58.0	45.2
2. Communal services	9.4	10.6	8.0	9.0	6.3	7.6	10.5	11.6
3. Government administration, including NKVD (MVD and MGB)	2.5	3.1	3.0	3.6	2.9	3.5	4.8	5.9
4. Defense (as recorded in budget)	6.0	7.7	12.4	15.6	28.3	34.2	8.2	11.7
5. Gross investment	19.2	22.9	13.7	16.6	11.5	13.5	18.5	25.6
6. Gross national product	100.0	100.0	100.0	100.0	100.0	100.0	100.0	100.0

a See Tables 6, 8, 9, 10. Minor discrepancies between calculated sums of items and indicated totals are due to rounding.

uation of collective farm market sales. Adhering to the terminology of
Soviet National Income, the results are referred to as being in terms of
"adjusted rubles."

As might have been expected, the data in adjusted rubles show a
distinctly smaller share going to household consumption than do those
in prevailing rubles. The shares of defense and investment are correspondingly increased. These relations obtain in all years, but the effect
of the adjustment is especially pronounced in 1948. So far as state and
cooperative retail prices are concerned, all adjustments together involve
a reduction of 39.1 percent in 1940, 30.5 percent in 1944, and 51.9 percent in 1948. The corresponding figure for 1937 was 45.4 percent.[23]

We have discounted previously the notion that under the ruble price
system the armed forces and defense industries obtain supplies at lower
prices than those paid for the same goods by other wholesale consumers.
At the same time, it was also indicated that defense activities might
benefit from ruble pricing nevertheless, insofar as they are favored
by the uneven impact on different commodities of other features, particularly the turnover tax and subsidies. Our calculation of the incidence of the turnover tax and subsidies by national product use category, and accordingly the revaluation in terms of adjusted rubles, it
remains to explain, rest on the assumption that defense activities, or
more precisely munitions production and procurement, are favored
in this way no less and no more than fixed-capital investment. In relation to the value of output, the total incidence of turnover taxes and
subsidies, both direct and indirect, is the same for the two types of
product outlays.

Barring differential pricing for the same goods, there clearly is some
a priori support for this assumption in the similarity of the two types
of product outlays and their common requirements for raw materials,

[23] It was said that the collective farm market prices are first reduced to the original
level of state and cooperative shop prices and then are further reduced in proportion to
the state and cooperative shop prices as these latter are corrected for the turnover tax
and subsidies. Strictly speaking, the decline in the state and cooperative shop prices is
itself calculated as the net resultant after allowance has been made both for the elimination of turnover taxes and subsidies and the rise in procurement prices needed to
offset the decline in collective farm market prices. As may readily be seen, to figure the
decline in state and cooperative shop prices only on the basis of the elimination of the
turnover tax and subsidies would involve us in an inconsistency.

etc. Beyond this, in the case of the turnover tax, available information on the rate structure makes it clear that the deviations from the assumed parity in incidence could not be important here. On the other hand, so far as it concerns subsidies, the actual relation is conjectural, and it probably is advisable to consider that our calculation may understate the incidence of this feature on defense.[24] The resultant understatement in our adjusted ruble figure on the share of defense in the national product, however, probably does not exceed one percent even in 1948 when subsidies are important.

Other adjustments. We have commented so far on the effects on our national product tabulation of the turnover tax, subsidies, and multiple prices in the consumers' goods market; it is necessary still to consider several other sources of divergence between ruble prices and Adjusted Factor Cost.

As a result of the Soviet treatment of the net charge for capital, there are two types of divergence between ruble prices and Adjusted Factor Cost to be considered: one due to the omission of such a charge and one due to the inclusion of a more or less arbitrary charge under the heading of profits. According to an illustrative calculation in *Soviet National Income*,[25] the total profits initially recorded in the national economic accounts for 1937, including the retained earnings of collective farms, amounted to 21.6 billion rubles, or to some 9.7 percent of the gross national product in adjusted rubles. The total stock of fixed capital

[24] According to *Gosudarstvennyi plan . . . na 1941 god*, pp. 11, 566, the marketable output of the defense industry commissariats was to be 40.3 billion rubles, whereas their costs of production (*sebestoimost'*) were fixed at 32.8 billion rubles. Since turnover taxes on the defense industry commissariats are believed to have been nominal, the difference between these two figures probably consisted almost entirely of profits. On this basis one is inclined to discount the possibility that there is an established policy to favor this sector specially, either directly or indirectly, through the use of subsidies. On the other hand, studies now in progress of price behavior in basic industries indicate that here as elsewhere under the five year plans inflationary forces were dominant. But in some instances there are notable disparities in the extent of the price increase between goods of an especially military sort and other basic industrial products; e.g., according to an unpublished study, A. Bergson and R. Bernaut, *Prices of Basic Chemical Products in the Soviet Union, 1928–1950*, the price of nitric acid rose only 5.5 percent from 1937 to 1948, whereas the prices of basic chemical products generally increased 109 percent in this same period. No doubt disparities of this sort are due mainly to a systematic policy of favoring defense-related industries with investment funds and advanced technology, but in part they may also reflect differential subsidies.

[25] Pages 79 ff.

of the USSR at the time studied was taken to be 325 billion rubles,[26] and, on the quite arbitrary assumption that an 8 percent return was appropriate from the standpoint of Adjusted Factor Cost, the total interest on fixed capital came to 26 billion rubles. Additional assumptions based on diverse information were that one-fifth of the initial profits figure of 21.6 billion rubles accrues to investment goods and that in terms of the proportion of fixed capital used currently in their production these goods should have been charged instead with one-third of the alternative total of 26 billion rubles interest corresponding to Adjusted Factor Cost. With a revaluation of the accounts to eliminate profits and to allow for interest on this basis, the share of gross investment in the gross national product, which amounted to 22.9 percent in adjusted rubles, is increased by 1.5 percent.

Coming now to the years of concern in this study, we set forth in Table 12 the results of an attempt to repeat for each year the sort of computation made previously for 1937. Because of the lack of data, the calculations do little more than reflect changes in total profits initially recorded and the share of investment in the national product, but they may be illuminating nonetheless.[27] Apparently the share of gross invest-

[26] This represents the stock of fixed capital, exclusive of cattle, but probably inclusive of housing and public buildings. It was assumed that the figure cited is net of depreciation, but the underlying Soviet sources are not explicit on this important point.

[27] The calculations rest in part on the following data:

YEAR	PROFITS INITIALLY RECORDED IN ACCOUNTS		STOCK OF FIXED CAPITAL, BILLION RUBLES IN CURRENT PRICES	INTEREST ON FIXED CAPITAL, ASSUMING 8 PERCENT RETURN
	Billion rubles	Percent of gross national product in adjusted rubles		
1937	21.6	9.7	325	26.0
1940	36.9	10.1	525	42.0
1944	33.1	8.1	525	42.0
1948	49.1	8.0	700	56.0

The figure on capital stock in current prices for 1937 was derived in *Soviet National Income* from a corresponding figure in terms of 1945 prices given in N. Voznesenskii, *Voennaia ekonomika SSSR v period Otechestvennoi voiny*, p. 12. An allowance for changes in investment goods prices between 1937 and 1945 was made on the basis of an index calculated in N. Jasny, *Soviet Prices of Producers' Goods*, p. 20. Voznesenskii also informs us that the stock of fixed capital amounted to 709 billion rubles in 1940. This again is in terms of 1945 prices, and for purposes of deriving a corresponding figure in terms of 1940 prices we allow for an increase in investment goods prices of 35 percent from 1940 to 1945. This is about the change calculated by Jasny. For purposes

ment in the gross national product is increased by the revaluation to a varying but generally limited extent. The largest increase is that for 1948: 2.1 percent. This calculation is based on the supposition that, in view of the large-scale subsidies, profits on investment goods production must have been quite limited in 1948.

In *Soviet National Income* the incidence of the revaluation for profits and interest was calculated only for gross investment. In Table 12 we set forth some corresponding figures compiled here for defense outlays. For all years, including 1937, the incidence of the revaluation on defense is taken to be the same as that on gross investment per adjusted ruble of product.

Insofar as depreciation is understated in our accounts, what is required, for present purposes, is an upward revision of prices all

---

of deriving a capital stock figure for 1944, we assume a wartime decline in fixed capital in "real" terms of one-fourth. See A. Bergson, J. H. Blackman, and A. Erlich, "Postwar Economic Reconstruction and Development in the U.S.S.R.," *Annals of the American Academy of Political and Social Science,* May, 1949, p. 53. Also, we take the 1944 price level to be the same as that for 1945. In the light of information such as was cited in Chap. I on the postwar recovery, we assume that the capital stock in 1948 was again nearly as large as that of 1940. On the other hand, relying on Jasny's index we take the 1948 prices to be somewhat greater than those of 1945. Accordingly, the 1948 stock in 1948 prices is about the same as the 1940 stock in 1945 prices.

For purposes of deriving the figures in Table 12, it is necessary to know also the share of profits initially recorded that accrues to gross investment and also the share of the existing stock of fixed capital that is used directly or indirectly to produce the gross investment. We assume that the share of total profits accruing to gross investment varies from 1937 onwards with the share of gross investment in the gross national product. For the year 1948, however, the amount of profits entering into gross investment is taken to be disproportionately low in view of the widespread subsidized losses in industry in that year. This comes to the same thing as assuming that relative profit margins as between investment and other goods are stable from year to year prior to 1948. So far as concerns the distribution of the existing stock of fixed capital, we proceed analogously on the assumption that in relation to the 1937 situation the disposition in subsequent years varies proportionately with the share of gross investment in the gross national product.

The shares of the initially recorded profits and the alternative interest total accruing to investment on these assumptions are as follows:

YEAR	SHARE OF TOTAL PROFITS INITIALLY RECORDED, PERCENT	SHARE OF COMPUTED INTEREST ON FIXED CAPITAL, PERCENT
1937	20	33.3
1940	15	25
1944	12	20
1948	10	35

TABLE 12

INCIDENCE OF VARIOUS OTHER ADJUSTMENTS, USSR, 1937, 1940, 1944, AND 1948[a]

(Percent of gross national product in adjusted rubles)

ITEM	SHARE OF GROSS NATIONAL PRODUCT INITIALLY	ADJUSTMENT FOR 8 PERCENT RETURN ON CAPITAL	ALLOWANCE FOR DEPRECIATION AT 3.5 PERCENT OF FIXED CAPITAL	REVALUATION OF FARM SERVICES	REVALUATION OF MILITARY SERVICES	SUM OF ADJUSTMENTS
Defense						
1937	7.7	+.5	+.1	n.a.[b]	n.a.	+.6
1940	15.6	+1.1	+.1	+.8	(−).3	+1.7
1944	34.2	+2.0	+.3	n.a.	+1.1	+3.4
1948	11.7	+.9	+.1	(−).4	(−)1.7	(−)1.1
Gross investment						
1937	22.9	+1.5	+.2	n.a.	n.a.	+1.7
1940	16.6	+1.1	+.1	+.8	...[c]	+2.0
1944	13.5	+.8	+.1	n.a.	(−).2	+.7
1948	25.6	+2.1	+.2	(−).7	+.5	+2.1

[a] See text.
[b] n.a. = no adjustment made (see text).
[c] ... = negligible.

around in order to provide for an increased depreciation charge. The
increase in prices for any category of final goods depends on the amount
of fixed capital used in their production. For purposes of appraising
the effect of such a revision, it was assumed in *Soviet National Income*[28]
that the correct depreciation charge might be on the order of double
that initially recorded, this magnitude being suggested by United States
data. The incidence of the revaluation on gross investment was then
calculated on the same premise as to the disposition of fixed capital
by use categories as was used in the revaluation for profits and interest.
As is shown in Table 12, the final adjustment is negligible, but for the
sake of completeness we nevertheless have calculated here corresponding figures, also shown in Table 12, for the years now studied. In the
latter calculation we assume that the correct depreciation charge is
3.5 percent of fixed capital, or approximately the 1937 relation. We
show also in Table 12 corresponding figures for defense. As before we
assume that the incidence of revaluation per adjusted ruble of product
is the same for defense as for investment. The revaluation for depreciation takes as a point of departure the tabulation of national income in
adjusted rubles and does not take into account the incidence of the
revaluation for profits and interest.

The initial and revised depreciation charges figuring in the foregoing
calculations are as follows (in billions of rubles):

YEAR	INITIAL	REVISED
1937	5.8	11.6
1940	13.0	18.4
1944	11.0	18.4
1948	14.0	24.5

As was explained earlier (p. 44), our initial depreciation charges for
1940, 1944, and 1948 are more comprehensive than that for 1937. This
partly explains the lower ratio of revised charge to initial charge for
the later years.

The reader will be allowed to speculate on his own as to the possible
effects on our accounts of changes in the relation of wage differentials
to productivity and Disutility that may have occurred in the years

[28] Pages 81–82.

studied. So far as concerns the changes in the relation between farm
and nonfarm incomes, we show in Table 12 the results of a revaluation
for this aspect. In the revaluation, we take the 1937 relation as a norm
and for subsequent years revalue farm procurements so as to yield
values for farm services more or less in accord with this standard. The
revaluation of procurements leads in turn to a revaluation of use categories utilizing farm goods.

Since farm and nonfarm earnings in 1944 are already nearly in accord
with the 1937 relation (due in part to the valuation of farm income in
kind at 1940 prices), no revaluation was made for this year. For 1940,
a reduction in procurement values of 25 percent yields approximately
the required change in farm income, while for 1948 an increase in farm
procurement prices of about the same magnitude seems to be indicated.
The rule-of-thumb procedure adopted to allocate this increase by use
categories may well understate the incidence on the shares of investment and defense in the gross national product.[29]

In Table 12 we show for the revaluation of farm services, as for other
adjustments previously considered, the incidence on defense services
as well as on investment. The 1937 relation of farm to nonfarm earnings
is taken as a norm throughout.

Insofar as the turnover tax in some part represents agricultural rent,
the complete elimination of this tax in our calculation of national
income in adjusted rubles tends to lead to an undervaluation of farm
services for 1937 as well as for later years. Furthermore, in the calculations just made the 1937 relation of farm to nonfarm earnings is taken
as a norm, and this is obviously arbitrary. These calculations indicate,
however, that further revaluations of farm services for these factors are
likely to have only a very limited effect.

In Table 12 we show, in addition to the foregoing, the results of a
revaluation of military services. As in the case of farm income, the
revaluation involves use of the 1937 relation to the earnings of hired
civilian workers as a norm.

[29] In more detail, we allow for the indicated changes in procurement prices, for
changes in state and cooperative retail prices due to the changes in procurement costs,
for proportional changes in collective farm market prices, for changes in income in kind
reflecting the changes in realized farm prices, and for changes in all other use categories
reflecting the changes in procurement costs. Farm earnings change as a result of the
changes in procurement values, collective farm market prices, and the value of income
in kind.

While farm procurement prices vary for different types of procurements, through the use of turnover taxes, prices to processors are made more or less uniform. In adjusting for turnover taxes, then, it might seem that we are again left with multiple prices, and consequently with a distortion in the relation of prices to Adjusted Factor Cost. This, however, is not the case. In adjusting for the turnover tax it was hardly possible to take account of the variation in the tax in dependence on the type of procurement. Accordingly, except by chance the deduction of the tax should leave the prices to processors no less uniform than they were to begin with.

While the prices of agricultural products to processors are made uniform by the use of taxes, the government levies no taxes on grain and possibly other products going into stockpiles. In the case of agricultural commodities, this probably means that they are valued in stockpiles at the very low obligatory delivery prices established for such goods. There is, therefore, an undervaluation of gross investment in our accounts to the extent that stockpile increments are included in this outlay category. The possible magnitude of this undervaluation may be appraised in the light of the magnitude of stockpiling outlays: in 1940, possibly some 2 billion rubles, or about one-half of one percent of the gross national product; in 1944, probably none to speak of; in 1948, perhaps as large a share of the national product as in 1940, if not larger.[30]

In the calculation in terms of adjusted rubles summarized in Table 11, we already have allowed for two other cases of multiple prices in the USSR: differences between collective farm market and state and cooperative retail shop prices and, during the war, differences between ration and "commercial shop" prices.

Each of the revaluations in Table 12 takes as a starting point our tabulation of national income in adjusted rubles. Accordingly, the summation of the various adjustments in the final column in the table is not entirely meaningful. On the other hand, the end result of a cumulative revaluation for the features covered in the table, together with the one needed for stockpiles, clearly would be to raise the share of gross investment in all years and also of defense in all years, with the possible exception of 1948. In that year the revaluation of military

[30] See Appendix B, pp. 204 ff.

services probably more than offsets the other adjustments suggested. In the case of gross investment, however, the increase for any one year probably would be limited to two or three percentage points. For defense, the increase might be of this order in 1940 and somewhat greater in 1944.

In the foregoing calculations we have concentrated on the incidence of the various revaluations on *gross* investment and defense. It may be of interest to append at this point corresponding figures derived in *Soviet National Income* for the incidence of certain of the revaluations on *net* investment in 1937:

	NET INVESTMENT, PERCENT OF NET NATIONAL PRODUCT
(i) Adjusted rubles	20.8
(ii) Adjusted for 8 percent return on fixed capital	+1.6
(iii) Allowance for increase in depreciation charge from 5.8 to 11.6 billion rubles	−1.8

It will readily be seen that while the increase in depreciation raises gross investment, it must have a contrary effect on net investment.

In *Soviet National Income,* priority was given to the tabulation of national income in adjusted rubles as a provisional representation of Adjusted Factor Cost. This was done because of the relatively nebulous character of the revaluations for profits, interest, depreciation, and the like. This consideration has if anything even more force in the years now studied, and accordingly we continue to give priority to the calculation in adjusted rubles. The reader is asked to bear in mind, however, that these figures are subject to the deficiencies noted. On balance they tend to understate gross investment and for the most part also defense. Furthermore, it may be advisable to recall here certain other shortcomings in our calculations which were referred to in Chapter II: the inclusion in consumption, rather than in investment, of farm household investment in kind, and the omission from investment of private investment in housing construction.

IV. ECONOMIC IMPLICATIONS

INTRODUCTION

It REMAINS to consider some economic implications of our calculations. Our discussion falls under three main headings to be referred to in turn: prices and finance; trends in Soviet resource allocation; and Soviet versus United States resource allocation.

PRICES AND FINANCE

Sources of finance. In Table 13 we recapitulate in summary terms the data previously compiled in Table 4, pp. 22 ff. Total income, however, is understood now to represent the total charges accruing to government and social and economic organizations *prior* to the deduction of subsidized losses. Previously we deducted this latter item. Also, as initially compiled, Table 4 showed only the total charges of any particular type, without regard to the ultimate payer. In Table 13 we show not only such totals but also the amounts paid ultimately by households alone. In the case of the charges to economic organizations for special funds, turnover taxes, and miscellaneous indirect taxes, the payments by households are supposed to represent the charges included directly or indirectly in the retail value of consumers' goods.

On this basis, Table 13 shows at a glance the structure of revenues drawn on by the government and social and economic organizations to finance all the various activities the costs of which were not covered immediately by market sales to households—i.e., social and cultural projects, government administration, internal security and defense, capital investments, subsidies, and pensions and the like paid to households. Insofar as the revenues are derived ultimately from households, they represent at the same time the diverse offsets that the government relied on to absorb the purchasing power created by these very same activities. The purchasing power, of course, had to be absorbed in one way or another.

TABLE 13

SOURCES OF SOVIET FINANCE, 1937, 1940, 1944, AND 1948[a]

A. In Billions of Rubles

ITEM	ALL PAYERS				HOUSEHOLDS ONLY			
	1937	1940	1944	1948	1937	1940	1944	1948
1. Net income of economic organizations	21.6	36.9	33.1	49.1	n.a.[b]	n.a.	n.a.	n.a.
2. Charges to economic organizations for social insurance and other special funds	8.8	11.2	10.8	19.3	3.6	4.3	2.8	6.6
3. Turnover tax	75.9	105.9	94.9	247.5	61.1	88.0	76.9	199.1
4. Miscellaneous indirect taxes	2.7	5.5	11.4	17.3	1.3	2.5	3.3	6.7
5. Custom duties; government receipts from sale of Lend-Lease, reparations	1.3	2.9	24.0	16.5	n.a.	n.a.	n.a.	n.a.
6. Depreciation	5.8	13.0	11.0	14.0	n.a.	n.a.	n.a.	n.a.
7. Net household savings	5.4	8.4	45.6	23.1	5.4	8.4	45.6	23.1
8. Direct taxes	4.0	10.8	48.8	37.5	4.0	10.8	48.8	37.5
9. Total income	125.5	194.6	279.6	424.3	75.4[c]	114.0[c]	177.4[c]	273.0[c]

B. In Percent of Total Income

ITEM	ALL PAYERS				HOUSEHOLDS ONLY			
	1937	1940	1944	1948	1937	1940	1944	1948
1. Net income of economic organizations	17.2	19.0	11.8	11.6	n.a.[b]	n.a.	n.a.	n.a.
2. Charges to economic organizations for social insurance and other special funds	7.0	5.8	3.9	4.6	4.8	3.8	1.6	2.4
3. Turnover tax	60.5	54.4	33.9	58.3	81.0	77.2	43.3	72.9
4. Miscellaneous indirect taxes	2.2	2.8	4.1	4.1	1.7	2.2	1.9	2.5
5. Custom duties; government receipts from sale of Lend-Lease, reparations	1.0	1.5	8.6	3.9	n.a.	n.a.	n.a.	n.a.
6. Depreciation	4.6	6.7	3.9	3.3	n.a.	n.a.	n.a.	n.a.
7. Net household savings	4.3	4.3	16.3	5.4	7.2	7.4	25.7	8.5
8. Direct taxes	3.2	5.6	17.5	8.8	5.3	9.5	27.5	13.7
9. Total income	100.0	100.0	100.0	100.0	100.0[c]	100.0[c]	100.0[c]	100.0[c]

[a] Basic data are taken from Tables 4 and 8. The share of the total charges for special funds that falls on households is taken to be the same as the share of consumption, exclusive of income in kind, in the gross national product, both consumption and the gross national product being expressed in adjusted rubles. With minor reservations, the share of miscellaneous indirect taxes falling on households is determined in the same way. Minor discrepancies between sums of individual items and specified totals are due to rounding.

[b] n.a. = not available.

[c] Represents sum of items for which data are cited.

The chief charge throughout, from both these standpoints, was the turnover tax, but other charges were important, and there are notable variations in the course of time. In the years 1937 and 1940 the turnover tax provided about three-fifths of the total revenue from all payers. The profits of economic enterprises, including both amounts paid into the budget and amounts retained, provided almost another fifth, while household savings and direct taxes represented 7.5 percent of the total revenue in 1937 and 9.9 percent in 1940.

As might be expected in view of the sharp curtailment in supplies of consumers' goods and the government's concern to hold the line on ration prices, the turnover tax suffered a major decline as a source of income during the war: in 1944 it provided but one-third of the total revenue from all payers. Profits too declined somewhat, the slack being taken up to a great extent by household savings and direct taxes. In 1944 these together matched the turnover tax as a source of Soviet finance.

In 1948 the supplies of consumers' goods were more abundant than during the war, but still relatively limited in comparison with prewar conditions. The government had restored the open market in December of the previous year, however, and in this connection it apparently found it expedient to reestablish turnover taxes in their prewar position. In 1948 these again constituted about three-fifths of the total revenue from all sources. Profits were a somewhat smaller share and household savings and direct taxes a somewhat larger one than before the war.

We have been citing here figures on the charges levied on all payers. So far as concerns the structure of charges ultimately paid by households alone, the trends over the years considered (as far as they may be ascertained from available data) were broadly similar. Interestingly, however, savings and direct taxes together in 1944 appreciably exceed turnover taxes when reference is made to the sums paid by households only.

The net savings in Table 13, it will be recalled, include additions to cash holdings. In the 1937 income study, these additions were assumed to be quite small.[1] We have taken them to be zero for the years now

---

[1] *Soviet National Income*, p. 111.

studied other than for 1944. In this latter year additions to cash holdings are estimated to be some 15 billion rubles.

The absence of any accumulation of cash balances means that excess
purchasing power was fully absorbed by fiscal devices such as taxes,
bond drives, etc., and this, one might suppose, would mean in turn that
something of a balance was achieved in the consumers' goods market,
in the sense that supplies in state and cooperative retail shops were
adequate to meet demand at established prices. This, however, is not
necessarily the case. A shortage in state and cooperative shops would
lead to the bidding up of prices in the collective farm market, with
the possibility that the resultant high farm incomes might be absorbed
through taxes and bond sales. Shortages would then prevail in the consumers' goods market without leading to any accumulation of excess
cash in the hands of the households. Considering the sizable margin
between collective farm market and state and cooperative retail shop
prices in 1940, our assumption that there was no change in cash balances
in that year would have to be understood in this light. Possibly, however, this belief is in error. Since prices in the two markets were more
or less proximate in 1937 and probably differed only to a limited extent
in 1948, there seemingly is no corresponding basis to question the
stated views on cash holdings in these years. The assumption of a sizable increment in hoards in 1944 is, of course, entirely consistent with
the comprehensive rationing and acute shortages of that year.[2]

Household tax burden. The question is sometimes raised as to the
burden of taxes on Soviet households. On the basis of Table 13 and other
data at hand,[3] we have compiled the following alternative measures
of this item:

	1937	1940	1944	1948
1. Total of charges for special funds, turnover taxes, miscellaneous indirect taxes and direct taxes, less subsidies, as percent of household income	34.1	32.2	36.6	44.3
2. Total of foregoing charges plus net bond purchases as percent of household income	35.6	34.7	44.2	48.2

[2] On the organization and operation of the consumers' goods market in the years
considered, see *ibid.*, pp. 63 ff., and the present study, above, pp. 12 ff.

[3] The underlying figures on subsidies are from Table 9.

We have calculated the tax burden here inclusive as well as exclusive of net bond purchases in view of the semicompulsory nature of these outlays. Under Soviet conditions still other concepts could no doubt be defended. Thus there probably is something to say for considering bookkeeping profits as an indirect tax rather than, as we have done above, as a factor charge, in which case the tax burden would be correspondingly increased. On the other hand, as has been previously explained, the turnover tax in some measure has the character of agricultural rent, and in any case an allowance might plausibly be made at this point for the absence under the *khozraschet* system of any explicit charge either for the latter item or for interest on fixed capital. With this allowance the tax burden would be reduced.

At a later point we refer to calculations of the national product and its components that we have made in terms of adjusted rubles. These calculations are intended to provide a basis on which to appraise resource allocation. By way of comment on the figures just cited on the household tax burden, it may suffice merely to call attention to the fact that these figures, broadly speaking, are still another measure of resource allocation. With the exclusion of transfer receipts from household income and the addition to the balance of total profits and depreciation, the denominator of our fraction would measure the national product at factor cost. It will readily be seen that the numerator, inclusive of bond purchases, is more or less indicative of the amount of this product going to "nonconsumption," i.e., to communal services, government, defense, and investment. Hence the tax burden as computed measures, albeit rather imperfectly, the share of the national product at factor cost going to "nonconsumption."[4]

[4] By implication, our calculation of the tax burden assumes that custom duties and government revenue from the sale of Lend-Lease and reparations are a part of factor cost. If so, these charges should be included, together with earned household income, profits, and depreciation, in the measure of national product at factor cost. If they are considered as charges over and above factor cost, however, they must be added to the numerator of the fraction representing the tax burden fraction. This is necessary in order that the latter serve as a measure of "nonconsumption." Beyond this, a further addition must be made for savings other than bond purchases and for profits, none of which are distributed to households; while from the sum total of these items it is necessary to deduct all transfer receipts of households.

In a forthcoming article ("The Burden of Soviet Taxation"), F. D. Holzman makes several alternative calculations of the household tax burden in the USSR for the period

Volume of excess purchasing power. Our measures of the tax burden bear also on the magnitude of excess purchasing power created in the years studied; but on this latter item the somewhat different calculations shown below may be more illuminating:[5]

	1937	1940	1944	1948
Money incomes of households (bil. rubles)	153.9	239.5	273.3	445.9
Less: consumers' goods purchases at factor cost (bil. rubles)	87.1	138.8	112.6	201.0
Excess purchasing power (bil. rubles)	66.8	100.7	160.7	244.9
Excess purchasing power as percent of household money income	43.4	42.0	58.8	54.9

In contrast to the procedure followed in the calculation of the tax burden, it now seems in order to include contributions to special funds, such as social insurance, as an element in factor cost. But, needless to say, now as before, the determination of the scope of factor charges is in general rather arbitrary. It will be readily understood, too, that the difference between household money income and the value of consumers' goods at factor cost, however defined, has more the character of a statistical than a theoretic category.[6] But it is of interest nonetheless, as a testimonial to the extreme inflationary pres-

---

of the five year plans. For the three years, 1937, 1940, and 1948, for which our own calculations overlap his, the results differ considerably. There are only limited differences in estimates of the various elements in the calculation; the divergence arises chiefly because of differences in methodology. Most importantly, in the absence of data on income in kind, Holzman relates the amount of taxes paid by households to household money income; instead, we have related the amount of taxes to total household income, including income in kind. Also, Holzman includes profits as a tax, whereas we treat this category as a factor charge. The writers are grateful to Dr. Holzman for permission to refer to his article prior to publication.

[5] The figures on household money income are calculated from Table 3. Consumers' goods purchases at factor cost represent consumers' goods at retail less turnover and miscellaneous indirect taxes plus subsidies. Data on the share of turnover taxes and subsidies falling on consumers' goods purchases are from Appendix Tables 37 and 39. These figures, it should be noted, differ somewhat from the corresponding ones in Table 13, since the former exclude, while the latter include, turnover taxes and subsidies on army subsistence. In the case of miscellaneous taxes, however, we use the same figures as appear in Table 13.

[6] From a theoretic standpoint, interest presumably attaches chiefly to the excess over factor cost of effective demand at prices equaling factor cost. This differs from excess purchasing power as computed by the amount of savings desired by households when prices equal factor cost. These savings in turn differ from the amount actually realized (Table 13), insofar as the latter, on the one hand, reflect a different price level and, on the other, include involuntary savings.

sures under the five year plans, that the computed excess purchasing power in the years 1937 and 1940 exceeds two-fifths of money income. In 1944 it amounts to nearly three-fifths. After the war the proportion declines, but in 1948 it still is far above the prewar level: 55 percent.

Scope of the budget. Table 13 includes revenues retained by nongovernmental organizations as well as revenues entering the government budget. The following data on the division of the total between these two sectors may be of interest.[7]

	SHARE IN TOTAL FINANCE, PERCENT		
YEAR	*Government*	*Nongovernment*	*Total*
1937	84.1	15.9	100.0
1940	85.5	14.5	100.0
1944	86.9	13.1	100.0
1948	91.6	8.4	100.0

In various connections, interest also attaches to the relation of the government budget to the national income. Percentage data on this matter are tabulated below, along with corresponding figures for the United States, compiled from calculations of the Department of Commerce:

YEAR	USSR[8]	USA[9]
1937	36.7	17.1
1940	38.4	17.6
1944	54.7	24.2
1948	49.9	23.1

The percentages, to be precise, represent the relation of total government budget revenue to the gross national product. In the case of the USSR, the gross national product is in established rubles. State and local as well as Federal government revenues are included in the total government revenue for the United States.

Considering the predominance of government ownership, it may seem surprising that the government budget in the USSR is not larger

[7] Compiled from data in Table 4.

[8] Calculated from Tables 5 and 7.

[9] Calculated from data in United States Department of Commerce, *National Income, 1951 Edition,* pp. 150, 154.

in relation to the gross national product than is shown here. As was explained in *Soviet National Income*,[10] however, this relation has to be read in the light of several factors: (i) under the *khozraschet* system the state enterprise is divorced from the government budget and operates financially more or less on its own; (ii) under collectivization Soviet agriculture also operates on an independent financial basis; (iii) this is also true of cooperatives; and (iv) a sizable amount of the gross national product consisting of income in kind is consumed by the households producing it.

While the budget is smaller in relation to the gross national product than is sometimes supposed, it is still far larger than that in the United States. Also, it increased during the war and, while the wartime peak has not been maintained, the postwar level remains relatively high. Interestingly, the Soviet and American experience during and since the war are broadly parallel.

The Russians often make comparisons between the Soviet Union and the United States regarding the share of defense expenditures in government budget outlays. Considering the difference in scope of the Soviet and American government budgets, the comparison obviously tends to minimize Soviet defense expenditures in comparison with our own.

Price formation. The data that have been compiled in this study provide a partial basis on which to appraise a significant aspect of Soviet price formation, namely, the relative importance of different elements in prices. To refer to an outstanding element, we present in Table 14 some information on the role of the turnover tax. More particularly, we cite data on the following: (i) The ratio of the total turnover tax yield to the gross national product in established prices. This indicates the status of the tax as an element in prices generally. (ii) The ratio of the total turnover tax yield to the total value at established prices of taxed components of the gross national product, i.e., the gross national product less services, income in kind, and the like. This indicates the status of the tax as an element in the prices of taxed goods. (iii) The ratio of turnover taxes levied directly or indirectly on consumers' goods sold at retail to the total volume of retail trade in

[10] Page 93.

state and cooperative shops. This indicates the role of the tax in consumers' goods prices.

Evidently the turnover tax represents throughout a major element in prices. In the case of retail prices, it constitutes in all years more than half of the final selling value, inclusive of the tax.

TABLE 14

THE TURNOVER TAX AS AN ELEMENT IN SOVIET PRICES,
1937, 1940, 1944, AND 1948

YEAR	TOTAL TAX RECEIPTS AS PERCENT OF GROSS NATIONAL PRODUCT[a]	TOTAL TAX RECEIPTS AS PERCENT OF TAXED SHARE OF GROSS NATIONAL PRODUCT[b]	TAXES ON GOODS SOLD AT RETAIL AS PERCENT OF STATE AND COOPERATIVE RETAIL TRADE[c]
1937	26.0	35.1	53.8
1940	23.1	32.7	52.5
1944	19.5	29.2	59.7
1948	30.5	42.1	62.5

[a] From Tables 4 and 5.
[b] See *Soviet National Income,* p. 137; in this study, see below, p. 217.
[c] *Ibid.,* p. 136; in this study, see below, p. 218.

The increase shown in the share of the turnover tax in retail prices from 1940 to 1944 may seem in conflict with indications that the government held the line on retail prices during the war. The increase probably is to be understood, however, in terms of (i) the fact that retail prices were raised somewhat in the period 1940–41; (ii) the fact that during the war the government held the line on ration prices but permitted "commercial shop" prices more or less to find their own level;[11] and (iii) the increased share in total retail trade of grain products, which are subject to relatively heavy taxes.

A further increase in the share of the turnover tax in retail prices occurs from 1944 to 1948, with the result that the 1948 share is appreciably above the prewar amount. This appears to fit in with the increases in consumers' goods prices which paved the way for the restoration of

[11] See above, pp. 12 ff., and below, p. 227.

the open market in December, 1947. The increases in prices were sizable, however, and accordingly would have to be explained largely in terms of changes in elements in prices other than the turnover tax, especially wages. In Moscow in January, 1948, food prices were more than three times higher than the January, 1939, level.[12]

The more significant variations shown in Table 14 in the relation of the turnover tax to the gross national product and to the taxed share of the national product may readily be understood in terms of the changes just referred to in the share of the tax in retail prices and the changes in the share of consumers' goods in the national product. The latter changes will be discussed in a moment.

Another element of special interest in Soviet prices is subsidies. According to the estimates that have been compiled here, these were of relatively limited importance in prices generally immediately before and during the war, their share in the gross national product in established prices amounting to but 2.7 percent in 1937, 3.1 percent in 1940, and 3.3 percent in 1944. The corresponding figure for 1948, however, was appreciably greater: 6.5 percent. The share of subsidies in the prices of fixed capital goods was sizable even in the earlier period: 5.0 percent in 1937, 6.2 percent in 1940, and 6.5 percent in 1944. But in the year 1948 the share of subsidies in the prices of such products came to the impressive total of 22.7 percent.

The rationale of subsidies in the Soviet planned economy, particularly as to why the Russians trouble with this device as an alternative to raising prices to cover costs, is an interesting question on which it does not seem possible to embark here. But it may be in order to recall that there were major changes in policy on this matter both before and after the period that we are studying, as well as during it. Subsidies were a major factor in prices in the early thirties, but the government greatly curtailed their role by a price reform in April, 1936. According to our calculations, subsidies again became important after the war, and indeed were allowed to rise to unprecedented levels. By a price reform in January, 1949, however, the volume of subsidy payments was once more greatly reduced.

[12] I. B. Kravis and J. Mintzes, "Food Prices in the Soviet Union, 1936–50," *Review of Economics and Statistics,* May, 1950.

TRENDS IN SOVIET RESOURCE ALLOCATION

Prewar allocation. Our calculations in adjusted rubles (Table 11, pp. 70–71; Chart 2, p. 92) provide a basis on which to appraise the interesting question of the degree to which the Russians mobilized before the German attack. Apparently this mobilization was on a sizable scale. In the period 1937–40 the government doubled the share of defense in total resource input. In the latter year this reached the respectable total of nearly 16 percent.

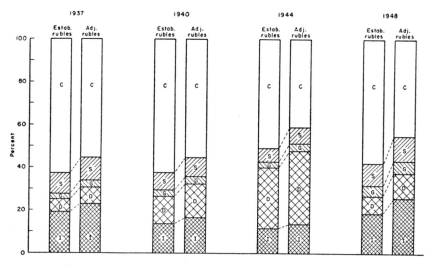

CHART 2. DISPOSITION OF THE GROSS NATIONAL PRODUCT OF THE USSR IN ESTABLISHED AND ADJUSTED RUBLES (IN PERCENT), 1937, 1940, 1944, AND 1948

C: household consumption; S: communal services; G: governmental administration; D: defense; I: gross investment

According to the data in adjusted rubles (Table 11), the share of resources going to civilian consumption hardly declined in the period 1937–40. Civilian consumption in these terms, however, is inflated somewhat in 1940 by various factors, particularly the overvaluation of farm services. Allowing for this, along the lines of Table 12, p. 000, the share of civilian consumption in 1940 amounts to 51.1 percent, which may be compared with the 54.9 percent allotted to this sector in 1937. Possibly the actual decline was still greater. To a limited extent, therefore, the increase in military expenditures was accomplished at the expense of consumption.

The increase in military expenditures, however, came also, and in good part, from investment. According to the calculations in adjusted rubles, the share of investment in the total resources allocated declined almost as much as the share of defense increased.

In view of familiar facts about Soviet economic policy, particularly the priority generally given to investment, this pattern of mobilization may seem surprising. A more plausible course, it might be supposed, would have involved the financing of mobilization primarily out of consumption. Without questioning the prevalent impression regarding the general nature of Soviet economic policy, however, it is believed that the pattern revealed might be understood in these terms: (i) A more sizable cut in the share of civilian consumption might have been politically awkward in conditions short of war. (ii) Given the limited development of consumers' durables in the USSR, rapid shifts between investment and defense may have been more feasible economically than rapid shifts between consumption and defense. (iii) The defense build-up was concurrent with the annexation of large areas, with an economic structure weighted relatively heavily in the direction of consumption.

Wartime allocation. According to the calculations in adjusted rubles (Table 11), the share of defense in the total resources allocated rose to 34 percent in 1944. As has been explained, this is probably an understatement. If account is taken of various deficiencies in ruble pricing beyond those considered in the adjusted ruble calculation, the share of defense in 1944 might be several points greater, say 38 percent (Table 12, p. 76). In the light of generally known facts about the Russian war effort, this may still appear to indicate an implausibly limited degree of mobilization. But for purposes of appraising the Russian war effort there is much to be said for coupling with defense outlays the sizable investments, which in 1944 must have been almost exclusively in support of defense activities. From this standpoint, then, the war effort absorbed a full half of the total resource input.

Evidently, the wartime increase in the share of resources going to defense was primarily at the expense of consumption rather than

investment. This reverses the pattern of the period 1937–40. This particular development, however, hardly calls for any special explanation.

Postwar allocation. A recurring question regarding the USSR
concerns the extent of that country's demobilization after the war.
So far as the share of resources going to defense is concerned, our
calculations show a considerable decline after the war but to a level
that was still notably high even by Russia's own peacetime standards.
Referring again to the data in adjusted rubles (Table 11, pp. 70–71),
the share of the total resource input going to defense was about 12
percent in 1948. This is far below the corresponding figure for 1944,
34 percent, but in peacetime it was only exceeded in the years immediately preceding the Nazi attack. The allocation to defense came to 8
percent in 1937 and to 16 percent in 1940.

Closely related to the question of the scale of Russia's demobilization
after the war is that concerning the allocation of the resources thus
freed as between investment and consumption. According to the
calculations in adjusted rubles, the shares of both consumption and
investment increased, but the latter to a greater extent. As a result,
the share of consumption in the total resource input in 1948 was still
well below that of 1940. On the other hand, the share of investment
in 1948, some 25 percent, far exceeded that of 1940 and was somewhat
greater than that of 1937.

This pattern of demobilization, like that of the pre-1941 mobilization,
presumably is to be understood in part in terms of the opportunities
for economical substitutions in the USSR being greater between defense
and investment goods production than between defense and consumers'
goods production. But the prompt reestablishment of the high investment rate of the prewar five year plans no doubt was also very much
a matter of policy. Considering the extreme privation of the Russian
civilian in wartime, the policy applied apparently was essentially the
same as that of the prewar five year plans. In the period up to 1948
at any rate, first consideration was given, as before the war, to the
expansion of over-all economic potential as distinct from current
consumption.[13]

[13] We are repeating here a conclusion reached on the basis of somewhat different
evidence in A. Bergson, "The Fourth Five Year Plan: Heavy versus Consumers' Goods
Industries," *Political Science Quarterly,* June, 1947.

Internal security. In Table 11 we combine outlays for government administration and the NKVD (MVD-MGB). In terms of adjusted rubles, the outlays for each of these two categories, taken separately, were as follows in the years studied:

YEAR	GOVERNMENT ADMINISTRATION		NKVD (MVD-MGB)	
	Billion rubles	*Percent of gross national product*	*Billion rubles*	*Percent of gross national product*
1937	4.1	1.8	2.8	1.3
1940	6.4	1.8	6.8	1.9
1944	7.5	1.8	6.6	1.6
1948	12.3	2.0	24.1	3.9

The NKVD outlays in 1937 evidently were somewhat less than those for government administration. In 1940 and 1944 the expenditures for these two categories were more or less comparable, whereas by 1948 there had been a marked expansion of NKVD to a level far exceeding government administration. The precise reasons for this increase in outlays from 1944 to 1948 are conjectural. Most of the gain is believed to have occurred in the years 1946 and 1947. Accordingly, it may represent simply a transfer of some military functions from the armed forces to the security ministries or an assignment to the security ministries of significant new civilian functions. For example, it is rumored that the NKVD takes a very active part in the Soviet atomic energy program. But one inevitably wonders whether there may not also be here a commentary on the postwar tensions resulting from such factors as the Soviet postwar economic policy on resource allocations just described, the return of Red Army men who had been in contact with the West, and the like.

Trends in "real" national product components. As has been explained, revaluation at Adjusted Factor Cost does not yield any measures of the changes over time in the "real" national product and its components. For this it is necessary to value national income in constant prices. On the other hand, our calculations do measure resource allocation and it may be shown that, given also data on the changes over time in the aggregate "real" national product, the changes over time in the components of the "real" national product can be determined as well. However, this is so only if the relative productivities of resources producing different components are unchanged; insofar as relative productivities change, it is necessary to know their magnitude also.[14] On the variation in "real" national product in the years studied here, we have available only the guesses ventured in Chapter I, and trends in the relative productivities of resources producing different components are similarly conjectural. But it may be of interest, nevertheless, to indicate the resultant implications regarding the trends in the components of "real" national income.

In Chapter I it was suggested that the "real" national product increased from 1937 to 1940, but by appreciably less than the officially claimed 33 percent. Assuming the actual increase was, say, 20 percent, and that there was no marked change one way or another in the relative productivity of resources in different sectors, "real" defense outlays in 1940 should have been nearly two and one-half times the 1937 level. Concomitantly, there was a limited decrease in "real" gross investment, say by one-seventh, and an increase of about the same order in aggregate civilian consumption. The "real" national product in 1944 was thought of in Chapter I as possibly being as much as one-

[14] Consider the following simple case, where labor is the only factor of production, where the wage rate is constant, and where accordingly the national income at Adjusted Factor Cost comes to the same thing as the wage bill, which in turn serves as a measure over time of total man-hours:

	OUTPUT AT CURRENT WAGE COST PER UNIT		"REAL" OUTPUT, I.E., OUTPUT AT YEAR 1 WAGE COST PER UNIT		OUTPUT PER UNIT OF LABOR, YEAR 1 = 100	
	Year 1	Year 2	Year 1	Year 2	Year 1	Year 2
Consumption	75	100	(75)	(125)	100	125
Defense	25	50	(25)	(75)	100	150
National product	100	150	100	200	100	133

For this example, what is contended is simply that given all the figures except those in parentheses one might determine the latter. That this is so is self-evident. If the money wage rate changed, the magnitude of this change might be determined from the comparative data on the national product in terms of base-year and given-year wage cost and on output per worker. On this basis, the figures on output in terms of current wage cost might be "deflated" for the change in the money wage rate, and then the figures in parentheses calculated as before. If the figures available initially on the "real" national product are in terms of constant prices rather than in terms of constant wage cost per unit, it is possible to proceed only insofar as the former may be supposed to approximate the latter.

fourth below that of 1940. Productivity in the defense industries must have increased greatly in comparison with that in other sectors after munitions production struck its gait during the war.[15] Under the priorities prevailing in war as in peace, however, the chief laggard presumably was consumption rather than investment. The implication is that "real" defense outlays by 1944 had increased by considerably more than three-fourths over 1940. "Real" gross investment in 1944 may have been on the order of one-third below the earlier year, while "real" civilian consumption may have been reduced at the same time by as much as one-half and possibly more. In the light of the supposition of Chapter I that the "real" national product of 1948 may have been on a par with that of 1940, we are inclined to think that "real" defense outlays in the later year were nearly as great as those in the earlier one. We assume here that the wartime gains in productivity were only partly lost with demobilization. "Real" gross investment in 1948 may have been half again as great as in 1940; civilian consumption, however, was still well below the prewar year.

The implication that civilian consumption increased, even if only to a limited extent, from 1937 to 1940, may again call in question our calculations on resource allocation for these years. In view of the evidences of growing shortages in the consumers' goods market, particularly the increasing gap between collective farm market and state and cooperative prices, one might have supposed that there was a decline. A limited increase, however, appears consistent with the data on the output of different consumers' goods in Table 2, pp. 9–10. Also, account has to be taken here of the 20 percent increase in population from 1937 to 1940, due mainly to the annexations. For per capita consumption, our calculations indicate a decline from 1937 to 1940.

We referred earlier to the possibility that our calculations on resource allocation for 1944 might tend to understate the magnitude of Russia's war effort. Given the implication just drawn that during the war there was a further vast increase in "real" defense outlays over and

---

[15] Thus there could hardly have been a parallel elsewhere to the gains in productivity reported in Voznesenskii, *Voennaia ekonomika SSSR . . . ,* pp. 114 ff., as having occurred in defense production. For a variety of armaments it is indicated that labor requirements declined by one-fifth to three-fourths in the years 1941 to 1943–44.

above that realized from 1937 to 1940, one might now be impelled to
the contrary notion. The wartime expansion, for example, appears
in direct conflict with the concomitant decrease in steel output from
18 to less than 12 million tons. The conflict probably could be resolved,
however, if allowance were made for the wartime decrease in investment, the probable increase in the "degree of fabrication" involved
in this shift from investment to defense, and, last but not least, Lend-
Lease imports.

SOVIET VERSUS UNITED STATES RESOURCE ALLOCATION

Comparative scope of Soviet and American national product categories.
In Table 15 are shown some data on the disposition of the United
States gross national product for the same years as have been studied
for the USSR. The data are taken mainly from United States Department of Commerce calculations, but they have been adjusted somewhat in order to make them more nearly comparable with those
that have been compiled here for the USSR. More particularly, we
have attempted to make possible comparisons on the following basis:

CATEGORY FOR UNITED STATES, IN TABLE 15	CATEGORY FOR USSR, IN TABLE 11
Consumption of households	Consumption of households
Government purchases of goods and services, etc.	Communal services; government administration, including NKVD
National security	Defense
Gross investment	Gross investment

On the other hand, the adjustment of United States data was only
very partial, and as a result the categories just paired are at best only
broadly comparable. To refer only to the main aspects:

In the USSR health care and education are distributed to the public
without charge to a relatively greater extent than in the United States.
For both countries, however, "Consumption of households" includes
only the amounts paid for, while the amounts distributed without
charge are included in "Government purchases . . ." in Table 15 and
in "Communal services" in Table 11. Accordingly, "Consumption of
households" tends to be more comprehensive in the United States than
in the USSR, while "Government purchases . . ." for the United States

TABLE 15

GROSS NATIONAL PRODUCT OF THE USA
BY USE, 1937, 1940, 1944, 1948[a]

ITEM	1937 BILLION DOLLARS	1937 PER-CENT	1940 BILLION DOLLARS	1940 PER-CENT	1944 BILLION DOLLARS	1944 PER-CENT	1948 BILLION DOLLARS	1948 PER-CENT
1. Consumption of households, including education and health care privately paid for	67.1	74.4	72.1	71.1	111.6	52.2	177.9	68.7
2. Government purchases of goods and services, including public education and health, and excluding defense and investment outlays classified below	7.3	8.1	8.1	8.0	8.0	3.7	15.7	6.1
3. National Security a. General	n.a.[b]	n.a.	n.a.	n.a.	n.a.	n.a.	11.1	4.3
b. Other national security, including foreign economic assistance	n.a.	n.a.	n.a.	n.a.	n.a.	n.a.	4.4	1.7
c. Total	1.0	1.1	2.2	2.2	82.8	38.7	15.5	6.0
4. Gross investment	14.8	16.4	19.0	18.7	11.3	5.3	50.0	19.3
5. Gross national product	90.2	100.0	101.4	100.0	213.7	100.0	259.0	100.0

[a] Minor discrepancies between indicated totals and sums of specified items are due to rounding. For the most part, the data in the table are obtained from United States Department of Commerce, *National Income, 1951 Edition*. The sources and methods in more detail are as follows:

1. Consumption of households, including education and health care privately paid for. This is "Personal consumption expenditures" in *ibid.*, p. 150.

2. Government purchases of goods and services, including public education and health, and excluding defense and investment outlays classified below. This is the end result of the following calculation (all figures in billions of dollars):

	1937	1940	1944	1948
"Government purchases of goods and services," in *ibid.*, p. 150	11.6	13.9	96.5	36.6
Less: "National security" as computed below	1.0	2.2	82.8	15.5
Less: "New public construction activity" other than "Military and Naval," in *ibid.*, pp. 198–99	3.1	3.2	2.2	4.7
Less: Government purchases of producers' durable equipment, according to tentative independent estimates	.2	.4	3.5	.7
Less: Total deductions	4.3	5.8	88.5	20.9
Equals: "Government purchases . . . " in Table 19	7.3	8.1	8.0	15.7

The cited estimates of government purchases of producers' durable equipment are meant to be exclusive of various items of transport equipment but are supposed to include federally financed wartime purchases of durable equipment for private use, such as war production, provided that the government retained title.

3. *National security.* This is obtained by the following calculation (all figures are in billions of dollars):

	1937	1940	1944	1948
For 1940 and 1944, "Government purchases of goods and services: Federal: War," in United States Department of Commerce, *National Income, 1951 Edition,* p. 150; for 1937, an estimate of corresponding outlays based on data in United States Bureau of the Census, *Statistical Abstract of the United States: 1952,* p. 306; for 1948, Federal "National security" purchases, in *Survey of Current Business,* July, 1952, pp. 12–13	1.0	2.2	88.6	16.1
Less: Government sales of goods and services, from United States Department of Commerce, *National Income, 1951 Edition,* p. 155	. . .*	. . .	1.1	.6
Less: Federal purchases of producers' durable equipment for war production, assuming all purchases of such equipment as previously estimated were for war production in 1944 and none in other years	. . .	. . .	3.5	. . .
Less: New public construction, industrial, for military purposes, assuming only the industrial construction listed in *ibid.*, p. 199, for 1944 was primarily for war purposes	. . .	. . .	1.2	. . .
Equals: "National security" in Table 19	1.0	2.2	82.8	15.5

In the *Survey of Current Business,* July, 1952, pp. 12–13, where we obtained the figure cited for 1948 in the first row of the foregoing tabulation, it is explained that this magnitude represents "National security" purchases. This in turn represents the sum of

* . . . = negligible.

outlays under two general headings: (i) "National defense" purchases, comprising in addition to purchases of the Defense Department various other purchases, including those for foreign military assistance under the Mutual Defense Assistance Program, programs of defense production and economic stabilization, the Atomic Energy Commission, the Maritime Administration, and stockpiles of strategic and critical materials; and (ii) "Other national security" purchases, which include among other things purchases for the National Security Council, National Security Resources Board, State Department, and various foreign economic assistance programs. As appears from our tabulation, our "National security" outlays in 1948 correspond to the "National security" purchases as thus defined after deductions for (i) government sales, which were mainly war surplus; (ii) purchases of equipment for war production; and (iii) industrial public construction for war purposes.

For the years 1940 and 1944, our "National security" outlays correspond (after similar deductions) to "Government purchases of goods and services: Federal: War" as given in the United States Department of Commerce, *National Income, 1951 Edition*, p. 150. The Department of Commerce explains that it is observing here the classification in the *Daily Treasury Statement*, and it is believed that as thus derived the category in question is broadly comparable with the "National security" category it defines in the *Survey of Current Business*, July, 1952, and this apparently is the assumption in the latter source. Among other things, "Federal: War" purchases include purchases for atomic energy research, development and production, purchases of the Maritime Commission, and purchases under the Lend-Lease Act. On the other hand, purchases of foreign raw materials for stockpiles are excluded.

As computed, our "National security" figure for 1937 is more or less comparable in scope with those for 1940, 1944, and 1948.

As derived, "National security" outlays in Table 15 include in all years purchases of a sort classified in United States Department of Commerce, *National Income, 1951 Edition*, p. 198, as "New public construction activity: Military and Naval." This, it is believed, consists primarily of the construction of military and naval installations.

In Table 15, we give a breakdown of "National security" outlays for 1948 between "General" and "Other national security . . . ." This corresponds to the breakdown between "National Defense" and "Other National Security" in the *Survey of Current Business*, July, 1952, pp. 12–13, after the deduction of sales of war surplus.

4. *Gross investment.* This is obtained as the following summation (all figures in billions of dollars):

	1937	1940	1944	1948
"Gross private domestic investment," United States Department of Commerce, *National Income, 1951 Edition*, p. 150	11.4	13.9	7.7	42.7
"Net foreign investment," *ibid.*, p. 150	.1	1.5	(−)2.1	1.9
"New public construction activity," other than "Military and Naval," *ibid.*, p. 198	3.1	3.2	2.2	4.7
Federal purchases of producers' durable equipment, as previously derived	.2	.4	3.5	.7
Gross investment	14.8	19.0	11.3	50.0

b n.a. = information not available.

tends to be understated in comparison with the combination of "Communal services" and "Government administration, including NKVD" for the USSR. So far as the latter comparison is concerned, there is also a relative understatement of United States "Government services" because of the classification of various civilian governmental agencies, e.g., various economic stabilization agencies and the State Department, under "National security" in Table 15. The counterparts of such agencies in the USSR are under "Government administration." Furthermore, while the American counterparts of certain NKVD expenditures, e.g., ordinary police, fire protection, etc., are classified under "Government purchases . . . ," the American counterparts (to the extent that such exist) of the NKVD quasi-military activities are mainly under "National security." Finally, the Soviet "Communal services" may include some outlays on military (including atomic energy) research. For the United States, these are classified as "National security."

As with "Defense" for the USSR, "National security" for the United States is exclusive of defense plant construction and military pensions. On the other hand, the American "National security" category includes a number of items which may only be covered in part, if at all, in the Soviet category, "Defense," particularly: (i) atomic energy outlays, other than capital construction; (ii) the support of troops quartered abroad; (iii) paramilitary activities comparable with those of the NKVD; (iv) for 1948, and to some extent for earlier years, the increment in stockpiles of strategic and critical materials; (v) the operating cost of various civilian agencies concerned with security, such as the economic stabilization agencies and the State Department.

The United States "National security" category also includes during the war years Lend-Lease shipments of both civilian and military goods and, in the postwar period, foreign economic as well as military assistance. In the case of the USSR, a counterpart of these outlays is to be found in the receipts of Lend-Lease and reparations, but presumably these were classified only in part as "Defense."[16] In any event, in endeavoring to compare the American and Soviet defense outlays, some interest may attach to the breakdown of the American "National

[16] We leave it to the reader to consider the implications for our comparison of the Soviet methods of accounting for Lend-Lease and reparations that were described above, pp. 43, 63.

security" figure for 1948 which is given in Table 15. The "Other national security" consists mainly of foreign economic assistance.

"Gross investment" for the United States is an aggregate of United States Department of Commerce categories referring to private domestic investment, net foreign investment, public construction, including defense plant construction, and government purchases of producers' durable equipment. To this extent, this class of outlay is broadly comparable with the Soviet "Gross investment." Many of the omissions just referred to in the Soviet "Defense" category, however, would find their way into the Soviet "Gross investment." Beyond this, the Soviet "Gross investment" embraces a variety of quasi-investment activities, including prospecting, resettlement, conservation, etc. Some of these activities, e.g., conservation, are included in the American "Gross investment," but it is believed that others are not.[17] Accordingly, the Soviet category tends to be overstated in some measure in comparison with the American one.

Defense. As a share in the total resource input, American defense outlays apparently were still of very limited dimensions as late as 1940. By 1944 the share of national income going to defense, understood as "National security," was 38 percent. Allowing for differences in coverage between this and our Soviet category of "Defense," the defense share for the two countries was probably about the same in that year. On the other hand, our subsequent demobilization proceeded well beyond that of the USSR. In terms of the share in resource input, the American defense outlays in 1948 were at most but one-half of those of the USSR. Allowing for differences in coverage in the pertinent statistical categories, and omitting from defense our foreign economic assistance, the American outlays were only about one-third of those of the Soviet Union.[18]

[17] American "Gross investment" as computed includes conservation but apparently not prospecting and presumably there is no counterpart either for such activities as industrial resettlement. On the inclusion of quasi-investment activities in the Soviet category, see above, p. 48, and below, pp. 205 ff. On the scope of the American category in this regard, see the notes to Table 15, and United States Department of Commerce, *National Income 1951 Edition*, pp. 36, 198.

[18] Here and in the subsequent pages we take at face value, as measures of resource input, American market prices. An allowance for American indirect taxes would tend to raise somewhat American defense and investment expenditures and reduce those for consumption correspondingly. According to a very rough calculation, the reduction in

In the absence of information on the comparative productivity of resources in different sectors and of comparative "real" gross national product in the two countries, it is not possible to proceed from the foregoing comparison of the share of resources going to defense to a calculation of the comparative defense outlays in the two countries in "real" terms. In "real" terms, of course, our gross national product far exceeds the Russian. For this reason the "real" defense outlays corresponding to each percent of the country's total resource input in all outlay categories together must be appreciably greater in the United States than in Russia. But the Russians under their five year plans have systematically favored munitions industries with advanced technology, so the resources allocated to this sector probably are considerably more productive than are Soviet resources generally. In the United States, in contrast, there is little basis to suppose that the resources allocated to munitions are especially superior in efficiency; and perhaps some reason to think to the contrary. For this reason, the excess of American over Russian "real" defense outlays per one percent of total resource input in all outlay categories together might be much less than proportional to the excess of American over Russian "real" gross national product.

We have been referring here only to a comparison, in an economic sense, of the "real" magnitude of Soviet and American defense output. The reader should bear in mind that, if the concern is rather with comparative "fighting power" or "military worth" in some sense or other, the matter is still more complicated. Assuming that defense outlays in both countries could be valued in terms of the prices of either one, it would still remain to consider whether one country might not obtain more "fighting power" per dollar (or per ruble) of expenditure than the other. Using conventional economic valuation procedures, Soviet military personnel presumably would be valued at a rate in dollars per man far below those of the United States. This would allow for the difference in Soviet and American labor efficiency generally. Obviously, however, such a valuation might be quite misleading if the concern is to compare "fighting power." In the case of munitions, too,

---

the latter category might have amounted to about 2.5 percent of the national product in 1944, about 1 percent in 1948, and probably less than 1 percent in 1937 and 1940.

it is readily seen that there might be many sources of a disparity between comparative dollar outlays and comparative "fighting power" in the two countries: for example, the reported differences in policy regarding personnel safety devices and model change and variety. Then again, if the concern is with "fighting power" not in the abstract but in a particular geographic area, there are still other complexities to reckon with, such as differences in transportation requirements.

Investment. In terms of adjusted rubles, gross investment in the USSR in 1937 amounted to 23 percent of the gross national product. The corresponding figure for the United States in the same year was 16 percent (Table 15). As has already been noted, the Soviet government in expanding its allocations to defense in the period 1937–40 curtailed, at the same time, the allocations to investment. As a result the margin between Soviet and American investment rates apparently had been entirely dissipated by the latter year; if anything, the American rate was higher. In the war year 1944, however, the Russians maintained their allocations to investment to a markedly greater degree than we did. In the postwar year 1948 both countries seem to have surpassed their 1937 allocations to investment, but the Russians succeeded in maintaining their previous margin over this country. For the USSR, gross investment amounted to about 26 percent in 1948; for the United States, the corresponding figure was 19 percent.

Of the foregoing comparisons, those for 1940 and 1944 obviously have a special character. If one accordingly focuses instead on those for 1937 and 1948, our results apparently corroborate the general impression as to the relatively high priority the Russians have been giving to investment under their five year plans. In this connection, the margin might be appreciably greater if allowance were made for a number of special features of ruble pricing that are not taken into account in our adjusted ruble calculation (see Table 12, p. 76). Allowance for the greater scope of the Soviet category of "Gross investment," in comparison with the American category, however, has a contrary effect.

It remains to observe, however, that some doubts are raised about these findings, nevertheless, as a result of a study by Norman Kaplan. Referring to fixed capital alone, Kaplan finds that the rate of investment in the USSR in peacetime has been virtually identical with that in the

United States.[19] Needless to say, this is a surprising result, and a question seems in order as to the reliability of this comparison as well as our own. But accepting Kaplan's finding, the implication is that as regards investment the Russians have maintained a margin over us not in the key fixed capital sector but in other sectors, such as working capital, stockpiles, conservation, etc. On the face of it this is by no means out of the question, and in any case it is hardly possible that the large margin that we have found between the Soviet and American rates of aggregate investment could be due entirely to statistical error or incomparabilities. But, pending further inquiry into the investment components, the possibility of an overstatement of the margin between the Soviet and American aggregate investment rates cannot be ruled out.[20]

From some standpoints one might wish to consider not so much the

[19] N. Kaplan, "Capital Formation and Allocation," in A. Bergson (ed.), *Soviet Economic Growth,* pp. 38 ff.; Kaplan's figures on the rate of fixed-capital investment, which are in adjusted rubles, are derived from data on national income, taxes, and subsidies given in an unpublished preliminary version of the present study, and for some years also from figures on fixed capital investment in current rubles that are slightly different from those accepted by the present writers (see Appendix Table 37, pp. 218 ff.). But the comparable rates of investment indicated by our final results on national income, taxes, and subsidies and the investment data in current rubles accepted here are scarcely different from Kaplan's for all years except for 1948, and for 1948 the recomputed rate exceeds his by only 1.5 percent. This, of course, does not materially affect his conclusion concerning the comparative Soviet and American rates.

[20] It may be useful to recall again at this point that our comparisons between the Soviet Union and the United States bear directly only on resource allocation. This is also true of Kaplan's data. Accordingly, depending on the relative productivity of resources in the investment sector, the calculated investment rates for each country are consistent with very diverse relations between the volume of investment goods and the gross national product in "real" terms. On a priori grounds it might be supposed that the technical superiority of the United States over Russia would be especially pronounced in the production of investment goods, and accordingly that in comparison with the general level of productivity in all sectors productivity in the investment sector would be distinctly greater in the United States than in Russia. A recent study of comparative industrial labor productivity for late prewar years by W. Galenson ("Industrial Labor Productivity," in Bergson, *ibid.*) is, however, suggestive to the contrary. Although the American productivity is greater than the Soviet in all sectors, the margin of superiority generally is considerably less in the case of machinery and metals than in the case of consumers' goods, such as textiles, shoe manufacturing, and the like. These findings of Galenson relate to industrial labor productivity alone. For a systematic appraisal of the comparative productivity of resources as a whole as between investment and other sectors, it would also be necessary to have information on diverse other elements, including the productivity of labor in sectors other than industry and the distribution of indirect labor and capital between sectors. But we venture to think, nevertheless, that such an appraisal might disclose a relatively high rate of productivity of investment resources in the USSR compared with that of the United States. If so,

share of national income going to investment alone as that going to investment and defense together. As the figures tabulated below show, there has been a notably large gap between the Soviet Union and the United States in this regard in all the years studied:

	DEFENSE PLUS INVESTMENT, PERCENT OF GROSS NATIONAL PRODUCT			
	1937	*1940*	*1944*	*1948*
USSR	30.6	32.2	47.7	37.3
United States	17.5	20.9	44.0	25.3

there is a basis for a reinterpretation of the Soviet investment rate. The Soviet rate of investment in fixed capital may be only comparable with ours as a share of total resource input, but it may possibly be greater as a share of the national product in "real" terms. Insofar as the relative Soviet superiority in resource productivity might not prevail in the case of working capital, conservation, etc., the observed difference in the volume of investment in these activities, compared with that of fixed-capital investment in the two countries, also becomes more understandable. This difference becomes more a matter of resource allocation than of the allocation of the national product in "real" terms.

The stated view concerning the relative productivity of investment resources in the USSR and the United States, it may be noted, may help resolve a paradox to which Kaplan draws attention in his essay. The rate of fixed-capital investment in the USSR under the five year plans has been about the same as that in the United States not only for the same years but also for the post-Civil War period generally. Yet the rate of industrial growth in the USSR under the five year plans appears to have considerably exceeded that in the United States in the period since the Civil War. In trying to explain these conflicting findings, Kaplan refers mainly to data which he has assembled on the allocation of investment. These show a persistently larger share of investment going to industry in the Soviet Union than in the United States. This no doubt was a major factor, but it would seem pertinent, too, that the Soviet investment rate, if measured in terms not of resource input but of "real" product disposed of, might to begin with have exceeded the American investment rate.

Of course, Galenson's productivity data, mentioned above, bear on the relative productivity of investment resources in the USSR and the United States where reference for both countries is only to the late thirties. What must be of concern at this point, however, is for the USSR the entire five year plan period and for the United States the entire post-Civil War period. But because of the lack of national product calculations for other years, Kaplan was able to compile investment rates for the USSR for only two nonwar years, 1937 and 1948, so how the Soviet investment rate for earlier five year plan years, measured in any terms, compares with that in the United States is as yet conjectural. So far as concerns the comparison of relative investment resource productivities in the Soviet Union in the late thirties and in the United States in early years, presumably the margin of the former over the latter is greater than that where reference is to the late thirties for both countries.

In trying to understand the comparative Soviet and American rates of growth, still another factor to consider is the comparative stocks of capital in the two countries. From data compiled by Kaplan, Professor Domar (in Bergson, *ibid.*, pp. 88–89) has

Consumption. The corollary of the relatively large Russian allocations to investment and defense has been the relatively small allocations
to household consumption. According to Tables 11 and 15, the Soviet
share of consumption in total resource input is far below ours throughout. This comparison is somewhat unfavorable to the USSR in view of
the smaller coverage of education and health care in our household
consumption data for that country. Even if all such goods are added
to the Soviet household consumption in the USSR, however, the share
of the national product absorbed is still less than the American share
of household consumption alone.

---

computed that the capital coefficient for the Soviet economy as a whole, i.e., the ratio
of the stock of fixed capital to the national product, is around 1.4. This figure apparently applies to the late thirties, and may be compared with a coefficient of 2.5–3.0
obtained for the United States. Such a disparity, of course, means that even the same
rate of investment might yield a much higher rate of growth in the USSR than in the
United States. Domar suggests, however, that the computed coefficient for the USSR
is implausibly low. But here again it is necessary to have in mind a possibly high relative productivity of investment resources in the USSR. Given this, investment goods
prices and hence the stock of fixed capital in terms of such prices tend to be relatively low.

Incidentally, the data on the Soviet capital stock cited above, p. 74, n. 27, when
taken together with our figures on the gross national product in adjusted rubles in the
same year, yield for the year 1937 a capital coefficient almost identical with that obtained
by Domar: 1.45; and for the year 1948 an even lower coefficient: 1.13. Because of the
similarity in underlying sources, however, this correspondence cannot be considered
as much of a check.

But while the assumption of a Russian margin over the United States in relative
investment resource productivity appears illuminating in numerous respects, it remains
to observe that on this reasoning it becomes difficult to explain still another incongruity
to which attention was called in *Soviet National Income,* pp. 86 ff.: calculations of
Soviet national income in dollar terms by Colin Clark and Julius Wyler indicate a
much lower rate of aggregate investment than do those in adjusted rubles. In *Soviet
National Income* it was suggested that this might be due to a relatively low level of
investment goods prices in the United States compared with those in the Soviet Union.
The reasoning of the preceding paragraphs suggests the opposite.

To come back to the question of the comparative structure of aggregate investment
in the USSR and the United States, it should be noted that a difference might be
expected in the share of working capital in "real" terms as well as in terms of resource
input. As was indicated above, given the low ratio of the stock of fixed capital to the
national product in the USSR, a given rate of fixed-capital investment in "real" terms
means a high rate of growth of the national product. Presumably the rate of working
capital investment in "real" terms is in proportion not to the rate of fixed-capital investment in "real" terms but to the rate of growth of the national product.

The foregoing comments on the relation of Kaplan's findings to those of the present
study are in part the outgrowth of a discussion on this subject between one of the
writers and Mr. Richard Moorsteen.

APPENDICES

APPENDIX A: NOTES TO TABLE 3

A. INCOMES

1. NET INCOME OF HOUSEHOLDS FROM AGRICULTURE

1a. Wages of farm labor

These consist of the wages earned by agricultural workers outside of collective farms, i.e., in government-owned agricultural enterprises (such as state farms, MTS, etc.), and the wages paid to hired workers by collective farms. The calculations are as follows:

1940. The wages earned by agricultural workers outside of collective farms are taken to amount to 7.40 billion rubles. This is the product of (i) the average annual wage of such workers in 1940, taken as 2,863 rubles, and (ii) the number of such workers that year, estimated as 2.583 million. The wage figure is the average annual wage in agriculture envisaged for 1942 by the Third Five Year Plan. See Gosplan, *Tretii piatiletnii plan razvitiia narodnogo khoziaistva Soiuza SSR (1938–42 gg.) (proekt)*, pp. 228–29. We assume that this was achieved in 1940, since the average annual wage of the general labor force reached 4,069 rubles by then, as compared with the 1942 planned goal of 4,100. See A. Bergson, "A Problem in Soviet Statistics," *Review of Economic Statistics,* November, 1947, p. 236. The figure for the size of the agricultural labor force outside of collective farms is interpolated from data in the Third Five Year Plan. According to the plan, the "labor force in agriculture" (taken here to include all hired agricultural workers except those on collective farms) was to expand from 2,482,600 in 1937 to 2,650,000 in 1942. See Gosplan, *Tretii piatiletnii plan . . . ,* pp. 228–29. Interpolation between these figures to estimate employment in 1940 is more or less justified by Soviet data on the planned and actual growth during the same period in the general labor force. This was to increase, according to the Third Five Year Plan, from 27 million workers in 1937 to 32 million in 1942. Its actual size in 1940 is given variously as: 30.4 million in D. Degtiar, *Zabota sovetskogo gosudarstva ob uluchshenii material'nogo polozheniia trudiashchikhsia,* p. 15; and N. Kozev, *Sotsialisticheskaia sistema khoziaistva i ee prevoskhodstvo nad kapitalisticheskoi sistemoi khoziaistva,* p. 27; 31.2 million in N. A. Voznesenskii, *Voennaia ekonomika SSSR v period Otechestvennoi voiny,* p. 13; and 31.5 million at the end of the year in Gosplan and TSU, "Ob itogakh vypolneniia chetvertogo (pervogo poslevoennogo) piatiletnego

plana SSSR na 1946–1950 gody," *Voprosy ekonomiki,* No. 5, 1951, p. 12. It
should be noted that our estimate of 7.40 billion rubles as the total wages
paid to the labor force in agriculture in 1940 is higher than the 7.139 billion
rubles of wages of MTS and state farm workers projected for 1941 in the
1941 national economic plan. See *Gosudarstvennyi plan razvitiia narodnogo
khoziaistva SSSR na 1941 god,* p. 512. The two figures are not, however,
equally comprehensive: the 1941 plan does not seem to have covered certain
categories of agricultural specialists, agronomists, etc., which presumably
have been included in our estimate.

Referring now to wages paid to hired workers by collective farms, these are
taken as 5.69 percent of the wages earned by agricultural workers outside of
collective farms. This ratio is taken from Bergson's estimates for 1937.

1944. According to the foregoing calculations, the wages of farm labor
totaled 7.82 billion rubles in 1940. This amounts to 4.99 percent of the total
civilian wage bill of that year, which is estimated in Appendix Table 8, below,
at 156.87 billion rubles. For purposes of calculating the total farm wages for
1944, we assume that the corresponding percentage for that year was 4.00.
Since the total civilian wage bill for 1944 is estimated in Appendix Table 8
at 161.02 billion rubles, this yields a figure of 6.44 billion rubles for total farm
wages. The reason for assuming that the share of farm wages in total civilian
wages had declined in 1944, compared with 1940, is that MTS activities
declined sharply during the war. The wages of workers in the MTS account
for a good part of total farm wages.

1948. Total civilian wages are estimated in Appendix Table 8 at 294.00
billion rubles. We assume that the prewar relation, i.e., 4.99 percent, of farm
to total civilian wages had been reestablished, so total farm wages amount
to 14.67 billion rubles.

1b. *Money payments to collective farmers on labor-day basis; salaries of collective farm executives; premiums*

For each year, the magnitudes of these different kinds of payments are
calculated from the estimates set forth in Appendix Table 1 of aggregate collective farm money income and the relative shares of the different kinds
of payments in this total. These latter figures are obtained as follows:

1. *Total money income of collective farms:*

1940. N. I. Anisimov, *Sel'skoe khoziaistvo SSSR za 30 let,* p. 14.

1944. This is calculated as the product of the average money income, per
collective farm, given as 114,100 rubles in 1944, and the number of collective
farms operating that year, taken as 190,722.

The average money income of a collective farm is from N. I. Anisimov,
Pobeda sotsialisticheskogo sel'skogo khoziaistva, p. 82. As given by Anisimov,

the figure on average money income for 1944 might be construed as referring only to income from the sale of agricultural products, and as exclusive of revenues from subsidiary enterprises, e.g., flour and vegetable mills, brickyards, etc. But the corresponding figure on average money income which he gives for 1937, when multiplied by the number of collective farms in that

APPENDIX TABLE 1

AGGREGATE COLLECTIVE FARM MONEY INCOME,
LABOR-DAY EARNINGS, EXECUTIVE SALARIES,
PREMIUMS, 1940, 1944, AND 1948

ITEM	1940		1944		1948	
	RELATIVE SHARE, PERCENT	BILLION RUBLES	RELATIVE SHARE, PERCENT	BILLION RUBLES	RELATIVE SHARE, PERCENT	BILLION RUBLES
1. Total money income of collective farms	100.00	21.00	100.00	21.76	100.00	20.00
2. Labor-day earnings of collective farmers	50.35	10.57	40.00	8.70	50.00	10.00
3. Salaries of collective farm officials and administrative personnel	1.65	.35	1.65	.36	2.00	.40
4. Money premiums paid to collective farmers	1.78	.36	3.45	.75	2.00	.40
5. Total payments for labor-days, executive salaries, premiums (sum of items 2, 3, 4)	53.78	11.28	45.11	9.81	54.00	10.80

year, yields a total for money income of 14.3 billion rubles. This latter figure is known to be comprehensive of income from subsidiary activities in that year. See *Soviet National Income,* pp. 103–4.

The number of active collective farms is calculated as a quotient by dividing the aggregate investments in 1944 in the collective farms' "indivisible funds" (i.e., assets belonging to the collective farm as such, to which additions are to be made annually according to decree), which amounted to 3.7 billion rubles, by the average amount of such payments that year, per collective farm, given as 19,400 rubles. For the total indivisible fund payments, see S. Nosyrev, "Ustav sel'skokhoziaistvennoi arteli i finansovoe khoziaistvo kolkhozov," *Sovetskie finansy,* No. 1, 1947, p. 21; for the average payments, per collective farm, see F. Koshelev, *Stalinskii ustav—osnovnoi zakon kolkhoznoi zhizni,* p. 24.

1948. This is calculated on the assumption that the aggregate cash payments to the collective farms' indivisible funds, amounting to 3.4 billion rubles in 1948 (I. A. Benediktov, *Izvestiia,* December 20, 1949, p. 2), constituted 17 percent of the total collective farm money income that year, as they did in 1944. According to decree, collective farms are to add annually between 12 and 20 percent of their cash income to their indivisible funds, the higher percentages being required of collective farms specializing in livestock. See *Sobranie postanovlenii i rasporiazhenii pravitel'stva Soiuza Sovetskikh Sotsialisticheskikh Respublik,* No. 55, December 26, 1938, p. 686; also, Ia. F. Mikolenko and A. N. Nikitin, *Kolkhoznoe pravo,* pp. 130–38. The 1944 percentage of 17 percent represents a downturn in the movement of the aggregate ratio, which rose from 12.4 percent in 1937 (see *Soviet National Income,* pp. 103–4, 112) to 19.2 percent in 1940 (calculated from data in V. Chuvikov, "O nedelimykh fondakh kolkhozov," *Sotsialisticheskoe sel'skoe khoziaistvo,* No. 4, 1948, p. 28). This downturn was accompanied by complaints in the Soviet press about underfulfillment of the legal ratios in 1944, it being said that the deficiency in allocations to indivisible funds in four republics alone that year totaled 568.8 million rubles (Nosyrev, *Sovetskie finansy,* No. 1, 1947, p. 24). This ratio is, of course, influenced by other factors, but apparently the underfulfillment of indivisible funds payments persisted until 1948, so we take the ratio to be the same that year as in 1944. Concerning underfulfillment of indivisible funds payments in 1948, see particularly *Sotsialisticheskoe zemledelie,* April 8, 1949, p. 3; and D. Dukel'skii, "Uluchshit' rabotu Sel'khozbanka po privlecheniiu nedelimykh fondov kolkhozov," *Sovetskie finansy,* No. 3, 1947, pp. 28–29. It is claimed that the situation with respect to indivisible funds payments was somewhat improved by 1948 as a result of the decree passed September 19, 1946, aimed at liquidating violations of the regulations governing collective farms. On this, see Chuvikov, *Sotsialisticheskoe sel'skoe khoziaistvo,* No. 4, 1948, p. 33; see also "Za dal'neishii pod"em sel'skogo khoziaistva," *Bol'shevik,* No. 5, 1948, p. 6.

2. Labor-day earnings of collective farmers: relative share in total collective farm money income:

1940. This is taken at 50.35 percent, which is the average of the 1937 and 1938 relative shares of labor-day payments in aggregate collective farm money income, given as 47.9 percent and 52.8 percent, respectively, in M. Nesmii,

"Finansovoe khoziaistvo kolkhozov," *Planovoe khoziaistvo*, No. 8, 1939, p. 92.

1944. The relative share of labor-day payments in aggregate collective farm money income is taken to be 40 percent, on the assumption that this proportion fell significantly between 1940 and 1944. Account is taken of the following: First, after all cash obligations are met, the residual of the collective farm's money income is distributed to the members on a labor-day basis. Second, whereas most of the cash obligations are fixed proportions of the money income, during the war there was apparently an increase in the proportion of collective farm money income going for taxes, fees, "voluntary" contributions to such patriotic funds as the Red Army fund and the fund for the Reconstruction of Liberated Areas, larger subscriptions to the state war loan, and the maintenance and assistance of invalid war veterans returning to the farm. See, for example, V. Chuvikov, "Raspredelenie dokhodov v kolkhozakh i avansirovanie kolkhoznikov," *Kolkhoznoe proizvodstvo*, No. 8–9, 1945. Accordingly, the residual share available for distribution to collective farm members should have been reduced.

1948. This is taken as 50 percent, or approximately the prewar porportion, on the basis of sample investigations covering postwar years, particularly one for 1948, published in *Sotsialisticheskoe zemledelie*, April 16, 1949, p. 3.

3. Salaries of collective farm officials and administrative personnel: relative share in total collective farm money income:

1940. This is taken as the average of this proportion in 1937 and 1938, given as 1.8 percent and 1.5 percent, respectively, by Nesmii, *Planovoe khoziaistvo*, No. 8, 1939, p. 92.

1944. This is taken to be the same as in 1940.

1948. This is simply the prewar figure, rounded for the sake of consistency with the other percentages cited for 1948.

4. Money premiums paid to collective farmers: relative share in total collective farm money income:

1940. This is arbitrarily taken as one-half of the percentage of total collective farm money income allocated to social funds, premiums, etc., in 1937 and 1938, given for both years as 3.45 percent (*ibid.*).

1944. This is taken as twice the 1940 ratio because of the greatly extended use of bonuses and premiums as incentives for high production rates during the war.

1948. This is assumed to be, on the one hand, somewhat higher than in 1940 in view of the more extensive postwar use of premiums and bonuses, and, on the other hand, somewhat lower than in 1944 because of the decreased importance of incentive payments in the postwar years, as compared with the period of wartime emergency.

1c. Net money income from sale of farm products

As appears in Appendix Table 2, this is the estimated money income realized by households from the sale of farm products to government and cooperative procurement agencies and in the open collective farm markets (the two kinds of outlets in the USSR for producers' farm products), minus an allowance for the households' money costs of production.

APPENDIX TABLE 2

CALCULATION OF NET MONEY INCOME OF HOUSEHOLDS FROM SALE OF FARM PRODUCTS, AT AVERAGE FARM PRICES, 1940, 1944, AND 1948

(Billions of rubles)

ITEM	1940	1944	1948
1. Sales of farm products by households			
(i) Sales to procurement agencies	5.02	4.00	4.06
(ii) Sales in collective farm markets	35.10	45.00	53.23
(iii) Total	40.12	49.00	57.29
2. Less: Households' money costs of production	5.11	5.00	6.77
3. Net money income of households from sale of farm products, at average farm prices	35.01	44.00	50.52

For purposes of compiling the data in Appendix Table 2, it was necessary first to carry out the calculations shown in Appendix Tables 3–5. Reference is made to each of these tables in turn.

In Appendix Table 3, the figures for 1937 are from *Soviet National Income,* pp. 103 ff. Those for 1944 are derived from data in Appendix Table 4 and are presented here only for the sake of completeness. In the case of the figures on item 1 for 1940 and 1948, on item 2 for 1940, and on item 4 for 1940 and 1948, it will be evident that we are assuming that the same ratios prevail as in 1937. This assumption is for the most part arbitrary, but reference may be made to some information in G. Chernyi, "Kolkhoznaia torgovlia i finansovoe khoziaistvo v kolkhozakh," *Sotsialisticheskoe sel'skoe khoziaistvo,* No. 2, 1949, p. 37. Chernyi states that close to 30 percent of the "prewar" total money income of collective farms was derived from collective farm market trade. We assume that Chernyi, like most other Soviet writers, applies "prewar" to the year 1940 or 1941. Assuming that the 1937 figures for items 2 and 1 apply in 1940, collective farm market trade in 1940 accounts for 34.3 percent of the collective farm money income from sales of farm products; while the latter, in turn, is 84.63 percent of total collective farm money income from all sources. Accordingly, our assumptions imply that the revenue of collective farms from sales in collective farm markets is 29.03 percent of the total collective farm money income from all sources, or about the same as Chernyi's figure.

For the rest, the data in Appendix Table 3 are obtained as follows:

1940. 3. Ratio between household sales and collective farm sales to procurement agencies. This is based on the 1937 percentage, which Bergson assumes is the same as the ratio in 1937 between the agricultural output of households

---

APPENDIX TABLE 3

SELECTED DATA ON MONEY INCOME OF COLLECTIVE FARMS
AND COLLECTIVE FARM HOUSEHOLDS,
1937, 1940, 1944, AND 1948

ITEM	1937	1940	1944	1948
1. Collective farm sales of farm products as percent of total collective farm money income	84.63	84.63	87.00	84.63
2. Collective farm sales on collective farm markets as percent of total collective farm sales of farm products	34.30	34.30	53.00	40.00
3. Ratio between household sales and collective farm sales to procurement agencies (percent)	36.60	43.00	44.00	40.00
4. Sales of households and collective farms to procurement agencies as percent of total sales to procurement agencies	68.50	68.50	72.00	68.50

---

and that of collective farms. But we take account here of the increase in the number of farm households as a result of the 1939–40 territorial annexations. A rural population of about 17.5 millions was added to the USSR in 1939–40, increasing the Soviet rural population of 114.5 millions (1939 census) by about 15 percent. Our estimate that household sales to procurement agencies in 1940 amounted to 43 percent of the collective farm sales to procurement agencies, instead of 36.6 percent as in 1937, is meant to reflect the absence of collectivization in the new territories, as well as a lower rate of agricultural output there than in the rest of the USSR.

1948. 2. Collective farm sales on collective farm markets as percent of total collective farm sales of farm products. We take this as somewhat larger than in 1940, in view of the probable increase, as compared with 1940, in collective farm market prices relative to procurement prices, and on the basis of early postwar data in Chernyi, *Sotsialisticheskoe sel'skoe khoziaistvo*, pp. 37 ff.

1948. 3. Ratio between household sales and collective farm sales to procurement agencies. This is roughly estimated as lower than in 1940, account being taken of the postwar collectivization of agriculture in the areas of the USSR annexed during 1939–40, which was well under way by 1948.

The data in Appendix Table 4 are obtained as follows:

1940 and 1948. 1. Sales by collective farms. Sales in all outlets are computed as the product of total collective farm money income in Appendix Table 1, and the percentage that collective farm sales of farm products constitute of this money income, as given in Appendix Table 3. Sales in collective farm

APPENDIX TABLE 4

SALES OF FARM PRODUCTS BY PRODUCERS AND OUTLETS,
1940, 1944, AND 1948

(Billions of rubles)

	SALES TO PROCURE-MENT AGENCIES			SALES IN COLLECTIVE FARM MARKETS			SALES IN ALL OUTLETS		
ITEM	*1940*	*1944*	*1948*	*1940*	*1944*	*1948*	*1940*	*1944*	*1948*
1. Sales by collective farms	11.67	9.00	10.16	6.10	10.00	6.77	17.77	19.00	16.93
2. Sales by households	5.02	4.00	4.06	35.10	45.00	53.23	40.12	49.00	57.29
3. Sales by state agricultural enterprises	7.67	5.00	6.54	...[a]	...	...	7.67	5.00	6.54
4. Sales by all organizations	24.36	18.00	20.76	41.20	55.00	60.00	65.56	73.00	80.76

[a] ... = negligible.

markets are computed as the product of the total sales in all outlets, as just calculated, and the percentage that collective farm sales on the collective farm market constitute of all collective farm sales, as given in Appendix Table 3. Sales to procurement agencies are computed as a residual.

1940 and 1948. 2. Sales by households. Sales to procurement agencies are computed as the product of collective farm sales to procurement agencies and the ratio of household to collective farm sales to these agencies, as given in Appendix Table 3. Sales on collective farm markets are calculated as a residual after sales by all other organizations have been deducted from total sales of all organizations on collective farm markets (see items 1, 3, and 4). Sales in all outlets are calculated as the sum of the foregoing.

1940 and 1948. 3. Sales by state agricultural enterprises. Sales to procurement agencies are computed from the following data: Sales to procurement agencies by collective farms and by households as already calculated; and the ratio of sales to procurement agencies by collective farms and households to the total sales of all organizations to procurement agencies, as given in Appendix Table 3. It is assumed that sales by state agricultural enterprises on the collective farm market are negligible.

1940 and 1948. 4. Sales by all organizations. Sales to procurement agencies are computed as the sum of the sales to these agencies by the different agricultural organizations. Sales on collective farm markets are from Appendix Table 18. Sales in all outlets are computed as the sum of the foregoing.

1944. For all items, the figures in Appendix Table 4 are rule-of-thumb estimates intended to take into account various aspects, particularly:

(i) The physical volume of agricultural production in 1944 probably was on the order of one-half of that in 1940. This is suggested by information in various sources, including H. C. Farnsworth and V. P. Timoshenko, *World Grain Review and Outlook,* pp. 102–9; the data on agricultural output and stocks in 1940 and 1945 in Table 2, above, pp. 9–10; and various other sources of information. In estimating from the data in Table 2, referring to 1940 and 1945, the change in real agricultural output between 1940 and 1944, we take account of Soviet claims as to the expansion of agricultural activity during 1945, which indicate that in 1944 the area sown to crops, the amount of tractor work performed, and the livestock population were substantially below their respective 1945 levels. Consideration is also given to the fact that harvesting and threshing losses are included in the Soviet grain crop figures cited, which represent the biological yield of grain in 1940 and 1945. These losses were probably greater under the difficult wartime conditions of 1944 than they were in 1940.

(ii) It is believed that the physical volume of sales to government and other procurement agencies did not decline at all in proportion to output. According to all indications, the government endeavored to obtain a maximum of produce from the farmers. Timely fulfillment of heavy delivery quotas was made a "first commandment" and a "sacred duty." No collective farm or farmer was permitted to sell its surplus products on the free collective farm market until the delivery quotas of the entire region had been filled. The result of this policy, to judge by a number of Soviet publications, appears to have been to maintain the physical volume of procurements at a relatively high level and to restrict that of collective farm market sales quite severely. For collective farm performance in particular areas, see N. I. Anisimov, "Velikaia sila kolkhoznogo stroia," *Sputnik agitatora,* No. 19–20, 1944, pp. 11–16; Chuvikov, *Kolkhoznoe proizvodstvo,* No. 8–9, 1945, pp. 9–11; and P. A. Granditskii, *Kolkhoz "Borets,"* pp. 86–89, 164–67.

(iii) Under the foregoing policy, deliveries from collective farms and farm households were probably maintained at a relatively higher level, compared with the prewar period, than those from state farms, which already must have been near the maximum before the war.

(iv) It is believed that farm procurement prices were stable during the war. Accordingly, the data in Appendix Table 4 imply the following relations between the physical volume of government procurements from different farm organizations in 1944 and 1940: from collective farms, 77 percent; from households, 80 percent; from state farms, 65 percent; from all organizations, 74 percent.

(v) The indications are that the subsidiary nonfarm activities of collective farms may have declined more than farm production during the war. Accord-

APPENDIX TABLE 5

CALCULATION OF MONEY COSTS OF PRODUCTION, INCURRED
BY HOUSEHOLDS IN THE OUTPUT OF FARM PRODUCTS,
1940, 1944, AND 1948

ITEM	1940	1944	1948
1. Nonwage income of households from agriculture			
(i) Labor-day payments (bil. rubles)	10.57	8.70	10.00
(ii) Premiums paid to households (bil. rubles)	.36	.75	.40
(iii) Total sales of farm products by households (bil. rubles)	40.12	49.00	57.29
(iv) Total (bil. rubles)	51.05	58.45	67.69
2. Ratio between households' money costs of production and households' total nonwage income from agriculture (percent)	10	10	10
3. Households' money costs of production (bil. rubles)	5.11	5.00	6.77

ingly, income from sales of farm products probably constituted a larger share of total collective farm money income than before the war. The latter has already been calculated at 21.76 billion rubles (Appendix Table 1). The figure for collective farm sales of farm products in 1944 in Appendix Table 4, 19.0 billion rubles, comes to 87 percent of collective farm money income. The corresponding percentage for 1937 and 1940 was 85 (Appendix Table 3).

(vi) Total collective farm market sales for all organizations are calculated elsewhere at 55.0 billion rubles in 1944 (Appendix Table 18).

In Appendix Table 5, the different elements in total nonwage income are taken from Appendix Tables 1 and 4.

As indicated in Appendix Table 5, the money costs of production incurred by households in the output of farm products are taken for all years as 10 percent of the households' total nonwage income from agriculture in those years. (The absolute figure for 1944 has been rounded.) This is done on the basis of calculations in *Soviet National Income*, pp. 103–4, and information in Nesmii, *Planovoe khoziaistvo*, No. 8, 1939, p. 100.

To come back now to Appendix Table 2, it will be evident that the basic data are all from Appendix Tables 4 and 5.

1d. Net farm income in kind

For all years farm income in kind is valued at average farm prices, gross of subsidies, but for 1940 and 1948 reference is to current prices, while for 1944 reference is to 1940 prices. Valued in these terms, farm income in kind is calculated as a residual in gross agricultural output after the deduction of the marketed share and production costs in kind. The elements of the calcu-

---

APPENDIX TABLE 6

DISPOSITION OF GROSS AGRICULTURAL OUTPUT,
VALUED AT AVERAGE REALIZED FARM PRICES
GROSS OF SUBSIDIES, 1940, 1944, AND 1948

(Billions of rubles)

ITEM	1940	1944[a]	1948
1. Marketed share	72.56	30.00	91.26
2. Production costs in kind	64.08	32.00	76.57
3. Net farm income in kind	54.31	33.00	60.32
4. Gross agricultural output	190.95	95.00	228.15

[a] In 1940 prices.

---

lation, together with the resulting figures for income in kind, are shown in Appendix Table 6. As to the derivation of the data used here, for convenience reference is made first to the marketed share, then to gross agricultural output, and finally to production costs in kind.

The calculation of the *marketed share* for all years is shown in Appendix Table 7. In the table, the figures on sales to procurement agencies for all years are from Appendix Table 4. (The figure in Appendix Table 4, on this item for 1944, as for other years, is in current rubles, but it is believed this may be taken as the corresponding sum in 1940 prices as well.) For the years 1940 and 1948, the figures on sales in collective farm markets are also from Appendix Table 4; for the year 1944, the figure on this item is a rule-of-thumb estimate derived in the notes to Table 3-B, item 1b. The figures on agricultural subsidies for 1940 and 1948 are from Appendix Tables 28 and 29; the figure for 1944 is obtained on the assumption that at 1940 prices, gross of subsidies, the total subsidies would bear the same relation to total sales to procurement agencies as in 1940.

The *gross agricultural output* of 1944 in terms of 1940 prices is obtained here from the assumption made previously that output in these terms in 1944 was one-half of that of 1940, in comparable prices (see above the comments on Table 3-A, item 1c). For 1940 and 1948, gross output is calculated from the value of the marketed share, as just computed, and the percentage that this share is of gross output, determined as follows:

According to *Soviet National Income,* p. 105, the marketed share constituted 36.15 percent of the gross output in 1937. On the basis of various data,

APPENDIX TABLE 7

CALCULATION OF MARKETED SHARE OF AGRICULTURAL
OUTPUT IN REALIZED PRICES, GROSS OF SUBSIDIES,
1940, 1944, AND 1948

(Billions of rubles)

ITEM	1940	1944[a]	1948
1. Sales to procurement agencies	24.36	18.00	20.76
2. Sales in collective farm markets	41.20	6.50	60.00
3. Agricultural subsidies			
(i) Subsidies to MTS	5.00	n.a.[b]	8.00
(ii) Subsidies to other state agriculture	2.00	n.a.	2.50
(iii) Total	7.00	5.00	10.50
4. Value of marketed share of agricultural output in realized prices, gross of subsidies	72.56	29.50	91.26

[a] In 1940 prices.
[b] n.a. = information not available.

we assume that the corresponding figure for 1940 was slightly higher, or 38 percent. According to official Soviet announcements, the total grain harvest of 1940 was somewhat smaller than that of 1937 (118.8 million metric tons in 1940, as compared with 120.3 million metric tons in 1937), while a slightly larger amount of grain was marketed in 1940 than in 1937 (38.3 million tons in 1940, as against 38.0 million tons in 1937). The gross production of the other principal crops in 1940 appears to have been about equal to, or slightly below, the 1937 level (except for potatoes, the output of which increased substantially). The amount of these products marketed, however, was probably greater in 1940 than in 1937. Effective in 1940, government procurement regulations were changed so as to require each collective farm to make its obligatory deliveries of agricultural products to the state on the basis of the total arable land assigned to it, and not, as heretofore, on the basis of the farm's actual plan for crop planting and livestock production. For a discussion of the avowed objectives of these decrees, see *Pravda,* May 8, 1940, pp. 3 ff. A translation appears in United States Department of Commerce, *Russian Economic Notes,* Vol. II, No. 14, July 30, 1940, pp. 2 ff. Judging by scattered data on procurements in 1940, this new procurement policy resulted in an immediate increase in total procurements of agricultural products. See on this S. F. Demidov, *Razvitie sel'skogo khoziaistva v poslevoennoi piatiletke,* p. 142; and *Sovetskaia torgovlia za XXX let,* pp. 98–99.

For 1948, we take the marketed share as a still higher percentage of the gross output: 40 percent. According to data in Table 2, pp. 9–10, the production of grain in the USSR in 1948 was still below the 1940 level. Yet Soviet reports claim that government procurements of grain in 1947 had already reached "approximately the level of the best prewar years" (V. Moskvin, "Sovetskaia torgovlia v tret'em godu piatiletki," *Bol'shevik,* No. 15, 1948, p. 33). Soviet statistics indicate that livestock herds were still below the prewar level in 1948. (See "Za skoreishee vosstanovlenie i pod"em sel'skogo khoziaistva," *Bol'shevik,* No. 4, 1947, p. 8.) It is said, however, that during 1948 "the prewar level of milk and butter procurements was exceeded and the 1940 level of meat procurements almost equaled" (*Pravda,* May 26, 1949). According to M. M. Lifits ("Razvitie sovetskoi torgovli v poslevoennyi period," *Voprosy ekonomiki,* No. 7, 1951, p. 79), a 22 percent increase in the volume of collective farm market trade between 1940 and 1948 "was made possible by a significant growth in the marketed output of agriculture."

Taken together with our estimate of the value of the marketed share in 1944 as 30.00 billion rubles in 1940 prices, the assumption that output in 1944 was one-half of that in 1940 means a marketed share in 1944 amounting to 31 percent of output. This may be compared with the figures just cited for other years: 36 percent for 1937, 38 percent for 1940, and 40 percent for 1948. In view of the generally known facts about the government pressure on marketings during the war, the indicated reduction in the marketed share in relation to output may seem rather puzzling, to say the least. But the data become more plausible if account is taken of several other aspects. First, in comparison with 1940, we assume only a limited reduction in sales to government procurement agencies, i.e., 25 percent. The decline in marketings occurs mainly in collective farm market sales (see the notes to Table 3-A, item 1c). Second, while collective farm market prices were high in 1944, there was hardly any opportunity for the farmer to dispose of extra income at reasonable prices; accordingly, the incentive to market produce must have been rather weak. Third, given the decline in total output, a severe reduction in those marketings over which the peasant had control was to be expected.

To come now to *production costs in kind,* these are understood here to include feed, fodder, seed, and also an allowance for certain losses in grain harvesting and threshing which the Russians deducted from their reported harvest prior to 1937 but did not deduct after that year. For all years, production costs in kind are taken to amount to 33.56 percent of the gross output, or the figure more or less implied in pertinent data compiled in *Soviet National Income,* pp. 105–7, for the year 1937. This figure is obtained as follows:

(i) During the period 1933–36, gross agricultural output included the grain harvest reported according to its biological yield (i.e., the amount of grain in the fields before harvesting), minus about a 10 percent allowance for harvesting and threshing losses, which thus figured neither as output nor as production costs. Beginning in 1937, however, the full biological yield, without any allowance for such losses, became the measure of the grain harvest covered in gross agricultural output. Since the grain crop, measured according to its biological yield, normally is about one-third of the gross agricultural output of the USSR, this means that, beginning in 1937, grain losses not deducted amount to about 3 percent of the total harvest of all agricultural products, according to the 1937 concept.

(ii) On the basis of data on annual production costs in agriculture during the years 1933–35, Bergson estimates in *Soviet National Income,* p. 105, that production costs in kind, not including any allowance for grain losses of the sort just referred to, but taken together with money outlays on agricultural inputs (e.g., fuel, lubricants, fertilizer, etc.), amounted to 35 percent of the gross harvest in 1937. Reference here is to the harvest under the Soviet pre-1937 concept, i.e., the 1937 concept less 3 percent. This means that the production costs referred to amount to 33.95 percent of the 1937 harvest under the Soviet 1937 concept, i.e., $35.00 \times 97.00 \div 100$.

(iii) On the basis of scattered information we assume that production costs in kind amounted to 90 percent of production costs in kind and in money taken together. (Strictly speaking, this assumption is framed to take account of conditions during the years studied here rather than in 1937. According to *Soviet National Income,* p. 106, production costs in kind were only about 80 percent of all costs in 1937.) Hence production costs in kind amount to 30.56 percent of the 1937 harvest (1937 concept). This is exclusive of the special allowance for grain losses of 3 percent, so the two together come to 33.56 percent.

In the foregoing calculation of net farm income in kind, that for 1944 has been valued at 1940 prices. While it has seemed in order to accord priority to this valuation here, interest attaches also to the corresponding figure in terms of current prices: 82.50 billion rubles. This is calculated as follows: According to Appendix Table 7, the total marketed share in 1944 amounted to 29.50 billion rubles in terms of 1940 farm prices, gross of subsidies. From data in Appendix Table 4 and in Appendix Tables 28 and 29, the corresponding figure in terms of current prices is 77.50 billion rubles, or about 2.5 times the figure in 1940 prices. Farm income in kind is taken to increase proportionately with revaluation.

In transferring the data on farm income in kind from Appendix Table 6 to Table 3 in the text, it has seemed in order to round to the nearest billion rubles. Also, we arbitrarily make the following allowances for income in kind retained by the collective farms for investment purposes: 2.0 billion rubles in 1944 and 4.0 billion rubles in 1948. It is believed there was no significant investment of income in kind in 1940. The corresponding figure for 1937, in prices which were probably lower than in any of the succeeding years, was 2.0 billion rubles.

2. WAGES AND SALARIES, NONFARM

For all years the total in Table 3-A, item 2c, is the wage bill for the whole national economy, minus the following earnings, which we itemize elsewhere in the table: wages of farm labor (Table 3-A, item 1a), earnings of cooperative artisans (included in Table 3-A, item 3), and military pay (Table 3-A, item 5a).

As pointed out in Bergson, *Review of Economic Statistics,* November, 1947, pp. 234 ff., two types of series are evident in Soviet statistics on the wage bill. The one most frequently presented in Soviet publications is compiled by TSUNKHU (at various times, TSU; see *ibid.,* p. 235, n. 4) from current reports prepared by economic organizations. This series is of limited coverage and excludes the wages paid to workers in certain local industries and other activities not provided for in the national economic plans, and also the wages paid to hired workers by collective farms, the earnings of cooperative artisans, and military pay. It is believed that the TSUNKHU series also excludes the wages paid to penal labor.

The other type of wage series consists of estimates of all wage and salary payments. Until 1941 such estimates were presented sporadically in Soviet publications on the basis of special statistical studies. Their comprehensiveness seems to be limited only by the particular writer's conception of wage and salary payments and the data he uses. Bergson takes the figures for the wage bill during the thirties, given in N. S. Margolin, *Voprosy balansa denezhnykh dokhodov i raskhodov naseleniia* and *Balans denezhnykh dokhodov i raskhodov naseleniia,* to include, in addition to the TSUNKHU wage bill, the wages paid to hired workers by collective farms, military pay, and other miscellaneous wage and salary payments not covered by the TSUNKHU wage bill. It is assumed, however, that Margolin's data exclude the earnings of cooperative artisans, these being given separately.

A comprehensive wage figure for 1940 was published in connection with the annual plan for 1941. This was apparently the first time that such data on the wage bill received full official sanction, and their application in planning seems to have been continued in the postwar period. In the 1944 handbook of statistical terms, published by the Central Statistical Administration, the comprehensive concept of the wage fund is defined and, as officially used, covers in addition to Margolin's concept the earnings of cooperative artisans. See TSU, *Slovar'-spravochnik po sotsial'no-ekonomicheskoi statistike,* 1944 ed., pp. 211–13.

In our calculations of nonfarm wages and salaries we make use of the following wage bill concepts:

$$\text{Comprehensive wage bill} = \begin{cases} \text{Comprehensive civilian wage bill} = \begin{cases} \text{TSUNKHU wage bill} \\ + \\ \text{Wages paid to hired workers by collective farms} \\ + \\ \text{Earnings of cooperative artisans} \\ + \\ \text{Miscellaneous earnings not covered by TSUNKHU wage bill} \end{cases} \\ + \\ \text{Military pay} \end{cases}$$

Appendix Table 8, below, summarizes the calculations upon which our estimates for all years of total wages and salaries are based, exclusive of farm wages, earnings of cooperative artisans, and military pay. The figures in Appendix Table 8 are obtained as follows:

1940. 1. Comprehensive wage bill. From Bergson (quoting Voznesenskii, *Voennaia ekonomika . . . ,*) in *Review of Economic Statistics,* November, 1947, p. 240.

1940. 2. Military pay. See Table 3-A, item 5a.

1940. 3. Comprehensive civilian wage bill. This is calculated as a residual by subtracting the military pay in item 2 from the comprehensive wage bill in item 1.

1940. 3 (i). TSUNKHU wage bill. See *ibid.,* p. 239.

1940. 3 (ii). Wages paid to workers by collective farms. See Appendix A, notes to Table 1-A, item 1a.

1940. 3 (iii). Earnings of cooperative artists. See Appendix Table 9, item 1.

1940. 3 (iv). Miscellaneous earnings not covered by TSUNKHU wage bill. This is calculated as a residual.

1940. 4 (i). Wages earned by agricultural workers outside of collective farms. See Appendix A, notes to Table 3-A, item 1a.

1940. 4 (ii). Wages paid to hired workers by collective farms. See Appendix A, notes to Table 3-A, item 1a.

1940. 4 (iii). Earnings of cooperative artisans. See Appendix Table 9, item 1.

1940. 5. Civilian nonfarm wages and salaries, exclusive of earnings of cooperative artisans. This is calculated as the difference between items 3 and 4.

APPENDIX TABLE 8

CALCULATION OF CIVILIAN NONFARM WAGES AND SALARIES, EXCLUSIVE OF EARNINGS OF COOPERATIVE ARTISANS, 1940, 1944, AND 1948

(Billions of rubles)

ITEM	1940	1944	1948
1. Comprehensive wage bill	161.00	175.18	308.00
2. Less: Military pay	4.13	14.16	14.00
3. Comprehensive civilian wage bill	156.87	161.02	294.00
(i) TSUNKHU wage bill	123.70	126.98	n.a.
(ii) Wages paid to hired workers by collective farms	.42	n.a.[a]	n.a.
(iii) Earnings of cooperative artisans	7.15	5.00	9.50
(iv) Miscellaneous earnings not covered by TSUNKHU wage bill	25.60	n.a.	n.a.
4. Less: Total of farm wages and earnings of cooperative artisans	14.97	11.44	24.17
(i) Wages earned by agricultural workers outside of collective farms	7.40 ⎫		
(ii) Wages paid to hired workers by collective farms	.42 ⎬	6.44	14.67
(iii) Earnings of cooperative artisans	7.15 ⎭ 7.15	5.00	9.50
5. Civilian nonfarm wages and salaries, exclusive of earnings of cooperative artisans	141.90	149.58	269.83

[a] n.a. = information not available.

1944. 1. Comprehensive wage bill. This is calculated as the sum of the comprehensive civilian wage bill in item 3 and the military pay in item 2.

1944. 2. Military pay. See Table 3-A, item 5a.

1944. 3. Comprehensive civilian wage bill. This is calculated on the assumption that our estimate of the 1944 TSUNKHU wage bill, given as 126.98 billion rubles in item 3 (i), below, is 78.86 percent of the 1944 comprehensive civilian wage bill. That is, we assume that the ratio between the 1940 TSUNKHU wage bill and that year's comprehensive civilian wage bill applies to 1944.

1944. 3 (i). TSUNKHU wage bill. We calculate this as the product of
the following: the labor force in branches covered by the national plan,
estimated as 22 million; and the estimated average annual wage in 1944 of
5,772 rubles. The labor force estimate is based on data pertaining to 1943 and
1945; i.e., the number of workers and employees in the economy are said
to have declined from 31.2 million in 1940 to 19.3 million in 1943 (Voznesenskii, *Voennaia ekonomika . . . ,* p. 109) and to have increased to 27.25
million by 1945 (G. Kosiachenko, "Povyshenie material'nogo i kul'turnogo
urovnia zhizni naroda v novoi piatiletke," *Planovoe khoziaistvo,* No. 2, 1946,
p. 137). The labor force in 1944, however, cannot be estimated by means of
a straight-line interpolation between 1943 and 1945 because of the heavy
demobilization that took place in 1945. Moreover, it seems clear from population data for 1944, and the fact of continuing mobilization in that year,
that the net addition to the labor force between 1943 and 1944 could not
have been large. Accordingly, it is taken roughly as one-third of the gain in
labor force claimed to have been made between 1943 and 1945 in the sources
cited above. It can be estimated from the data in Farnsworth and Timoshenko, *World Grain Review and Outlook, 1945,* pp. 105–6, and in E. M.
Kulischer, *Europe on the Move,* pp. 260 ff., that between 20 and 30 million
persons were added to the population of the USSR during 1944 through the
liberation of occupied areas by the Red Army. While this represents between
10 and 15 percent of the total prewar Soviet population, the share of nonagricultural workers in this group must have been quite small. Voznesenskii,
in *Voennaia ekonomika . . . ,* pp. 56–57, indicates that in the liberated areas
of the Russian and Ukrainian Republics only 17 percent of the prewar
number of workers remained after the German withdrawal, and in the
Byelorussian Republic only 6 percent.

The estimate of the average annual wage in 1944 is obtained as follows.
According to Voznesenskii *(ibid.,* p. 118), the average monthly wage of
workers in all industries of the USSR had increased in 1944 by 42 percent
over the 1940 level. The average monthly wage of all workers and employees
in the USSR was 339 rubles in 1940 (Bergson, *Review of Economic Statistics,*
November, 1947, p. 236). By taking the increase in industrial wages as typical
of the movement of all wages in the USSR, the average monthly wage in
1944 is estimated as 481 rubles, and the annual wage as 5,772 rubles.

1944. 3 (iii). Earnings of cooperative artisans. See Appendix Table 9,
item 1.

*1944. 4 (i). Wages earned by agricultural workers outside of collective
farms* and *4 (ii). Wages paid to hired workers by collective farms.* See
Appendix A, notes to Table 3-A, item 1a.

1944. 4 (iii). Earnings of cooperative artisans. See Appendix Table 9,
item 1.

1944. 5. Civilian nonfarm wages and salaries, exclusive of earnings of cooperative artisans. This is calculated as the difference between items 3 and 4.

1948. 1. Comprehensive wage bill. This is calculated as 10 percent larger than the comprehensive wage bill of 1947, which is taken as 280 billion rubles. This rate of growth in the wage bill between 1947 and 1948 is given in *Pravda,* January 20, 1949, p. 2. The magnitude for the 1947 wage bill is the goal of the 1947 annual plan, which we assume was fulfilled. See Sovet Minis- trov SSSR, *O gosudarstvennom plane vosstanovleniia i razvitiia narodnogo khoziaistva SSSR na 1947 god,* p. 24. From information on average wages and the labor force it is clear that the 1947 plan refers to the comprehensive wage bill rather than to the TSUNKHU series. Our estimate of 308 billion rubles for the 1948 comprehensive wage bill is supported by a statement in P. Vladimirov, "Za rentabel'nuiu rabotu predpriiatii," *Voprosy ekonomiki,* No. 8, 1948, p. 23, that the 1948 wage bill is "almost double that of 1940." The 1940 wage bill amounted to 161 billion rubles.

1948. 2. Military pay. See Table 3-A, item 5a.

1948. 3. Comprehensive civilian wage bill. This is calculated as a residual, by subtracting the military pay in item 2 from the comprehensive wage bill in item 1.

1948. 3 (iii). Earnings of cooperative artisans. See Appendix Table 9, item 1.

1948. 4 (i). Wages earned by agricultural workers outside of collective farms and *4 (ii). Wages paid to hired workers by collective farms.* See Appendix A, notes to Table 3-A, item 1a.

1948. 4 (iii). Earnings of cooperative artisans. See Appendix Table 9. item 1.

1948. 5. Civilian nonfarm wages and salaries, exclusive of earnings of cooperative artisans. This is calculated as the difference between items 3 and 4.

The magnitudes obtained in Appendix Table 8 for the civilian nonfarm wage bill, exclusive of cooperative earnings, depend chiefly on the magnitudes of the comprehensive wage bill and the comprehensive civilian wage bill. For the year 1940 the comprehensive wage bill is given in a Soviet source, while the comprehensive civilian wage bill can readily be calculated from this figure. On the other hand, one or the other of these two totals had to be estimated for the years 1944 and 1948, and in the case of 1944 particularly, the estimate seems somewhat arbitrary.

Under the circumstances, some interest attaches to the further data assem- bled below concerning the relation of social insurance contributions to the comprehensive civilian wage bill. The figures on social insurance contribu- tions are from Table 7, p. 26; those on the wage bill are from Appendix Table 8.

	1940	1944	1948
Comprehensive civilian wage bill (bil. rubles)	156.87	161.02	294.00
Social insurance funds (bil. rubles)	8.50	9.00	16.20
Ratio between social insurance funds and comprehensive civilian wage bill (percent)	5.40	5.60	5.50

Virtually the entire income of the social insurance fund is derived from payments by enterprises, the payment of each being calculated as a fixed percentage of its total payroll. The income of the social insurance fund, therefore, may be expected to bear a more or less stable ratio to the total civilian wage bill. Such a relationship is, in fact, indicated by the figures cited.

In the foregoing paragraphs the concern has been to explain the derivation of Table 3-A, item 2c, representing the total civilian nonfarm wage bill exclusive of cooperative earnings. For the year 1940, though not for the years 1944 and 1948, a breakdown of this total is given in Table 3-A between two categories: "As recorded in current statistical reports" and "Other." The first category is obtained simply as the difference between items 3 (i) and 4 (i) in Appendix Table 8. The second category is the same as item 3 (iv) in Appendix Table 8.

3. INCOME OF ARTISANS; OTHER MONEY INCOME CURRENTLY EARNED

This item is the sum of the earnings of cooperative artisans and certain money income currently earned which has not been itemized elsewhere in Table 3-A, particularly the earnings of independent handicraftsmen, domestic employees, repair servicemen, barbers, etc. The estimates of these different kinds of earnings for the years studied, together with comparable data for 1937, are shown in Appendix Table 9. The data for 1937 are taken from *Soviet National Income,* p. 108. The figures for the years studied are obtained as follows:

1. Earnings of cooperative artisans:

1940. This is based on percentage data in Margolin, *Balans . . . ,* p. 8, and Bergson's conversion of these data into absolute figures in current rubles, *Soviet National Income,* p. 108. On this basis, the income of cooperative artisans increased from 2.05 billion rubles in 1934 to 5.45 billion rubles in 1938, i.e., by an annual increment of .85 billion rubles. We assume that the same absolute annual amount of increase prevailed until 1940.

1944. We estimated this from data presented in Norman C. Stines, Jr., *Cooperatives in Soviet Industry,* especially pp. 38–41. On the basis of this study it appears that the industrial cooperative system was successfully converted to war production and may have been producing at a fairly high level in 1944. Also, we assume that average earnings in cooperatives rose appreciably during the war.

1948. This is calculated on the assumption that in 1948 these earnings were 32.8 percent higher than in 1940. That is, we assume that between 1940 and 1948 they increased at the same rate as the gross output of the industrial cooperatives in the RSFSR, which account for more than one-half of the cooperative output in the USSR. See P. V. Evseev, *Kooperativnaia i mestnaia promyshlennost' v poslevoennoi piatiletke,* p. 13; and *Izvestiia,* June 1, 1949, p. 2.

2. *Other money income currently earned.* According to data in *Soviet National Income,* pp. 107–8, this category totaled 8.6 percent of the comprehensive civilian wage bill in 1937. The implied figure on the comprehen-

---

APPENDIX TABLE 9

ESTIMATES OF INCOME OF ARTISANS AND OTHER MONEY
INCOME CURRENTLY EARNED, 1937, 1940, 1944, AND 1948
(Billions of rubles)

ITEM	1937	1940	1944	1948
1. Earnings of cooperative artisans	4.60	7.15	5.00	9.50
2. Other money income currently earned	9.10	13.49	8.00	25.28
3. Incomes of artisans; other money income currently earned	13.70	20.64	13.00	34.78

---

sive civilian wage bill is 105.8 billion rubles. Bergson's own figure for the comprehensive wage bill is 102.7 billion rubles, but unlike our comprehensive civilian wage bill this includes 1.5 billion rubles of military pay and excludes 4.6 billion rubles of earnings of cooperative artisans. In this connection, see Appendix A, notes to Table 3-A, item 2.

For purposes of calculating other money income in the years now studied, we arbitrarily assume that the same relation to the comprehensive civilian wage bill prevailed in 1940 and 1948 as in 1937. The corresponding figure for 1944 is taken to be about 5 percent. This latter figure for 1944 is intended to allow for a probable severe wartime cut in employment of independent artisans, domestics, etc.

4. IMPUTED NET RENT OF OWNER-OCCUPIED DWELLINGS

For each year this is calculated as the product of the estimated number of square meters of owner-occupied dwelling space and the estimated average annual rental paid by urban workers, per square meter of government-owned housing. Valuation on this basis, of course, is something of an expedient. What is desired here presumably is not the gross value of the housing services received, but the net return after allowing for operating expenses and depreciation. On the other hand, the government rental rates have tended to be very low, and may not much exceed such a net return after all.

In estimating the amount of privately owned housing, we assume that all housing in rural areas is privately owned, as well as part of the urban housing, the remainder being government-owned. The floor space occupied by kitchens, bathrooms, porches, halls, closets, etc., is not included, since it is not covered by Soviet data on dwelling space. The calculation of owner-occupied dwelling space is shown in Appendix Table 10.

APPENDIX TABLE 10

DWELLING SPACE IN THE USSR, 1940–48

(Millions of square meters)

		URBAN				TOTAL
	TOTAL, USSR	Total	Govern- ment- owned	Pri- vately owned	RURAL	PRI- VATELY OWNED
ITEM	(1)	(2)	(3)	(4)	(5)	(6)
1. Available, 1940	677	272	168	104	405	509
2. Less: Allowance for war losses	(−)119	(−)66	(−)41	(−)25	(−)53	(−)78
3. Available, 1944	558	206	127	79	352	431
4. Added, 1944–48	85	55	47	8	30	38
5. Available, 1948	643	261	174	87	382	469

For each year the figure for total privately owned dwelling space in the USSR, shown in column (6) of Appendix Table 10, is obtained as the sum of the privately owned urban dwelling space in column (4) and the rural dwelling space in column (5). The figures for total dwelling space in column (1) are the sums of total urban dwelling space in column (2) and rural dwelling space in column (5). This latter total is not needed in the calculation of imputed rent, but it will be used in other connections.

The estimates of urban and rural dwelling space for 1940 in Appendix Table 10 are based on the following sources and calculations.

Urban. According to V. L. Kobalevskii, *Organizatsiia i ekonomika zhilish-chnogo khoziaistva SSSR,* p. 106, there were in urban localities of the USSR in 1937 215 million square meters of housing space, including 131 million square meters government-owned and 84 million square meters privately owned. According to Degtiar, *Zabota sovetskogo gosudarstva . . . ,* p. 16, the government-owned urban housing had increased 28 percent by 1940, which comes to 37 million square meters. According to Gosplan, *Tretii piatiletnii plan* . . . , pp. 188–89, privately owned urban housing was to increase by 10 million square meters over the period of the plan, 1938–42. We assume the actual increase in the years 1938 through 1940 was 5 million square meters.

Degtiar's figure cited above on the increase in government-owned housing during the years 1938 through 1940 is taken here to include housing seized in the territories annexed in 1939 and 1940. Our figure on the increment in privately owned housing in this same period, however, would not include the privately owned housing of these territories; accordingly, a separate allowance must be made for this item, which is taken to amount to 15 million square meters on the following assumptions: The urban population of the annexed territories was about 5 million, or less than one-quarter of the total; one-half of these persons lived in privately owned dwellings; the average space per person was 6 square meters, or somewhat more than in the USSR within the pre-1939 boundaries.

Rural. On the basis of data in Voznesenskii, *Voennaia ekonomika* . . . , pp. 157, 161, on the proportion of the total population and the number of rural homes falling under wartime German occupation, it is calculated that the total number of rural homes in the USSR as a whole before the war was 27 million. Assuming a floor space of 15 square meters as average for Soviet rural houses, predominantly one-room huts, the total rural dwelling space may be calculated at 405 million square meters.

As is indicated in Appendix Table 10, the estimates of the urban and rural housing space for 1944 are derived from those for 1940 by deducting an allowance for wartime losses. This allowance is made on the following basis.

Allowance for urban losses, 1940–44. According to Degtiar, *Zabota sovetskogo gosudarstva* . . . , p. 20, and Voznesenskii, *Voennaia ekonomika* . . . , p. 165, 66 million square meters of urban housing were destroyed during the war. This is 24 percent of the prewar stock. The losses in government-owned and privately owned urban housing are assumed to be in the same proportion.

Allowance for rural losses, 1940–44. According to Voznesenskii, *ibid.,* p. 161, 3.5 million rural houses were destroyed during the war. At 15 square meters per house, this comes to 53 million square meters.

During the war there was a limited amount of reconstruction and new construction of housing both in the city and in the country. In the liberated regions alone, 12.8 million square meters of urban housing space and 839 thousand rural houses were built in the years 1943 and 1944 (*ibid.,* p. 62). For present purposes it is supposed that this construction offset normal losses.

In Appendix Table 10, the figures on urban and rural housing available in 1948 are obtained by adding to the corresponding figures for 1944 the increments in the different kinds of housing in question from 1944 through 1948. The increments in the different kinds of housing shown in Appendix Table 10 are estimated from information in A. Bergson, J. H. Blackman, and A. Erlich, "Postwar Economic Reconstruction and Development in the U.S.S.R.," *Annals of the American Academy of Political and Social Science,* May, 1949, pp. 64 ff.; and *Pravda,* June 9, 1948, p. 1.

We have referred so far to the estimates of housing space used in our estimates of the imputed net rent of owner-occupied dwellings. It remains to explain the imputed annual rental, per square meter. For each year this is calculated from the average monthly wage and from a formula established by law for calculating rentals for government-owned urban housing. See Ministerstvo Kommunal'nogo Khoziaistva RSFSR, *Zhilishchnye zakony,* pp. 158 ff., and D. L. Broner, *Kurs zhilishchnogo khoziaistva,* pp. 99–106. The formula, which has remained essentially unchanged since 1928, establishes basic rental rates for a monthly wage of 145 rubles as 30 to 44 kopeks, varying according to the locality. We take the average basic rental rate for the USSR as a whole as 38 kopeks per square meter. For every 10 rubles of average monthly wages above 145 rubles, an additional rental of 3.3 kopeks per square meter is charged.

The calculation of the average monthly rental for the whole USSR, then, may be made by means of the following equation, where R is the average monthly rental in kopeks, per square meter, and W is the average monthly wage in rubles:

$$R = 38 \text{ kopeks} + 3.3 \left(\frac{W - 145}{10} \right) \text{kopeks,}$$

which may be reduced to

$$R = .33 \ W - 9.85.$$

In Appendix Table 11, below, we obtain in this manner for each year the average monthly rental per square meter in kopeks (R) in column (3); reduce it to rubles (R/100) in column (4); and multiply by 12 to get the average annual owner-imputed rental per square meter in rubles, shown in column (5).

The average annual rentals shown in column (5) of Appendix Table 11 probably overstate somewhat the rentals charged for government-owned housing because we cannot take account of deductions allowed for dependents and substandard housing. These are presumably reflected in data on the average rental and the average wage in Moscow, presented by D. L. Broner in *Ocherki ekonomiki zhilishchnogo khoziaistva Moskvy,* p. 38: the 1940 average annual rental of 13.32 rubles which he indicates for Moscow is lower than our equation gives (16.64 rubles) for the 1940 average monthly wage of 450 rubles in Moscow. However, our 1940 USSR rental of 12 rubles, calculated for the lower monthly USSR wage of 339 rubles, is less than the rental given by Broner for Moscow alone.

The sources of the figures for the average monthly wage in the USSR, shown in column (1) of Appendix Table 11, are as follows:

1940. See 1944 notes to item 3 (i) of Appendix Table 8.

1944. The same as for 1940.

1948. According to Appendix Table 8, the comprehensive civilian wage bill amounted to 294 billion rubles in 1948, or to 187 percent of the corresponding figure for 1940, 157 billion rubles. The labor force in 1948 amounted to 33.4 million compared with 31.2 million in 1940. The 1948 figure is 107 percent of that for 1940. The data on the labor force are from Voznesenskii,

APPENDIX TABLE 11

CALCULATION OF AVERAGE ANNUAL RENTAL
PER SQUARE METER, 1940, 1944, AND 1948

YEAR	W (average monthly wage, rubles)	.33W (kopeks)	R (col. [2] minus 9.85 kopeks)	$\frac{R}{100}$ (average monthly rental per sq. meter, rubles)	$12 \times \frac{R}{100}$ (average annual rental per sq. meter, rubles)
	(1)	(2)	(3)	(4)	(5)
1940	339	111.87	102.02	1.00	12.00
1944	481	158.73	148.88	1.50	18.00
1948	593	195.69	185.84	1.90	22.80

Voennaia ekonomika . . . , p. 13; Bergson *et al., Annals . . . ,* May, 1949, p. 56; and the privately circulated Appendix to this article, pp 1–2. Thus the increase in average annual money wages may be calculated at 75 percent. The figures on the labor force cited here are limited in coverage; in scope they are to be compared with the TSUNKHU wage bill as distinct from the comprehensive civilian wage bill. See the notes to Table 3-A, item 2. But it is believed that the figures may serve well enough for present purposes to indicate the change in the employed labor force generally.

5. INCOME OF ARMED FORCES

5a. Military pay

These figures are calculated from the estimates of troop strength and average military pay rates in Appendix Table 12.

The basic data are from the following sources.

1940. 1. Military personnel. Estimated on the basis of scattered data, including an unpublished estimate by Hanson W. Baldwin, military editor, New York *Times.*

1940. 2. Annual rates of pay. The average rates of the new pay scale introduced in 1940 are estimated from information presented by K. Voroshilov
to the XVIII Party Congress in *XVIII S"ezd VKP(b)*, p. 198; in Walter
Kerr, *The Russian Army*, p. 7; and in W. H. Hutt, "Two Studies in the
Statistics of Russia," *The South African Journal of Economics,* March, 1945,
pp. 41–42.

1944. 1. Military personnel. The total is based on the following estimates
of the wartime peak strength of the Red Army: 10 to 12 million men (Han-

APPENDIX TABLE 12

MILITARY PERSONNEL AND PAY, 1940, 1944, AND 1948

ITEM	*1940*	*1944*	*1948*
1. Military personnel (millions)			
(i) Enlisted personnel	3.15	10.80	3.50
(ii) Officers	.35	1.20	.50
(iii) Total	3.50	12.00	4.00
2. Annual rates of pay (rubles)			
(i) Enlisted personnel	200.00	200.00	1,500.00
(ii) Officers	10,000.00	10,000.00	17,500.00
3. Military pay (bil. rubles)			
(i) Payments to enlisted personnel	.63	2.16	5.25
(ii) Payments to officers	3.50	12.00	8.75
(iii) Total	4.13	14.16	14.00

son W. Baldwin, New York *Times,* April 17, 1946, p. 14); 12.5 million men
(General Deane, New York *Herald Tribune,* October 31, 1945, p. 18). As
in 1940, enlisted personnel are taken as 90 percent, and officers as 10 percent,
of the total military personnel.

1944. 2. Annual rates of pay. It is assumed that the military pay rates
introduced in 1940 remained unchanged throughout the war. This assumption may not be entirely realistic, even though no changes in pay rates were
announced by the Soviet government until September, 1946. In the interim
a number of regulations were introduced concerning higher pay rates for
elite troops ("guard" units) of the Red Army and special remuneration and
privileges for the recipients of decorations. Furthermore, it is likely that the
military pay bill was inflated by general up-grading in the course of the
war and by higher longevity pay for increased length of service. These
changes are not taken into account here, since no data are available concerning them.

1948. 1. Military personnel. The total is the estimate generally made by non-Soviet writers regarding Soviet military strength in 1948, excluding the internal security forces of the MVD. See, for example, the estimates of Hanson W. Baldwin in New York *Times,* March 27, 1949, p. 5E, and May 16, 1949, p. 6. Possibly this figure on military strength is too high. Official Soviet statements imply a much smaller one; but this is widely discounted and we therefore do not accept it for purposes of the present calculation. In a Soviet foreign ministry reply to a British note in 1951 (*Pravda,* February 25, 1951, p. 3), for example, the current aggregate strength of the Soviet army, navy, and air force is stated to be about 2.5 million. Since it is also indicated that demobilization was completed early in 1948, this figure would apply to that year as well.

The ratio of officers to enlisted personnel is taken as 1:7, instead of the 1:9 ratio of 1940 and 1944. There are indications that the enlisted ranks were demobilized more rapidly than officers in the postwar period, with a larger share of the career officers, who serve indefinitely in the Soviet army, being retained on active duty.

1948. 2. Annual rates of pay. These are estimated from scattered data, including the pay scale by ranks, shown in Louis B. Ely, *The Red Army Today,* p. 223. The new military pay rates decreed at the time of the general wage-price revision of September, 1946 (see *Izvestiia,* September 16, 1946), have not been published in available Soviet sources.

5b. Military subsistence

This is calculated from the estimates of military strength just derived, and from very rough estimates in current rubles of the average cost, per man, of the food and clothing provided the armed forces. The calculations are summarized in Appendix Table 13, p. 138. The figures in Table 3 correspond to those in Appendix Table 13 after rounding.

In estimating the average cost of subsistence we assume that its real cost did not change after 1937, when, as estimated in *Soviet National Income,* p. 109, it was 1,500 rubles .To take account of subsequent price rises, we inflate the 1937 cost by means of a crude retail price index. Using an index of state retail prices of consumers' goods as an indicator of changes in the cost of military subsistence does not seem to be inappropriate under Soviet conditions. It appears from data in Narkomfin SSSR, Upravlenie Gosdokhodov, *Spravochnik po stavkam naloga s oborota i biudzhetnoi raznitse po prodo-vol'stvennym tovaram,* pp. 22–74, that the "wholesale" prices paid by the Soviet defense ministries for troop food rations include the turnover tax and probably differ from ordinary retail prices by little more than the retail trading margin, which is only about 7 or 8 percent of the wholesale price. Whether this is true of all military subsistence is conjectural; but assuming that it is, changes in the retail prices of these goods, whether due to increases in wholesale prices or turnover tax, would be reflected in the average cost of military consumption. And changes in the price index of consumers' goods as a whole would probably not greatly misrepresent changes in the average cost of military subsistence, since food and clothing predominate in both groups of goods.

The retail price index is obtained as follows:

1940. This is calculated from the retail price index for food in S. N. Prokopovicz, *Quarterly Bulletin of Soviet-Russian Economics,* May, 1941, p. 130. The order of magnitude of the indicated price change is confirmed by

APPENDIX TABLE 13

CALCULATION OF MILITARY SUBSISTENCE, 1940, 1944, AND 1948

ITEM	*1940*	*1944*	*1948*
1. Total military personnel (millions)	3.50	12.00	4.00
2. Average cost of subsistence, per man, in 1937 rubles	1,500	1,500	1,500
3. Retail price index (1937 = 100)	155	171	317
4. Average cost of subsistence, per man, in current rubles $\left(\text{item } 1 \times \dfrac{\text{item } 2}{100} \right)$	2,325	2,565	4,755
5. Total cost of military subsistence (bil. rubles)	8.14	30.78	19.02

data on changes in the prices of food and clothing between 1936 and 1941 in I. B. Kravis and J. Mintzes, "Food Prices in the Soviet Union, 1936–50," *Review of Economics and Statistics,* May, 1950, pp. 166–67.

1944. This is based on our estimate of a 10 percent rise in the retail prices of rationed goods between 1940 and 1944. This estimate rests on the following data: (i) the price quotations in the *Monthly Labor Review* (February, 1941, pp. 474–76; May, 1941, pp. 1294–96; and July, 1947, p. 28), indicating that by June, 1941, state retail prices were 10 percent higher than their average 1940 level; (ii) Voznesenskii's statement (*Voennaia ekonomika* . . . , p. 128) that the index of state retail prices for rationed goods hardly changed during the war years. According to Voznesenskii, the index in 1943 was 100.5 percent of its prewar level. We take this prewar level to mean the period immediately preceding the outbreak of war, i.e., June, 1941.

1948. This is based on scattered data concerning the prices charged by Moscow's retail stores for comparable articles of food and clothing in 1937 and 1948. Included among the sources is the unpublished United States Bureau of Labor Statistics circular, LS 49–3420, dated March 22, 1949.

According to our estimates, the total outlays on military pay and sub-sistence in 1948 are almost one-half of that year's budget appropriation for defense, whereas in 1944 the proportion was one-third, and in 1940, less than one-fourth. See Table 4-B, item 4, for defense appropriations. Although this ratio depends on many variables besides troop strength, pay rates, and cost of subsistence, the large ratio for 1948 raises some doubts about our estimates of these items. Evidence supporting the magnitudes we have arrived at, how-ever, may be found in the 1947 budget speech of A. G. Zverev, the USSR Minister of Finance (*O gosudarstvennom biudzhete SSSR na 1947 god,* p. 17). In speaking of the decline in the defense appropriation from 72.6 billion rubles in 1946 to 67.0 billion rubles in 1947, he noted that the decrease of 5.6 billion rubles was to occur "notwithstanding the increase in food prices and servicemen's pay, introduced in the latter part of 1946," and that the reduction would have amounted to 24 percent if these increases had not taken place. The difference of 11.8 billion rubles between a 24 percent reduction in the military appropriation of 1946 and the actual reduction of 5.6 billion rubles may be ascribed to the increased cost of military pay and subsistence due to the pay and price increases. This, it is believed, represents only a fraction of the 1947 outlays on military pay and subsistence. Accordingly, the magnitude of these outlays in 1947 may well have been of the order indi-cated by our estimates for 1948. With demobilization continuing until early in 1948, however, the outlays on military pay and subsistence were probably higher in 1947 than in 1948.

6. STATISTICAL DISCREPANCY

For all years this is the difference between the sum of all incomes, both earned and unearned, itemized in Table 3-A, and the sum of the outlays itemized in Table 3-B.

8. PENSIONS AND ALLOWANCES

Soviet public welfare payments are disbursed through three programs: "social insurance" (*sotsial'noe strakhovanie*), under which old-age pensions and sick benefits are paid; "social assistance" (*sotsial'noe obespechenie*), which provides disability pensions to war invalids, "invalids of labor," and their families; and assistance to mothers of many children and unmarried mothers. For each year, our estimate of pensions and allowances is calculated as the sum of the pensions, sick benefits, and allowances paid under these three programs. The pertinent data are shown in Appendix Table 14.

The foregoing expenditures do not comprise all the outlays of the govern-ment budget under the headings of "social insurance" and "social assistance." Of the budget appropriations for social insurance and social assistance, a part is used not for transfer payments, but for the maintenance of rest homes, sanitariums, camps, veterans' rehabilitation centers, war invalids' homes, etc., and therefore is not included in the present calculation. See notes to Table 4-B, item 1c, and N. N. Rovinskii, *Gosudarstvennyi biudzhet SSSR,* 1944 ed., pp. 239 ff.

The figures on the different kinds of pensions and allowances in Appendix Table 14 are obtained as follows:

1940. 1. Pensions and sick benefits paid under social insurance program. This is taken as 60 percent of the total budget outlays on social insurance, which amounted to 5.01 billion rubles, according to K. N. Plotnikov, *Biudzhet*

APPENDIX TABLE 14

PENSIONS AND ALLOWANCES, 1940, 1944, AND 1948

(Billions of rubles)

ITEM	1940	1944	1948
1. Pensions and sick benefits paid under the social insurance program	3.01	3.00	5.22
2. Disability pensions paid under the social assistance program	2.83	15.80	18.42
3. Allowances paid to mothers of many children and unmarried mothers	1.23	.90	2.50
4. Total pensions and allowances	7.07	19.70	26.14

sotsialisticheskogo gosudarstva, 1948 ed., p. 329. The remaining 40 percent of the social insurance expenditures, amounting to 2.00 billion rubles, constitute nontransfer outlays for the maintenance of rest homes, sanitariums, etc. The ratio of transfer to nontransfer payments in the social insurance expenditures is based on information in V. P. D'iachenko, *Finansy i kredit SSSR,* p. 382.

1940. 2. Disability pensions paid under the social assistance program. Total disbursements under this program amounted to 3.13 billion rubles (Plotnikov, 1948 ed., p. 329), of which .30 billion rubles are assumed to have been for nontransfer payments.

1940. 3. Allowances paid to mothers of many children and unmarried mothers. See *ibid.*

1944. 1. Pensions and sick benefits paid under social insurance program. Total outlays on social insurance amounted to 3.72 billion rubles. See *ibid.* Of this, .72 billion rubles are estimated to have been for the maintenance of rest homes, rehabilitation centers, etc. See *Trud,* June 1, 1944, p. 3.

1944. 2. Disability pensions paid under the social assistance program. See Plotnikov, 1948 ed., p. 329.

1944. 3. Allowances paid to mothers of many children and unmarried mothers. See *ibid*.

1948. 1. Pensions and sick benefits paid under social insurance program. Total outlays on social insurance amounted to 8.70 billion rubles. See A. G. Zverev, "Gosudarstvennyi biudzhet chetvertogo goda poslevoennoi stalinskoi piatiletki," *Planovoe khoziaistvo,* No. 2, 1949, p. 48. Of this sum, we take 60 percent as pension and sick benefit payments, i.e., the same ratio as in 1940. The other 3.48 billion rubles are nontransfer payments, including 1.2 billion rubles for the maintenance of rest homes and sanitariums, and .7 billion rubles for pioneer camps. See *V pomoshch FZMK,* No. 7, 1949, pp. 8–9. The order of magnitude of this division between transfer and non-transfer payments in the postwar social insurance budget is supported by a detailed budget for the year 1950, published in 1951. See A. S. Krasnopolskii, "O prirode sovetskogo gosudarstvennogo sotsial'nogo strakhovaniia," *Sovet-skoe gosudarstvo i pravo,* No. 6, 1951, pp. 62 ff. A translation of this article appears in *The Current Digest of the Soviet Press,* Vol. III, No. 46, December 29, 1951.

1948. 2. Disability pensions paid under the social assistance program. This is the total amount spent on social assistance, according to Zverev, *Planovoe khoziaistvo,* No. 2, 1949, p. 48. We assume that all of it constitutes pensions, although a small part may have been spent on the maintenance of institutions for veterans' rehabilitation and war invalids' homes.

1948. 3. Allowance paid to mothers of many children and unmarried mothers. See *ibid*. These grants were sharply reduced from 5.9 billion rubles in 1947, in accordance with a decree "on the reduction of motherhood grants," dated November 25, 1947. See *Trud,* November 26, 1947.

9. STIPENDS AND SCHOLARSHIPS

This is intended to comprise stipends paid to students in higher educational institutions and technicums and tuition scholarships granted to students in these schools and in the senior classes of secondary schools. The data on these different items, which are set forth in Appendix Table 15, were obtained as follows:

1. Stipends: 1940. The point of departure is given by the estimates below of stipend payments in billions of rubles during 1934–38:

YEAR	TOTAL STIPENDS
1934	1.0
1937	2.2
1938	2.6

These estimates are from the computations in *Soviet National Income,* p. 109, which are based in turn on data in Margolin, *Balans* . . . , p. 8. We take the stipends in 1940 to be 2.4 billion rubles, or .2 billion less than in 1938 in order to allow for a probable decline in enrollment in higher educational institutions and technicums during this period. See the data on enrollments in higher educational institutions alone in Stalin's report to the XVIII Party Congress (*XVIII S"ezd* . . . , p. 28); and in *Finansy SSSR za XXX let*, pp. 220–23.

1944. These are taken as 85 percent of the 1940 stipend payments. According to *Odinnadtsataia sessiia Verkhovnogo Soveta SSSR* . . . *1945 g.,* p. 17, the number of students in higher educational institutions and technicums declined from 1.505 million in 1940 to 1.158 million in 1944, or about 25

APPENDIX TABLE 15

STIPENDS AND SCHOLARSHIPS, 1940, 1944, AND 1948

(*Billions of rubles*)

ITEM	1940	1944	1948
1. Stipends	2.40	2.04	2.90
2. Tuition scholarships	.03	.10	.10
3. Total stipends and scholarships	2.43	2.14	3.00

---

percent. It is believed that the decline in stipends must have been less than proportional to the decline in enrollment. According to Voznesenskii, *Voennaia ekonomika* . . . , p. 116, during the war "the Soviet government increased the number of stipends in higher educational institutions." Also, changes in rates in 1943 resulted in a small increase in the average stipend.

1948. According to *Odinnadtsataia sessiia Verkhovnogo Soveta SSSR* . . . *1945 g.,* p. 17, enrollment in higher educational institutions and technicums in 1948 was 1.806 million, or 20 percent above 1944. Stipends are assumed to have increased proportionately.

2. Scholarships. These are more or less arbitrary estimates, based mainly on data in A. Bergson, *The Structure of Soviet Wages,* pp. 234 ff.; Ministerstvo Vysshego Obrazovaniia SSSR, *Vysshaia shkola,* pp. 547 ff.; *Shestaia sessiia Verkhovnogo Soveta RSFSR,* pp. 26 and 196; *Zasedaniia Verkhovnogo Soveta RSFSR (vtoraia sessiia)* . . . *1948 g.,* p. 196. Tuition fees were introduced in the USSR in 1940 and were payable only during the second half of the 1940 school year. This is the main reason for the fact that the 1940 figure on scholarships in Appendix Table 15 is low compared with that for 1944 and 1948.

10. INTEREST RECEIPTS

This comprises interest receipts of households on state bonds, including net winnings on lottery bonds, and on savings deposits. The two types of receipts are shown in Appendix Table 16. Referring to each in turn, the figures cited are obtained as follows:

1. Interest paid to households on state bonds: 1940. Plotnikov, 1948 ed., p. 292. Plotnikov is ambiguous as to the nature of the figure which we cite here, but it is believed that this figure represents interest paid to households on government bonds.

1944. See *ibid.*

1948. See *Pravda,* May 4, 1949, p. 1.

APPENDIX TABLE 16

INTEREST RECEIPTS, 1940, 1944, AND 1948

(Billions of rubles)

ITEM	1940	1944	1948
1. Interest paid to households on state bonds	1.16	2.84	1.40
2. Interest on savings deposits	.23	.42	.44
3. Total interest receipts of households	1.39	3.26	1.84

---

2. Interest on savings deposits. This must be calculated from data on the amount of savings deposits and the interest rate paid on these deposits. We take 3.25 percent to be the average annual rate of interest on savings deposits in all years. This rate of interest is implied by the following data: Savings deposits averaged 6.5 billion rubles during 1939. See M. Bodrov, "Narodnye sberezheniia v SSSR," *Bol'shevik,* No. 3–4, 1941, p. 76. These deposits yielded a total of .20 billion rubles in interest. See A. G. Zverev, *Gosudarstvennye biudzhety Soiuza SSR, 1938–1945 gg.,* p. 73. No changes in interest rates on savings deposits have been introduced since 1939. See L. B. Valler, *Sberegatel'noe delo v SSSR,* p. 63. The implied average annual interest rate of 3.25 percent may be compared with the interest rate structure: regular savings accounts earn 3 percent and, since 1939, long-term accounts, 5 percent. See *Finansy SSSR za XXX let,* p. 308.

The average amount of savings deposits for the years studied is obtained as follows:

1940. The average savings are taken as 7.16 billion rubles on the basis of data in Plotnikov, 1948 ed., pp. 201–2.

1944. The average savings deposits are taken as 12.82 billion rubles, or the sum of: (a) the average of savings deposits held by the population on January 1, 1944, and January 1, 1945, as listed in *ibid.,* p. 298, which comes to 4.82 billion rubles; and (b) the assumed average for 1944 of the special deposits which were opened for employees beginning in 1942 in compensation for accumulated wartime leave. According to A. K. Suchkov, *Dokhody gosudarstvennogo biudzheta SSSR,* pp. 185–86, about 4 billion rubles were paid into these accounts during 1944, and it is mainly on this basis that we take the average amount of such deposits held in 1944 as 8 billion rubles.

Soviet sources do not state explicitly that the special deposits just referred to, i.e., item (b) above, are not included in statistics on deposits of the sort cited by Plotnikov, i.e., item (a) above, but we believe that we are right in assuming this is the case. There may also be other omissions, particularly the deposits made by military personnel in the so-called "field banks." See Plotnikov, 1948 ed., p. 297.

1948. The average savings deposits are taken as 13.55 billion rubles. This is the average of the total savings deposits of 12.8 billion rubles at the beginning of 1948 and the deposits of 14.3 billion rubles expected by the end of the year. See A. G. Zverev, *O gosudarstvennom biudzhete SSSR na 1948 god,* p. 17. The anticipated increase of 1.5 billion rubles in savings deposits during 1948 was proabably fulfilled, since in Moscow alone savings deposits increased by .34 billion rubles between January, 1948, and April, 1949. See New York *Times,* April 23, 1949.

B. OUTLAYS

1. RETAIL SALES TO HOUSEHOLDS

1a. In government and cooperative shops and restaurants

This is calculated as the difference between the total retail turnover in state and cooperative shops and restaurants, and the sales in those outlets to institutional buyers. The calculations are summarized in Appendix Table 17.

To refer first to the sales to institutional buyers: For 1940 it is assumed that such sales amounted to 7.5 percent of the total sales to all buyers. This is based on the fact that near the end of 1938, when the relative share of institutional purchases in the total state and cooperative retail turnover was approximately 11 to 12 percent, the government ordered the curtailment of such buying. See Margolin, *Balans . . . ,* p. 89; *Sobranie postanovlenii . . . SSSR,* No. 52, December 9, 1938, p. 670. According to data in the 1941 national economic plan, the sales to institutions were to amount to only 3.4 percent of the total state and cooperative turnover that year. See *Gosudarstvennyi plan . . . na 1941 god,* p. 590. This, however, may have been a wishful understatement, or the government's data on such sales may have been incomplete. This latter hypothesis appears likely from a reading of Margolin, *Balans . . . ,* pp. 88–89.

Sales to institutional buyers are believed to have been small in 1944 because of rationing and the existence of "workers' supply sections" within enterprises; accordingly we assume that in relation to total sales these sales fell to 5 percent in that year. Because of the lack of postwar data, the percentage is taken to be the same in 1948 as in 1940.

Referring now to the total sales in state and cooperative outlets, the data on this category in Appendix Table 17 are obtained as follows.

1940. Voznesenskii, *Voennaia ekonomika . . . ,* p. 13.

APPENDIX TABLE 17

CALCULATION OF TOTAL RETAIL SALES AND RETAIL SALES TO HOUSEHOLDS IN STATE AND COOPERATIVE SHOPS AND RESTAURANTS, 1940, 1944, AND 1948

(Billions of rubles)

ITEM	1940	1944	1948
1. Total sales of state and cooperative retail shops	175.10	119.11	330.00
2. Less: Sales to institutions by state and cooperative retail outlets	13.13	5.95	24.80
3. Retail sales to households in state and cooperative shops and restaurants	161.97	113.16	305.20

1944. Total sales of state and cooperative outlets have just been taken as 175.1 billion rubles for the year 1940. This total comprises sales of state and cooperative restaurants, which according to *Sovetskaia torgovlia za XXX let,* p. 114, amounted to 23 billion rubles, and sales of other outlets, which may be calculated at 152.1 billion rubles. According to M. M. Lifits (ed.), *Ekonomika sovetskoi torgovli,* p. 106, the turnover of state and cooperative restaurants in 1944 was 24.4 percent greater than in 1940, while the turnover of other state and cooperative shops in 1944 was only 59.5 percent of the 1940 figure. Lifits does not say explicitly that he is referring to "state and cooperative" outlets here, but it is believed that this is so, and our figure on the total sales of state and cooperative outlets for 1944 is calculated on the basis of his percentages, taken together with the absolute figures for 1940 just cited. Thus, restaurant sales in 1944 amount to 28.61 billion rubles, i.e., 1.244 × 23; sales by other outlets, to 90.50 billion rubles, i.e., .595 × 152.1; and total sales, to 119.11 billion rubles.

According to the foregoing data, restaurant sales amounted to about 24 percent of sales by all outlets in 1944. This result may be compared with the corresponding ratio, 25 percent, given in Voznesenskii, *Voennaia ekonomika . . . ,* p. 125, for the year 1943.

1948. According to information set forth shortly, the total retail sales of state and cooperative outlets probably amounted to some 320.0 billion rubles in 1947. We assume that the corresponding figure for 1948 was only 10.0 billion rubles greater than this, or 330.0 billion rubles. Turnover tax receipts, derived mainly from consumers' goods, increased from 1947 to 1948, but only by about 3 percent, i.e., from 239.9 to 247.5 billion rubles. As a result of cuts instituted in December, 1947, retail prices in 1948 probably were somewhat below the 1947 level. Insofar as these cuts were due to a reduction in turnover tax rates rather than costs, the apparent implication is that the physical volume of trade increased more than proportionately to the price cut, but it is difficult to credit fully large Russian claims in this regard, as for example, in B. I. Gogol', *Sovetskaia torgovlia i ee rol' v narodnom khoziaistve,* p. 65; and Moskvin, *Bol'shevik,* No. 15, 1948, pp. 32 ff. Actually, so far as the retail sales turnover is concerned, the Russians themselves have made no large claims. Rather, they have contented themselves with the unusually modest statement that "in 1948 the retail trade turnover increased in comparison with 1947" (*Pravda,* March 13, 1949, p. 4).

As to the total retail sales of state and cooperative shops in 1947, this is calculated from two items of information in A. Klimov, "Sovetskaia potrebitel'skaia kooperatsiia na sovremennom etape," *Voprosy ekonomiki,* No. 6, 1948, pp. 99, 100; (i) the total retail turnover of consumers' cooperatives amounted to 70.4 billion rubles in 1947; and (ii) the share of consumers' cooperatives in the total sales turnover "of the country" is 22 percent. Klimov does not indicate the period to which this latter percentage refers, and there is a further ambiguity as to whether the total sales turnover "of the country" is understood as exclusive or inclusive of collective farm trade. We assume provisionally that the period is 1947 and that the turnover is exclusive of collective farm trade.

The resulting estimate of the total retail sales of state and cooperative outlets in 1947, 320.0 billion rubles, may be compared with the goal of the annual plan for that year: 324.6 billion rubles (see Sovet Ministrov SSSR, *O gosudarstvennom plane . . . na 1947 god,* p. 25). Also, the indicated limited underfulfillment is corroborated by a corresponding underfulfillment of the goal for turnover tax revenue. The actual turnover tax receipts were 239.9 billion rubles, whereas the goal was 254.7 billion rubles.

On the other hand, reference is also to be made to some other information that is somewhat at variance with the foregoing. According to Gogol', *Sovetskaia torgovlia . . . ,* p. 65, state retail trade in 1947 constituted 76.7 percent of state and cooperative trade taken together. The share of cooperative trade, then, was 23.3 percent of the total. We have already cited a figure of 70.4 billion rubles for the trade of consumers' cooperatives in 1947. In addition, cooperative trade in the USSR also comprises the trade of producers' and invalids' cooperatives. According to P. V. Evseev, "Reservy uvelicheniia vypuska tovarov shirokogo potrebleniia v mestnoi i koopera-tivnoi promyshlennosti," *Planovoe khoziaistvo*, No. 4, 1948, p. 52, the sales of these latter cooperatives amounted to 7.65 billion rubles in 1947. Accord-ingly, the total sales of all cooperatives come to 78.05 billion rubles, and the total trade of state and cooperative outlets together, 335.00 billion rubles, i.e., 78.05 billion rubles ÷ 23.3 percent.

What is the explanation of the inconsistency? It is probable that, contrary to a supposition in the foregoing calculation, the figure cited on sales of producers' and invalids' cooperatives includes some wholesale as well as retail sales. The Soviet source is not explicit on this aspect; it is said only that the "trade turnover" of the producers' and invalids' cooperatives amounted to 7.65 billion rubles. According to Lifits (ed.), *Ekonomika sovet-skoi torgovli*, p. 143, a "serious deficiency in the work of the producers' cooperative" that had already appeared in the prewar period was the "cur-tailment by it of its own retail network and the transition only to the whole-sale realization of the goods produced by it for personal consumption." Lifits adds that the government took steps to change this situation in 1946. But very likely it still obtained to a considerable extent in 1947. Assuming that the retail sales of producers' and invalids' cooperatives amounted only to 4.2 rather than to 7.65 billion rubles, it is readily seen that the inconsistency vanishes, i.e., 74.6 billion rubles ÷ 23.3 percent = 320 billion rubles.

Another possibility is that our calculation is affected by rounding errors. We cited above a figure from Klimov on the share of consumers' coopera-tives in all state and cooperative retail trade: 22 percent. If the share before rounding had been 21.5 percent, total retail sales would have come to 327 instead of 320 billion rubles. But apparently there is still a sizable discrepancy to be reckoned with.

In the foregoing we have been concerned primarily with the magnitude of the total retail sales of state and cooperative trade. In various connections it is also useful to have at hand the following tabulation of this total by organization (all figures in billions of rubles):

	1947 (Plan)	1947	1948
1. Retail sales by cooperatives			
(i) By consumers' cooperatives	n.a.[a]	70.4	n.a.
(ii) By cooperatives of producers and invalids	n.a.	4.2	n.a.
(iii) Total	73.0	74.6	70.0
2. Retail sales by state shops	251.6	245.4	260.0
3. Total	324.6	320.0	330.0

[a] n.a. = information not available.

The sources and methods used in deriving the breakdown of the planned

and realized sales in 1947 already have been indicated. As to the breakdown
for 1948, it is believed that price cuts in cooperative trade (induced, it is
claimed, by the December, 1947, reductions in state retail prices) must have
caused a small decline in the 1948 value of cooperative sales, as compared
with 1947. This is in spite of the "real" increase of 18 percent claimed in
Pravda, March 21, 1949, p. 2. According to Gogol', *Sovetskaia torgovlia . . . ,*
pp. 55–56, and S. Gurevich and S. Partigul, *Novyi pod"em narodnogo
khoziaistva SSSR v poslevoennoi piatiletke,* p. 131, prices in urban consumers' cooperative markets were 45 percent lower in the first quarter of
1948 than in the same quarter of 1947. The price declines in all cooperative
outlets, however, may not have been so steep.

1b. In collective farm markets

As indicated in Appendix Table 18, this is calculated as the difference
between the total sales in collective farm markets and the sales there to
institutional buyers.

APPENDIX TABLE 18

CALCULATION OF RETAIL SALES TO HOUSEHOLDS IN
COLLECTIVE FARM MARKETS, 1940, 1944, AND 1948

(Billions of rubles)

ITEM	1940	1944	1948
1. Total sales in collective farm markets	41.20	55.00	60.00
2. Less: Sales to institutions in collective farm markets	6.18	5.00	12.00
3. Retail sales to households in collective farm markets	35.02	50.00	48.00

To refer first to the sales to institutional buyers: According to Margolin,
Voprosy . . . , p. 63, these amounted to about 10 percent of the total sales in
collective farm markets in the late thirties. In view of the attempt at the end
of 1938 to limit the purchases of institutions in state and cooperative retail
outlets (see the notes to Appendix Table 17, item 2), it seems probable that
these purchasers may have acquired a larger share of the collective farm
market produce in 1940 than hitherto. Accordingly, we take the share for
this year to have been 15 percent. On the other hand, collective farm market
prices were exorbitant during the war; so for the year 1944 we assume this
share to be about the same in relation to total sales as it had been in the late
thirties. For the year 1948, the relative share is taken to be 20 percent. This
takes into account information in Moskvin, *Bol'shevik,* No. 15, 1948, pp.
40–41, indicating that cooperative organizations purchased a larger share of

collective farm market goods in the postwar period than before the war, e.g., 48 percent of all meat, 11 percent of all vegetables, 6 percent of all potatoes, 58 percent of all butter.

Referring now to the total sales in collective farm markets, the figure for 1940 is taken from M. M. Lifits, *Sovetskaia torgovlia,* p. 33. The figure for 1944 requires lengthy explanation; we shall return to this in a moment.

The 1948 figure on collective farm sales is calculated on the basis of information in *Pravda,* March 1, 1949, p. 1, and April 23, 1949, p. 1, that "the proportion of collective farm and cooperative goods in the total mass of goods sold to the population in the course of a year amounts to about 33 percent." Since all domestic retail trade in the USSR falls into the three categories of state trade, cooperative trade, and collective farm market trade, we take this statement in *Pravda* to mean that the combined value of sales in cooperative outlets and in collective farm markets in 1948 was 50 percent of the value of sales in state retail stores. We have already estimated that the retail sales of cooperative shops amounted to 70.0 billion rubles in 1948, while those of state shops amounted to 260.0 billion rubles (see notes to Table 3-B, item 1a). It follows that cooperative and collective farm market sales together should have amounted to 130.0 billion rubles, and, accordingly, that collective farm market sales alone amounted to 60.0 billion rubles.

This estimate of collective farm market sales may be low in view of other available information concerning collective farm trade in 1948. According to Lifits, *Voprosy ekonomiki,* No. 7, 1951, p. 79, the volume of goods sold in collective farm markets was 22 percent greater in 1948 than in 1940. With the collective farm market sales in 1940 amounting to 41.2 billion rubles, this statement indicates that the 1948 sales in collective farm markets, valued in 1940 prices, amount to 50.26 billion rubles. Data cited by Kravis and Mintzes, *Review of Economics and Statistics,* May, 1950, p. 167, indicate an increase in the unweighted average of collective farm market prices of over 100 percent between January, 1940, and January, 1948. However, according to an unpublished study of Soviet retail prices, undertaken as part of a doctoral thesis by Mrs. Janet Chapman, Columbia University, collective farm market prices increased markedly in the course of 1940 and decreased markedly in the course of 1948, so that the index of their average all-year 1940 level was probably some 20 percent higher than their level in January, 1940, and the index of their average all-year 1948 level was probably some 20 percent lower than their level in January, 1948. These two items of information, then, suggest an increase between 1940 and 1948 of approximately 33 percent in the average all-year level of collective farm market prices. Assuming the 22 percent increase in physical volume indicated above, collective farm market sales in 1948 come to 66.9 billion rubles.

We refer finally to collective farm market sales for the year 1944. Because

APPENDIX TABLE 19

MONEY INCOMES AND OUTLAYS OF RURAL
AND URBAN HOUSEHOLDS, 1944
(*Billions of rubles*)

A. INCOMES	ALL HOUSEHOLDS	RURAL HOUSEHOLDS	URBAN HOUSEHOLDS
1. Wages of farm labor	6.4	6.4	. . .[a]
2. Money payments to collective farmers on labor-day basis, etc.	9.8	9.8	. . .[a]
3. Net money income from sales of farm products			
(i) Sales to state and cooperative procurement agencies	4.0	4.0	. . .[a]
(ii) Sales to collective farm markets	45.0	45.0	. . .[a]
(iii) Less: Money costs of farm production	5.0	5.0	. . .[a]
(iv) Total	44.0	44.0	. . .[a]
4. Wages and salaries, nonfarm	149.6	15.0	134.6
5. Incomes of artisans; other money income currently earned	13.0	3.3	9.7
6. Military pay	14.2	7.1	7.1
7. Pensions and allowances			
(i) Social insurance benefits	3.0	.4	2.6
(ii) Social assistance benefits	15.8	7.9	7.9
(iii) Benefits to mothers of many children	.9	.6	.3
(iv) Total	19.7	8.9	10.8
8. Stipends and scholarships	2.1	. . .	2.1
9. Interest receipts	3.3	1.0	2.3
10. Statistical discrepancy	11.2	6.2	5.1
11. Total incomes	273.3	101.6	171.7

of the utter lack of data on these sales in Soviet sources, the writers had to appraise their magnitude from an involved and also highly tenuous calculation. In Appendix Table 19 are shown aggregative data on the money incomes and outlays of Soviet households in 1944. The incomes and outlays are tabulated for all households taken together, and for rural and urban households separately. The derivation of the data on all income and outlay categories other than collective farm sales and the income of households

APPENDIX TABLE 19 (*Continued*)

B. OUTLAYS	ALL HOUSEHOLDS	RURAL HOUSEHOLDS	URBAN HOUSEHOLDS
1. Retail sales to households in government and cooperative shops and restaurants	113.2	35.7	77.5
2. Retail sales to households in collective farm markets	50.0	15.0	35.0
3. Rent	2.3	. . . [a]	2.3
4. Services	11.6	3.5	8.1
5. Trade-union and other dues	1.8	.2	1.6
6. Net bond purchases	26.2	11.8	14.4
7. Increment in savings deposits	4.8	.7	4.1
8. Other savings, including increment in cash holdings	14.6	12.6	2.0
9. Direct taxes, etc.			
(i) Income tax	8.5	1.3	7.2
(ii) War tax	20.7	7.7	13.0
(iii) Tax on bachelors, etc.	2.2	1.1	1.1
(iv) Agricultural tax	5.6	5.6	. . . [a]
(v) Net lottery subscriptions	4.6	2.9	1.7
(vi) Cash donations to patriotic funds	3.3	1.6	1.7
(vii) Other charges	3.9	1.9	2.0
(viii) Total	48.8	22.1	26.7
10. Total outlays	273.3	101.6	171.7

[a] . . . = negligible.

from these sales will be explained in a moment. So far as collective farm sales and the income from these sales are concerned, these are derived more or less as residuals. More particularly, the calculation is as follows:

(i) Exclusive of collective farm market sales and the incomes derived from such sales, the incomes of the urban population exceed their outlays by some 29.9 billion rubles. At the same time, rural outlays exceed incomes by some 36.1 billion rubles.

(ii) Contrary to a general impression that collective farm market sales are almost exclusively in urban localities, it is believed that a substantial fraction of such sales actually are in rural localities. Thus, in an "illustrative" tabulation of household money incomes and outlays in Margolin, *Balans . . . ,* pp. 115–21, it is assumed that rural sales amount to 29.5 percent of the total of all sales. For present purposes it is assumed provisionally that the rural share of collective farm market sales in 1944 was about the same as in Margolin's tabulation, or 30 percent.

(iii) Let us assume provisionally that collective farm market sales to households amount to 50 billion rubles. Taking 70 percent of these sales as being made to urban households, this amounts to 35 billion rubles, or something more than the excess of urban incomes over urban outlays referred to in (i). At the same time, collective farm market sales to rural households amount to 15 billion rubles, while, as is explained below, these households derive some 45 billion rubles income from collective farm market sales, or 30 billion rubles more than their outlays in this market. This compares with the excess of rural outlays over incomes of 36.1 billion rubles referred to in (i). As to the incomes derived by rural households from collective farm market sales, the calculation is as follows: Assuming that total sales to households amount to 50 billion rubles, total sales to households and institutions come to 55 billion rubles (Appendix Table 18). Of these, 10 billion are sales by collective farms (Appendix Table 4), leaving 45 billion rubles as sales by farm households.

(iv) The foregoing indicates that a figure of 50 billion rubles for collective farm market sales to households is broadly correct, given the residuals to be explained and the assumed division of collective farm market sales between urban and rural households, i.e., 70 percent to the former and 30 percent to the latter. In view of the uncertainty regarding this latter aspect, however, it may be of interest to note the results of an alternative hypothesis: Suppose collective farm sales to urban households were 90 percent and collective farm sales to rural households 10 percent of the total. Assume provisionally that total sales to households amounted to 40 billion rubles; then sales to the urban households would come to 36 billion rubles, or about the same as before. Sales to rural households would be 4 billion rubles, while the incomes of such households from collective farm market sales might amount to about 34 billion rubles. Accordingly, the excess of rural incomes over outlays would come to 30 billion rubles, which is the same as before.

In Appendix Table 19, the figures on money incomes and outlays (other than collective farm market sales and the incomes therefrom) for all households taken together generally are taken directly from Table 3, p. 20. On the other hand, the figures on several items are taken from other sources, as follows:

A. Incomes:

3 (i). Sales to state and cooperative procurement agencies. Appendix Table 2.

3 (iii). Money costs of farm production. Appendix Table 2.

7 (i). Social insurance. Appendix Table 14.

7 (ii). Social assistance. Appendix Table 14.

7 (iii). Mothers of many children. Appendix Table 14.

B. Outlays:

3. Rent. Appendix Table 20.

4. Services. Appendix Table 20.

9 (i). Income tax. The total yield, 8.5 billion rubles, is calculated on the assumption that on the average the tax amounts to 5 percent on a total tax base of 169 billion rubles. The income tax rate varies not only with income but also as between different categories of the population; e.g., the rate is higher for cooperative artisans than for wage earners and salaried workers. The assumed average tax rate is about the rate levied on wage earners and salaried workers earning an estimated average wage of 481 rubles a month. The assumed tax base represents the sum of incomes of persons subject to the tax, or in Appendix Table 19, the total of farm wages, nonfarm wages, and the incomes of artisans, etc. For details on the income tax, including the tax scales, see Suchkov, *Dokhody . . . ,* pp. 133 ff.; on the estimated average wage, see the notes to Table 3-A, item 4. Our estimate of the income tax yield in 1944 may be compared with the corresponding figure for 1945, given in Plotnikov, 1948 ed., p. 281: 10.6 billion rubles.

9 (ii). War Tax. See *ibid.,* p. 277.

9 (iii). Tax on bachelors, etc. See *ibid.,* p. 278.

9 (iv). Agricultural tax. This is calculated as a residual in the total "taxes and levies on the population" of 37.0 billion rubles given in *ibid.,* p. 253.

9 (v). Net lottery subscriptions. See the notes to Table 3-B, item 7.

9 (vi). Cash donations to patriotic funds. See the notes to Table 3-B, item 7.

9 (vii). Other charges. See the notes to Table 4-A, item 3e.

Referring now to the breakdowns in Appendix Table 19 between urban and rural households, it will be noted that in a number of instances the sum of incomes or outlays, as the case may be, is allocated exclusively either to rural or to urban households. Here it should not be supposed that the division is in fact of just this sort; in some cases, e.g., income from collective farm sales, it is known that some part of the total accrues to the households assigned a zero share. But in view of the general nature of the income and outlay categories in question, it is believed that the assumed allocation may not be seriously in error for present purposes.

For the rest, the breakdowns as between rural and urban households are obtained as follows:

A. Incomes:

4. *Wages and salaries, nonfarm.* According to data in TSUNKHU, *Chislennost' i zarabotnaia plata rabochikh i sluzhashchikh v SSSR*, pp. 8–13, some 19.5 percent of the nonagricultural civilian wage bill was paid out in rural localities in March, 1936. Since March may be a somewhat favorable month for seasonal rural industries, e.g., lumbering and fishing, and since the war saw a great decline in such industries, it is assumed that the corresponding figure for the year 1944 was 10 percent.

5. *Incomes of artisans; other money income currently earned.* We assume that 25 percent of the total income in these categories is rural and 75 percent urban. This takes into account the following information on the prewar situation: (i) According to data in *ibid.*, pp. 12–13, of the total income earned by cooperative artisans in March, 1936, about 25 percent was earned in rural localities and 75 percent in urban localities. (ii) According to data in Plotnikov, 1948 ed., p. 195, of the total income of other artisans in 1938, 25 percent was earned by rural persons and 75 percent by urban.

6. *Military pay.* The fifty-fifty division is arbitrary.

7 (*i*). *Social insurance benefits.* Since only wage earners and salaried workers are covered by this insurance, we have taken the breakdown to be proportional to that of the wage bill, including farm wages, i.e., 13.7 percent rural and 86.3 percent urban.

7 (*ii*). *Social assistance benefits.* These benefits are paid to all social groups, but probably a major part in 1944 went to disabled veterans. The fifty-fifty division between rural and urban households assumed here is arbitrary, but account is taken of the fact that the urban population at the time studied probably was about one-third of the total, while, according to information in Rovinskii, *Gosudarstvennyi biudzhet SSSR*, 1944 ed., p. 229, the rates of social assistance payments were on the average about twice as high for wage earners and salaried workers as for other social categories.

7 (*iii*). *Benefits to mothers of many children.* The division is taken to be proportional to that of the population.

9. *Interest receipts.* Of the total interest receipts, 2.84 billion rubles consists of interest on bonds; .16 billion rubles, of interest on ordinary savings deposits; and .26 billion rubles of interest on the special deposits created for employees in compensation for unutilized vacations. See the notes to Table 3-A, item 10. We assume that two-thirds of the total bond interest accrues to the urban population. As of January 1, 1938, some 75 percent of the bonds outstanding were held by wage earners and salaried workers and 25 percent by peasants and others. See A. Baykov, *The Development of the Soviet Eco-*

nomic System, p. 380. Allowing for the fact that some 20 percent of the wage earners were in rural localities before the war, this indicates that about three-fifths of the bonds may have been held in urban localities before the war. During the war the share of peasants in current bond subscriptions increased, but we assume that the share of the urban population in total holdings increased somewhat due to the decline in rural wage earners. On the basis of diverse information, the bulk of the ordinary savings deposits is assumed to have been urban. So far as concerns the special deposits compensating workers for unutilized leave, we take the division between urban and rural households to be proportional to that obtaining for the civilian wage bill, including nonfarm wages, i.e., 13.7 percent rural and 86.3 percent urban.

B. Outlays:

1. Retail sales to households in government and cooperative shops and restaurants. Of the total sales made by state and cooperative retail shops in 1944, 26 percent were made by outlets of the consumers' cooperatives. See N. Riauzov and N. Titel'baum, *Kurs torgovoi statistiki*, pp. 64–65. At the time studied, it is believed these outlets functioned almost exclusively in rural localities; accordingly, their sales are taken here as rural sales. At the same time, the state shops also sold in rural areas to a limited extent. Thus, in 1940 total rural retail sales amounted to 47.9 billion rubles, while the total retail sales of consumers' cooperative outlets were only 42.4 billion rubles. See Lifits (ed.), *Ekonomika sovetskoi torgovli*, pp. 139, 236. We therefore assume that rural sales as a whole amounted to 30 percent of all retail sales in 1944. All retail sales are understood here to include sales to both households and institutions, i.e., 119.11 billion rubles in Appendix Table 17, but we assume finally that the rural sales are exclusively to households. Since sales to institutions amount to 5.95 billion rubles (Appendix Table 17), sales to urban households may be computed as a residual. In the USSR an appreciable volume of *urban* retail sales is probably made to *rural* households; insofar as this is so, we are overstating here the volume of sales to urban households and understating the volume of sales to rural households.

4. Services. We take the share of rural households to be 30 percent of the total for all households, or about the same as in the case of retail sales. The sales to rural households were assumed to be 30 percent of the total sales to all households and institutions; this means that sales to rural households come to 31.5 percent of total sales to households alone.

5. Trade-union and other dues. The division is assumed proportional to that obtaining in the case of the wage bill, including farm wages.

6. Net bond purchases. Purchases by rural households are taken at 45 percent of the total. According to Plotnikov, 1948 ed., p. 290, peasant households subscribed to 35 percent of the total bonds issued in 1944. We assume that

about one-seventh of the balance of 65 percent was subscribed to by rural
wage earners and other rural nonpeasant households. As was calculated
above, 13.7 percent, or about one-seventh, of the civilian wage bill (including
farm wages) is earned in rural localities.

7. *Increment in savings deposits.* This comprises 8.0 billion rubles of
ordinary savings deposits and 4.0 billion rubles of special deposits compensating employees for unutilized vacations. We arbitrarily assume that one-
fourth of the former are rural. The rural share of the special deposits is
taken as 13.7 percent.

8. *Other savings, including increment in cash holdings.* From generally
known facts on the Soviet war economy, it is believed that the bulk of the
cash hoarding must have been by peasants.

9 (*i*). *Income tax.* The rural share in total payments is taken as 15 percent. This represents the proportion of the previously computed income tax
base consisting of rural incomes.

9 (*ii*). *War tax.* From the tax schedule for taxpayers other than peasants
given in Plotnikov, 1948 ed., p. 275, the average rate for such persons seems
to amount to about 9 percent. The tax base for the urban population may be
calculated as about 154 billion rubles, or the sum of the urban wage bill
and the urban share in the incomes of artisans, etc. On the incomes subject
to tax, see *ibid.,* pp. 274–77.

9 (*iii*). *Tax on bachelors, etc.* The fifty-fifty division is arbitrary.

9 (*v*). *Net lottery subscriptions.* Wage earners and salaried workers subscribed to 42 percent of the "Fourth Lottery," i.e., the one issued in 1944,
and peasants subscribed to the remainder. See *ibid.,* p. 295. We take the subscriptions by wage earners and salaried workers to represent the urban
share generally, after allowing for the fact that 13.7 percent of the wage
bill is rural. In other words, urban subscriptions are taken as 36 percent
of the total.

9 (*vi*). *Cash donations to patriotic funds.* The fifty-fifty division is arbitrary.

9 (*vii*). *Other charges.* The fifty-fifty division is arbitrary.

The foregoing attempt to allocate money incomes and outlays between
urban and rural households (we fear a not especially successful one) may
call for one or two methodological comments. First, our basis for distinguish-
ing between urban and rural households generally must be the one implied
in the Soviet sources used. The nature of this distinction, however, is not
always made explicit in these sources, and there is the possibility that Soviet
usage varies in this regard. Second, as was already indicated regarding the
extent of purchases in the city by rural households, the breakdown of retail
sales between urban and rural shops is not the same as that between urban
and rural households. The desideratum, however, is the latter. Only on this

basis may one suppose that the urban and rural incomes and outlays balance separately.

The figure derived here for collective farm market sales, 55.0 billion rubles, may seem much too large in view of the general contraction of the civilian sector of the economy during the war. This impression, however, neglects the fantastic wartime rise in collective farm market prices; taking account of this aspect, our estimate implies a drastic decline in the "real" volume of these sales from the 1940 level. According to data in Voznesenskii, *Voennaia ekonomika . . .* , p. 129, collective farm market prices seem to have averaged in 1943 some 1,290 percent of 1940. According to data in B. Sukharevskii, *Sovetskaia ekonomika v velikoi Otechestvennoi voine,* p. 28, and Chernyi, *Sotsialisticheskoe sel'skoe khoziaistvo,* No. 2, 1949, p. 38, the corresponding index for early 1945 was some 645 percent. Taking the average level for 1944 to have been around 850 percent, collective farm sales come to 6.5 billion rubles in 1940 prices. This may be compared with sales of 41.2 billion rubles in 1940 in the prices of that year.

2. HOUSING (INCLUDING IMPUTED NET RENT OF OWNER-OCCUPIED DWELLINGS); SERVICES

As shown in Appendix Table 20, this item is calculated as the sum of the following: imputed net rent of owner-occupied dwellings; rent for government-owned housing; outlays for utilities and other services; and tuition payments. The other services include amusements and personal services. The data on imputed net rent are taken from Table 3-A, item 4. The rent for government-owned housing is calculated from data on government-owned housing in Appendix Table 10 and on rental rates in Appendix Table 11.

For purposes of calculating the outlays on utilities and other services, we take as a point of departure the following data for 1937: (i) As is indicated in Table 3-B, Bergson's figure on retail sales to households (other than in collective farm markets) in 1937 is 111.5 billion rubles. (ii) According to *Soviet National Income,* p. 110, total household money outlays on housing, utilities, and other services in 1937 amounted to 15.94 billion rubles. (iii) According to the same source, the average annual rental on government-owned housing in 1937 amounted to 9 rubles per square meter. (iv) Government-owned housing amounted to 131 million square meters in 1937. See above, Appendix A, notes to Table 3-A, item 4.

From the foregoing it follows that household money outlays on utilities and services, exclusive of housing, amounted to 13.76 billion rubles in 1937, or 12.34 percent of retail sales to households, other than in collective farm markets. We arbitrarily assume that the corresponding figures for 1940, 1944, and 1948 were, respectively, 12, 10, and 8 percent. Utility prices and the compensation rates for personal services in 1948 probably had not risen nearly as much over the prewar level as retail prices. The relation of outlays on utilities and other services to retail sales is assumed to have been considerably reduced on this basis. The data on utilities and other services in Appendix Table 20 follow from the stated assumption as to their relation to retail sales and estimates already derived for retail sales.

APPENDIX TABLE 20

HOUSEHOLD EXPENDITURES ON HOUSING,
UTILITIES, AND SERVICES,
1940, 1944, AND 1948
(*Billions of rubles*)

ITEM	1940	1944	1948
1. Imputed net rent of owner-occupied dwellings	6.00	8.00	10.50
2. Rent for government-owned housing	2.02	2.28	3.97
3. Utilities; other services	19.44	11.32	24.42
4. Tuition payments	.20	.30	.60
5. Total expenditures on housing; utilities and other services; tuition	27.66	21.90	39.49

Finally, the figures on tuition payments in Appendix Table 20 are arbitrary estimates based on the same information as has been cited previously in connection with our estimates of scholarship. See Appendix A, notes to Table 3-A, item 9.

3. TRADE-UNION AND OTHER DUES

Trade-union, Communist Party, and other dues paid by the population are estimated at one percent of the comprehensive wage bill, i.e., in Appendix Table 8, item 1. This is supported by data in U. Cherniavskii and S. Krivetskii, "Pokupatel'nye fondy naseleniia i roznichnyi tovarooborot," *Planovoe khoziaistvo,* No. 6, 1936, p. 112, which indicates that all dues paid out by the population in 1935 amounted to about one percent of the total wage bill for that year. In 1940 trade-union dues alone amounted to .90 billion rubles, according to a speech by K. I. Nikolaeva, chairman of the budget commission of the Sovnarkom, USSR, as reported in *Izvestiia,* February 27, 1941, p. 3. This compares with our estimate of 1.61 billion rubles for all dues in that year.

4. CONSUMPTION OF FARM INCOME IN KIND; ARMY SUBSISTENCE

For all years this is the sum of net farm income in kind and military subsistence. These two items already have been recorded as items 1d and 5b, respectively, of Table 3-A.

6. NET SAVINGS

6a. Net bond purchases

This is calculated as gross bond purchases of households, minus the estimated payments made by the government budget for retirement of the public debt. The data on gross purchases and retirements of debt held by households are shown in Appendix Table 21, along with corresponding figures for economic organizations. The latter data, which were obtained in the process

---

APPENDIX TABLE 21

BOND PURCHASES AND RETIREMENTS OF HOUSEHOLDS
AND ECONOMIC ORGANIZATIONS, 1940, 1944, AND 1948

(*Billions of rubles*)

ITEM	1940	1944	1948
1. Gross bond purchases			
(i) By households	9.44	26.24	22.30
(ii) By economic and financial organizations	2.77	6.36	1.63
(iii) Total	12.21	32.60	23.93
2. Debt retirement			
(i) Retirement of debt held by households	1.72	. . .[a]	1.70
(ii) Retirement of debt held by economic and financial organizations	.68	. . .	.10
(iii) Total	2.40	. . .	1.80
3. Net bond purchases			
(i) By households	7.72	26.24	20.60
(ii) By economic and financial organizations	2.09	6.36	1.53
(iii) Total	9.81	32.60	22.13

[a] . . . = negligible.

---

of deriving the figures for households, will be needed subsequently in another connection. The economic organizations include savings banks.

In the table, the figures on bond purchases and debt retirement are obtained as follows:

1940. The figures in part are taken directly from Soviet sources and in part are estimates based on available information for prior years. Use was made of the following sources: D'iachenko, *Finansy i kredit SSSR*, pp. 337–40; A. Gordin, "Zaimy v sotsialisticheskom gosudarstve," *Planovoe khoziaistvo*, No. 7, 1940, pp. 18–21; Plotnikov, 1945 ed., p. 86, and 1948 ed., p. 199; and the 1940 budget message of A. G. Zverev, Commissar of Finance, in *Shestaia sessiia Verkhovnogo Soveta SSSR . . . 1940 g.*, p. 71.

1944. 1. Gross bond purchases. The total and purchases by households are given in Plotnikov, 1948 ed., pp. 259, 292. Purchases by economic organizations are calculated as a residual.

1944. 2. Debt retirement. There appears to have been no repayment of principal in 1944.

1948. 1. Gross bond purchases. The total and purchases by households are given in *Pravda,* March 11, 1949, pp. 1–2. Bond purchases by economic organizations are calculated as a residual.

1948. 2. Debt retirement. The total loan service planned for 1948 amounted to 3.5 billion rubles. See Zverev, *O gosudarstvennom biudzhete SSSR na 1948 god,* p. 18. Of this, the figure of 1.7 billion rubles is taken as interest payments (see 1948 notes to item 1b of Table 7-B), while the residual of 1.8 billion rubles presumably constitutes repayment of principal. The breakdown of the debt retirement as between debt held by households and debt held by economic organizations is arbitrary.

6b. *Increment of savings deposits*

These estimates are obtained as follows:

1940. Plotnikov, 1948 ed., p. 201.

1944. According to data in *ibid.,* p. 298, the savings deposits of the population increased by .8 billion rubles during 1944. It is believed that Plotnikov is referring here to savings deposits of an ordinary sort as distinct from the special accounts opened for workers beginning in 1942 in compensation for unused vacations. Accordingly, in order to derive a comprehensive total for the increment in savings deposits in 1944, we add to the figure cited above a sum of 4.0 billion rubles, which according to Suchkov, *Dokhody . . . ,* pp. 185–86, is the approximate amount of the deposits made in compensation for unused vacations in 1944. Very possibly the figure of .8 billion rubles derived from Plotnikov does not include still another type of deposit, namely, that made by military personnel in special "field banks." See Plotnikov, 1948 ed., p. 297. No information is at hand, however, on the magnitude of these deposits.

1948. This is the planned increase in savings deposits during 1948. See notes to item 2 of Appendix Table 16.

6c. *Other, including increment in cash holdings*

This item is the sum of the increment in cash holdings during each year and other savings, such as voluntary life insurance premiums paid to the State Insurance Administration (*Gosstrakh*), initiation payments to cooperatives, etc. The data on these different items are presented in Appendix Table 22.

The sources and methods are as follows:

1. Increment in cash holdings during the year:

1940. In view of Voznesenskii's statement that a decrease in cash holdings took place, and in view of the lack of more precise data, this is taken as zero. See *Voennaia ekonomika . . . ,* pp. 67–68, 136.

1944. This is calculated as 34 percent of the amount of money in circulation on January 1, 1944, which is taken to amount to 42.96 billion rubles. Money in circulation on January 1, 1941, is estimated by G. Grossman as of the order of 17.9 billion rubles (in an unpublished essay, "Efforts toward Monetary Stability in the USSR"). In Voznesenskii, *Voennaia ekonomika . . . ,* p. 139, it is stated that "during three years of the Patriotic

APPENDIX TABLE 22

INCREMENT IN CASH HOLDINGS AND OTHER SAVINGS, 1940, 1944, AND 1948

(Billions of rubles)

ITEM	1940	1944	1948
1. Increment in cash holdings during the year	. . .[a]	14.61	. . .
2. Other			
(i) Voluntary life insurance premiums	.32	. . .	n.a.[b]
(ii) Initiation payments to cooperatives, etc.	.18	. . .	n.a.
(iii) Total	.50	. . .	1.00
3. Total	.50	14.61	1.00

[a] ...... = negligible.
[b] n.a. = information not available.

War currency circulation in the USSR increased 2.4 times." We take this to refer to the first three years of the war, that is, 1941–43. Voznesenskii's statement implies an average annual rate of growth of 34 percent in the amount of circulating money during the war, which we assume also applies to the year January 1, 1944, to January 1, 1945.

1948. Under normal circumstances, there probably would have been an increase during 1948 in the cash holdings of the public to the extent of several billion rubles. This would have been in connection with the growth in money incomes, which in the case of the wage bill might have amounted to about 10 percent. The increment in cash holdings by the public is assumed nevertheless to have been negligible chiefly in view of the notably large budget surplus. We comment on this aspect subsequently. See Appendix C, notes to Table 7-B, item 8.

2. Other, consisting of *2 (i). Voluntary life insurance premiums* and *2 (ii). Initiation payments to cooperatives, etc.:*

1940. Item 2 (i) is taken from D'iachenko, *Finansy i kredit SSSR,* p. 372. Item 2 (ii) is a rough estimate.

1944. Apparently of negligible magnitude.
1948. A guess.

7. DIRECT TAXES

As indicated in Appendix Table 23, reference here is to the following items:
(i) The revenue item in the government budget, "taxes and levies on the population" (*nalogi i sbory s naseleniia*). This in turn comprises the income tax so-called (*podokhodnyi nalog*) paid by wage and salary earners; the tax for "cultural and housing construction," for all practical purposes another

APPENDIX TABLE 23

DIRECT TAXES, 1940, 1944, AND 1948

(*Billions of rubles*)

ITEM	1940	1944	1948
1. Budget item, "taxes and levies on the population"	9.4	37.0	33.2
2. Miscellaneous charges	1.4	3.9	4.3
3. Net lottery subscriptions	. . .[a]	4.6	. . .
4. Cash donations to patriotic funds	. . .	3.3	. . .
5. Total direct taxes	10.8	48.8	37.5

[a] . . . = negligible or not applicable.

income tax, which was levied on both farm and nonfarm persons in 1940 but had been abolished by 1943; the "agricultural tax" (*sel'khoznalog*) paid by the farm population broadly on the basis of income; in 1944 and 1948, the special tax on the incomes of unmarried persons and persons with small families (*nalog na kholostiakov . . .*); and in 1944, the "war tax" (*voennyi nalog*), also levied on the basis of income.

(ii) A variety of other governmental charges, e.g., license fees, notarial fees, and property taxes, which generally are classified under other Soviet budgetary headings.

(iii) For 1944, net subscriptions to the state lottery and cash contributions to patriotic funds, such as the "Red Army" fund, fund "for defense," etc. Although these contributions were allegedly voluntary, it is believed they are properly classified here as direct taxes rather than with the bond subscriptions previously listed.

The data in Appendix Table 23 are obtained as follows:
1940. 1. Budget item, "taxes and levies on the population." From Plotnikov, 1948 ed., p. 181.
1940. 2. Miscellaneous charges. See the notes to Table 4-A, item 3e.

1944. 1. Budget item . . . . From Plotnikov, 1948 ed., p. 253.

1944. 2. Miscellaneous charges. See the notes to Table 4-A, item 3e.

1944. 3. Net lottery subscriptions. This is calculated from data on the fourth wartime lottery, i.e., that of 1944, in Plotnikov, 1948 ed., pp. 293–95.

1944. 4. Cash donations to patriotic funds. The figure cited represents donations to two funds: the fund "for defense" and the "Red Army" fund. See *ibid.,* p. 259. In Soviet sources reference has been found also to still another fund, namely, one for "the reconstruction of areas liberated from the German occupation," and according to *Desiataia sessiia Verkhovnogo Soveta SSSR . . . 1944 g.,* p. 247, this fund, together with those just mentioned and certain "other incomes," the nature of which is not explained, was planned to yield a grand total of 17.8 billion rubles in 1944. As between these different funds, however, donations by the population as distinct from economic organizations were probably made primarily to those for defense and the Red Army. Accordingly, we record in Appendix Table 23 only the contributions to these latter funds.

The figure cited on these funds probably includes donations not only of cash but also of various other property, particularly government bonds, precious metals, and ordinary commodities, such as grain. But, strictly speaking, only the cash donations ought to be shown at this point. The other payments presumably represent either transactions on capital account, which have no place in our accounts, or offsets to household consumption. Accordingly, the cited figure on donations to patriotic funds represents an overstatement of cash donations to an unknown extent.

1948. 1. Budget item . . . . See *Pravda,* March 11, 1949, p. 3.

1948. 2. Miscellaneous charges. See the notes to Table 4-A, item 3e.

APPENDIX B: NOTES TO TABLE 4

A. INCOMES

1. NET INCOME RETAINED BY ECONOMIC ORGANIZATIONS

1a. Retained income in kind of collective farms

See notes to Table 3, item 1d.

1b. Retained money income of collective farms

As is indicated in Appendix Table 24, this comprises the money income retained by collective farms for social and cultural measures and for their "indivisible funds" (*nedelimye fondy*). The money income used for social and cultural measures is the retained part of the collective farms' "social funds," the residual being distributed as premium payments to the collective farmers.

APPENDIX TABLE 24

NET MONEY INCOME RETAINED BY COLLECTIVE FARMS,
1940, 1944, AND 1948

(*Billions of rubles*)

ITEM	1940	1944	1948
1. Money income retained for social and cultural measures	.36	. . . [a]	.40
2. Payments to "indivisible funds"	3.97	3.70	3.40
3. Total net money income retained by collective farms	4.33	3.70	3.80

[a] . . . = negligible.

In Appendix Table 24, it is assumed that the "social funds" are divided between these two uses evenly in 1940 and 1948, and that they are allocated exclusively to premiums in the war year 1944. The allocation to premiums is taken from Appendix Table 1.

"Indivisible funds" are used mainly for capital investments and debt repayments. In the appendix table, the total amount allocated to these funds in 1940 is calculated as the product of (i) the average amount of such payments per collective farm, amounting to 16,800 rubles (see Anisimov, *Pobeda* . . . ,

p. 83); and (ii) the number of collective farms in 1940, given as 236,300 in
D. Shepilov, "Kolkhoznyi stroi SSSR," *Problemy ekonomiki,* No. 1, 1941,
p. 35. For 1944 and 1948, the corresponding figures are cited in the notes
to Table 3-A, item 1b.

1c. Retained profits of state and cooperative enterprises

Under Soviet financial practice, state enterprises pay into the government
budget a part of their profits as "deductions from profits" (*otchisleniia ot
pribylei*), and cooperative enterprises are subject to the same type of levy

---

APPENDIX TABLE 25

PROFITS OF STATE AND COOPERATIVE ENTERPRISES
AND THEIR DISPOSITION, 1940, 1944, AND 1948
(*Billions of rubles*)

ITEM	1940	1944	1948
1. Profits earned by economic organizations			
(i) State enterprises	28.80	24.40	35.26
(ii) Cooperatives	3.00	2.00	4.00
(iii) Total	31.80	26.40	39.26
2. Payments to government budget			
(i) "Deductions from profits" of state enterprises	21.72	21.40	26.48
(ii) Income taxes of cooperatives	1.79	1.50	2.00
(iii) Total	23.51	22.90	28.48
3. Retained profits			
(i) State enterprises	7.08	3.00	8.78
(ii) Cooperatives	1.21	.50	2.00
(iii) Total	8.29	3.50	10.78

---

under the more familiar name of "income taxes" (*podokhodnye nalogi*).
Retained profits are understood here as the balance remaining after these
payments, and correspondingly are computed as a residual from data, compiled in Appendix Table 25, on total profits, deductions from profits, and
income taxes. These latter data are obtained as follows:

1940. 1. Profits earned by economic organizations:

(*i*) *State enterprises.* Calculated as a residual.

(*ii*) *Cooperatives.* From M. I. Bogolepov, *The Soviet Financial System,*
p. 14.

(*iii*) *Total.* From Zverev, *Gosudarstvennye biudzhety Soiuza SSR, 1938–
1945 gg.,* p. 97.

1940. 2. Payments to government budget:

(*i*) *"Deductions from profits"* of state enterprises. From Plotnikov, 1948 ed., p. 181.

(*ii*) *Income taxes of cooperatives.* From *ibid.*, p. 268.

(*iii*) *Total.* This is calculated as the sum of (i) and (ii).

1944. 1. Profits earned by economic organizations:

(*i*) *State enterprises.* This figure is from the budget report presented in *Odinnadtsataia sessiia Verkhovnogo Soveta SSSR . . . 1945 g.,* p. 11. Although Soviet budget reports usually refer to the profits of all economic organizations, this one mentions specifically only the profits of state enterprises in connection with the figure cited. It is believed, therefore, that the profits of cooperatives are not included.

(*ii*) *Cooperatives.* This is estimated on the basis of the following: the comparative income tax revenues collected from cooperative enterprises in 1940 and 1944, shown in item 2 (ii), and a statement in V. M. Buzyrev, *Vosstanovitel'nye raboty i ikh finansirovanie,* p. 111, that consumers' cooperatives alone earned profits of almost one billion rubles in 1944.

(*iii*) *Total.* This is calculated as the sum of (i) and (ii).

1944. 2. Payments to government budget:

(*i*) *"Deductions from profits"* of state enterprises. From Plotnikov, 1948 ed., p. 259.

(*ii*) *Income taxes of cooperatives.* From *ibid.*, p. 268.

(*iii*) *Total.* This is calculated as the sum of (i) and (ii).

1948. 1 Profits earned by economic organizations:

(*i*) *State enterprises.* This is calculated as a residual.

(*ii*) *Cooperatives.* This is estimated as one-third more in 1948 than in 1940. We assume here that profits increased at approximately the same rate during that period as the gross output of industrial cooperatives, which, in the notes to item 1 of Appendix Table 9, we take to be 32.8 percent larger in 1948 than in 1940.

(*iii*) *Total.* See *Pravda,* March 11, 1949, p. 3.

1948. 2. Payments to government budget:

(*i*) *"Deductions from profits"* of state enterprises. This figure is given as the amount of "deductions from profits" in 1948 in *ibid*. It is believed that this does not include the income taxes paid by cooperatives.

(*ii*) *Income taxes of cooperatives.* This is estimated as one-half of the cooperatives' profits in 1948, taken as 4 billion rubles in item 1 (ii). This estimate is based on the assumption that the ratio between cooperative income taxes and cooperative profits is the same for 1948 as our estimates indicate for 1940.

(*iii*) *Total.* This is calculated as the sum of (i) and (ii).

The Soviet data compiled in Appendix Table 25 on the total profits earned by economic organizations are generally construed as true net profits figures in a conventional sense. This, however, is not the case. Rather they represent the total profits of economic organizations before the deduction of certain losses. The balance of this section explains the different kinds of losses we have in mind and the reasons why we think that the Soviet aggregative profits figures are gross of these losses. At a subsequent point, i.e., in reference to Table 4-A, item 6, an attempt is made to appraise the magnitude of the losses and to correct the tabulation of charges in Table 4 for the resulting overstatement. The losses, it will become clear, are of a type that should have been deducted in the first place in order to obtain a profits figure appropriate to Table 4.

One kind of loss which is not deducted in Soviet figures on total profits comprises the losses of economic organizations covered by subsidies from the government budget. Reasons for believing this to be the case are found partly in the nature of Soviet financial plans. As part of their system of financial planning, Soviet planners compile data not only on the incomes and expenditures of the government but also on the sources and disposition of Soviet finance generally. Published summary tabulations of the latter are in general very much like our own consolidated account of the incomes and outlays of government, economic organizations, etc., in Table 4. Significantly, however, the Soviet tabulations include subsidies as an outlay. Since the total of all outlays balances the total of all incomes, it seems to follow at once that the profits figures included among the incomes must represent profits before the deduction of subsidized losses; under the alternative procedure the incomes would fall short of outlays, including subsidies, by the amount of subsidized losses. In this connection reference is made particularly to the summary tabulation of the financial plan for 1936 in Gosplan, *Narodnokhoziaistvennyi plan na 1936 god,* 2d ed., pp. 376, 381; and to the corresponding tabulation for 1937 in A. Smilga, "Finansy sotsialisticheskogo gosudarstva," *Problemy ekonomiki,* No. 2, 1937, p. 115.

In these two tabulations the Russian terms taken here to mean subsidies are respectively *raskhody po osvoeniiu* and *raskhody po osvoeniiu proizvodstva.* Literally translated, the former term means "outlays on mastering," and the latter, "outlays on mastering production." As is explained in *Soviet National Income,* p. 115, these were conventional Soviet euphemisms for subsidies at the time to which the tabulations relate. More recently the more exact term for subsidies, *dotatsiia,* has come into increasing use.

The two Soviet summary tabulations referred to represent planned rather than actual incomes and outlays, but it is believed that the profits figure cited in them is otherwise of essentially the same scope as the realized ones considered in this study.

Regrettably, details on the Soviet financial plan of the type just cited for 1936 and 1937 are not available for more recent years. On the other hand, the same conclusion regarding Soviet figures on total profits seems to follow from the data on profits and their disposition in 1948 and 1949, shown in Appendix Table 26. The data are from Zverev, *Planovoe khoziastvo*, No. 2, 1949, p. 43. Zverev does not make the scope of his data entirely clear; however, it is believed that reference is to government economic organizations. In other words, cooperatives may not be included. The stated goal for total profits for 1948, 34.8 billion rubles, may be compared with the figure cited in Appendix Table 25, which refers to the realized profits for all economic organizations, both government and cooperative: 39.3 billion rubles.

In Appendix Table 26 the amount of profits allocated to different uses falls short of total profits by 4.2 billion rubles in 1948 and 6.3 billion rubles in 1949. These sums, it is believed, represent amounts allocated to various other uses not itemized, e.g., payments to the so-called Director's Fund. In any case, they clearly could not represent subsidized losses. According to calculations made subsequently, subsidies totaled some 42.7 billion rubles in 1948 and were planned to total 8.1 billion rubles in 1949. See Appendix Table 29.

With this aspect in mind, the data in the table should be read in the light of an interesting feature of Soviet budgetary practice: In the calculation of the profits to be paid into the government budget by economic organizations, the practice is to use as a base only a partially consolidated profits figure. More particularly, profits and losses of different enterprises are consolidated only to the level of regional and branch administrative units under the Ministry. Generally this means consolidation to the level of the so-called Chief Administration, or *glavk*, but apparently in cases where the trust or individual enterprise is directly subordinated to the Ministry, the consolidation proceeds only to the level of the trust or of the individual enterprise.

According to S. M. Kutyrev, *Analiz balansa dokhodov i raskhodov khoziaistvennoi organizatsii*, p. 49: "For the 'deductions' from profits there is established a centralized arrangement of accounts: the payments are determined not on the basis of the profits of separate enterprises, but on the basis of the general sum of profits of trusts or of glavki, after deduction of possible planned losses of individual enterprises. The enterprises make the payments from profits into the budget directly, but in accordance with the allocation of the trusts or *glavki*." While Kutyrev is not fully explicit here that the consolidation proceeds only to the *glavk* level, this is clearly implied.

Similarly, according to Rovinskii, *Gosudarstvennyi biudzhet SSSR*, 1949 ed., p. 185: "Deductions from profits . . . are made by *glavki* and not by individual enterprises. The 'deductions' are made from the net profits of *glavki*, derived from the sum of profits of profitable enterprises after deducting the losses of unprofitable enterprises."

The same arrangement prevails in the planning of subsidies. According to

Kutyrev, *Analyz balansa* . . . , p. 110: "Government subsidies are paid as compensation for planned losses of *glavki* or trusts as a whole, after taking into account any possible profits earned by some enterprises."

Thus, *within* each *glavk*, the losses of the unprofitable enterprises are deducted from the profits of the profitable enterprises to obtain a net profit or loss figure for the *glavk*. On this basis a calculation is made of the amount of profits to be paid into the budget. In other words, the calculation is made

---

APPENDIX TABLE 26

PROFITS EARNED BY ECONOMIC ORGANIZATIONS
AND THEIR DISPOSITION, PLANNED GOALS,
1948 AND 1949

(*Billions of rubles*)

ITEM	PLANNED GOALS	
	1948	*1949*
1. Total profits	34.8	69.6
2. Payments into government budget (*otchisleniia ot pribylei*)	22.0	32.2
3. Retained for		
(i) Investments in fixed capital	3.9	15.4
(ii) Investments in working capital	4.7	11.4
(iii) Capital repairs	. . .[a]	4.3

[a] . . . = negligible.

---

on the basis of the net profit of each profitable *glavk*, without regard to net losses of other unprofitable *glavki*, and accordingly not on the basis of a consolidated net profits figure for the Ministry as a whole, and still less for the whole economy.

Seemingly, then, to come to the point of concern here, the total profits figures cited in Appendix Table 26 must represent profits before the deduction of subsidized losses rather than true net profits figures. On the one hand, the itemized uses of profits, including the payments into the government budget, practically exhaust the totals, which is what might be expected if the totals represent profits before the deduction of subsidized losses. On the other hand, if subsidized losses had been deducted, the total profits should have been considerably less than the total payments into the budget together with the other itemized uses.

According to Soviet fiscal theory, budget subsidies are generally to be used to cover only planned losses and not losses in excess of the plan. In practice, however, this may not always be the case; quite possibly, the subsidies are increased to cover unplanned losses as well. On the other hand, some unplanned losses of *glavki* that are in the red are believed to be financed in other ways, particularly through bank-credit creation. In any event, insofar as this is the case, there is another category of charge which the Russians fail to deduct in calculating their figures on total profits. Actually, all that was said in previous paragraphs to show that they fail to deduct subsidized losses goes to prove equally well that they also fail to deduct *glavki* losses financed by bank credit.

Finally, reference so far has been to economic organizations operating on the so-called *khozraschet* basis, involving among other things a more or less independent financial status. As is explained in the text of this study and, in greater detail, in *Soviet National Income,* pp. 13 ff., 24 ff., this is the system that has long been generally operative in the USSR. But at various times there have been important exceptions where an economic enterprise or industry is attached fully to the government budget. Expenses are covered in the same way as are those of a government department, i.e., through budgetary appropriations. Furthermore, in some cases such expenses greatly exceed any revenues from sales. Thus, to cite an outstanding case in the period studied, the MTS have been attached to the government budget since 1938. Because of the low accounting values of the MTS income in kind, expenses generally have greatly exceeded earned income.

The losses of these economic organizations attached to the government budget, it is believed, must constitute still another category not deducted in Soviet figures on total profits. Since the organizations do not operate on a *khozraschet* basis, the Russians would hardly include their net return (assuming it is computed at all, which is doubtful) in compiling data on the profits of economic organizations.

2. CHARGES TO ECONOMIC ENTERPRISES FOR SPECIAL FUNDS

2a. For social insurance budget

According to Soviet administrative procedure, the total revenue of the social insurance budget is provided by economic enterprises. Our data on these contributions out of the enterprises' incomes are taken from the following sources:

1940. Plotnikov, 1948 ed., p. 181.
1944. Ibid., p. 259.
1948. Zverev, *Planovoe khoziaistvo,* No. 2, 1949, p. 40.

2b. For special funds for workers' training and education

This includes expense charges for contributions to special funds for workers' training and education, particularly the operation of factory apprentice schools and of courses for more advanced training. The contributions, which are fixed by law, are taken here to amount to one percent of the comprehensive wage bill as given in Appendix Table 8. See M. V. Nikolaev, *Bukhgalterskii uchet,* pp. 421 ff., where the amounts of contributions by different commissariats are stated as a percentage of the wage bill. While the percentages cited by Nikolaev average more than one percent, apparently only the funds levied on the wages of workers engaged in production were an expense charge before profits. In the absence of any information to the contrary, it is assumed that the funds referred to in this 1936 source continued in operation throughout the period studied.

The foregoing remarks apply primarily to the years 1944 and 1948. For the year 1940, reference is made here not only to the contributions just described but also to certain contributions which enterprises were called on to make at that time to the trade-union budget. These amounted to 1.05 billion rubles according to *Izvestiia,* February 27, 1941, p. 3. The support of trade unions by enterprises was discontinued during the war and not revived afterward. See the statutes and bylaws of the trade unions, as approved by the Tenth Congress of Trade Unions of the USSR, held April 27, 1949, in *Trud,* May 11, 1949; also, the trade-union budget, presented in A. Rothstein, *Workers in the Soviet Union,* p. 54. The resources of trade unions are now derived only from initiation fees, monthly membership dues, income from cultural, educational, and athletic institutions, the sale of publications, and their own subsidiary enterprises.

3. INDIRECT TAXES; OTHER PAYMENTS OUT OF INCOMES BY ECONOMIC
    ENTERPRISES TO GOVERNMENT BUDGET

3a. Taxes on incomes of collective farms

1940. From Bogolepov, *The Soviet Financial System,* p. 16.

1944. This is calculated as a residual by subtracting from the "taxes on incomes of enterprises and other receipts from economic organizations and institutions," given as 3.8 billion rubles in *Desiataia sessiia Verkhovnogo Soveta SSSR . . . 1944 g.,* p. 246, the cooperative income taxes, given in Appendix Table 25 as 1.5 billion rubles; the tax "on noncommodity operations," shown as .5 billion rubles in Appendix Table 27; and the machine-tractor station revenue, given as .8 billion rubles below, p. 210. Although it is not altogether clear from Soviet sources, the Soviet budget category "taxes on incomes of enterprises and other receipts from economic organizations" is probably exhausted by these various revenue items, including the collective farm income tax. The residual figure of one billion rubles, representing the 1944 collective farm income tax, appears to be consistent with what is known concerning the low level of 1944 collective farm income in comparison with 1940, and the rise in tax rates introduced March 1, 1941.

1948. This is a very rough estimate, based on the assumption that taxable collective farm income in 1948 was of about the same magnitude as in 1940 (money income of collective farms was roughly equal in the two years) and that the effective tax rates on farm income in 1948 were roughly two and one-half times as high as in 1940. On changes in the farm income tax, see G. L. Mar'iakhin, *Nalogi i sbori s naseleniia i kolkhozov,* pp. 46 ff.

3b. Payments from profits of state enterprises to government budget
   For all years, see Appendix Table 25.

3c. Taxes on incomes of cooperative organizations
   For all years, see Appendix Table 25.

3d. Turnover tax
   1940. From Plotnikov, 1948 ed., p. 181.
   1944. From *ibid.,* p. 259.
   1948. From *Pravda,* March 11, 1949, p. 3.

3e. Miscellaneous
   This consists of the items shown in Appendix Table 27, below.
   The figures in Appendix Table 27 are obtained as follows:
   1. Local taxes and fees. According to Soviet budgetary practice in the years studied, the category "local taxes and levies" (*mestnye nalogi i sbory*) comprises a variety of revenues, including taxes on buildings and houses, ground rent, taxes on the owners of automobiles, horses, and other means of transportation, etc. As is implied, these taxes are levied on both private citizens and economic organizations. We assume here that the division between the two types of payers is even, and accordingly record in Appendix Table 27 only one-half the total "local taxes and fees" recorded in Soviet sources. The other half is included with other direct taxes under the outlays of households in Table 3.
   As to the total "local taxes and fees," the data for the years studied are from the following sources:
   1940. Bogolepov, *The Soviet Financial System,* p. 29.
   1944. Plotnikov, 1948 ed., p. 349.
   1948. Zverev, *Planovoe khoziaistvo,* No. 2, 1949, p. 40.
   For a discussion of the local taxes and fees, see Suchkov, *Dokhody . . . ,* chap. xiv.

   2. Tax "on noncommodity operations":
   1940. Ibid., p. 79.
   1944. Plotnikov, 1948 ed., p. 268.
   1948. This is estimated as being in about the same ratio to turnover tax revenue as in 1940 and 1944.

The tax "on noncommodity operations" (*s netovarnykh operatsii*) is an analogue of the turnover tax, levied on such activities as custom clothiers, barbers, etc. For further details, see Suchkov, *Dokhody* . . . , chap. iii.

3. Stumpage fees and other budget charges for use of state forests:

1940. D'iachenko, *Finansy i kredit SSSR,* p. 441.

1944. Plotnikov, 1948 ed., p. 269.

1948. This is the planned figure for 1949 in Rovinskii, *Gosudarstvennyi biudzhet SSSR,* 1949 ed., p. 70. It represents only levies collected by local gov-

---

APPENDIX TABLE 27

MISCELLANEOUS CHARGES PAID TO GOVERNMENT BUDGET
BY ECONOMIC ORGANIZATIONS, 1940, 1944, AND 1948

(*Billions of rubles*)

ITEM	1940	1944	1948
1. Local taxes and fees	1.0	2.9	2.9
2. Tax "on noncommodity operations"	.6	.5	1.3
3. Stumpage fees and other budget charges for use of state forests	.6	.6	1.5
4. Notarial and other legal registration fees, fines, passport fees, etc.	1.4	3.1	5.5
5. Other revenues	1.9	4.3	6.1
6. Total miscellaneous charges	5.5	11.4	17.3

---

ernment units. Some additional income of the same sort was probably collected by superior government agencies. If so, this is included in the residual category "other income" referred to below.

4. Notarial and other legal registration fees, fines, passport fees, etc. According to Soviet budget practice in the years studied, the budget heading "nontax incomes and various levies" (*nenalogovye dokhody i raznye sbory*) includes a great variety of government revenues, such as mintage charges, fines, charges for checking weights and measures, automobile levies by the "automobile inspection," revenues from the "realization of state funds, securities, and confiscated property," passport fees, notarial fees, and revenue from the sale of unclaimed property left with railways, etc. For purposes of this study it is assumed arbitrarily that the totals recorded under this general heading comprise charges on the population to the extent of .5 billion rubles in 1940, 1.0 billion rubles in 1944, and 1.5 billion rubles in 1948. For the rest there is an even division between charges paid by economic organizations on current account and budgetary transactions on capital account. For present purposes we believe we are right in thinking of the coinage charges as properly classified with capital transactions.

We show in Appendix Table 27 only the amount paid by economic organizations on current account. The amounts paid by individuals are included with direct taxes in Table 3, while the balance, representing capital transactions, appears neither in Table 3 nor Table 4.

The figures on "nontax incomes and various levies" are obtained as follows:

1940. This is a planned goal from D'iachenko, *Finansy i kredit SSSR,* p. 441. There is no indication of any important overfulfillment or underfulfillment of the budget goals for 1940.

1944. The planned figure in *Desiataia sessiia Verkhovnogo Soveta SSSR . . . 1944 g.,* p. 246, has been raised somewhat to allow for a probable overfulfillment.

1948. The planned figure in *Zasedaniia Verkhovnogo Soveta SSSR (chetvertaia sessiia) . . . 1948 g.,* p. 279, which refers only to Union and Republican collections, has been raised to allow for local collections. There is no indication of any important overfulfillment or underfulfillment of the budget goals for 1948.

On the levies grouped under the budget heading "nontax incomes and various levies," see Suchkov, *Dokhody . . . ,* pp. 168 ff.

5. Other revenues. As is explained in Appendix C, pp. 207 ff., the individual revenue items which have been recorded so far either as household outlays in Table 3 or charges of economic organizations in Table 4, taken together with certain other revenue items which may be classified broadly as capital transactions, total somewhat less in each of the years studied than the figure given in Soviet sources for total revenue. This still obtains after allowance is made for certain special aspects, particularly the inclusion in the Soviet budget of gross income from the MTS and gross revenues from loans. We arbitrarily assume that one-half of this residual represents charges to economic organizations and one-half represents transactions on capital account.

The residual in some part may represent revenues of still another type, namely, the gross income of economic enterprises other than the MTS which are attached to the government budget, but except for the part of this revenue consisting of profits, it will readily be seen that this income has to be treated here in any case in the same way as transactions on capital account.

4. CUSTOM DUTIES; 5. GOVERNMENT RECEIPTS FROM SALE OF LEND-LEASE
AND REPARATIONS

1940. The figure for custom duties is taken from Bogolepov, *The Soviet Financial System,* p. 29. The revenues from Lend-Lease, etc. were, of course, nonexistent in 1940.

1944. The combined total given for items 4 and 5 is the expected amount of "custom receipts" in 1944 referred to in *Desiataia sessiia Verkhovnogo Soveta SSSR . . . 1944 g.,* p. 246. The large magnitude of 24 billion rubles is due, apparently, to the inclusion of revenues from Lend-Lease transactions in "custom receipts." Presumably the Soviet government sold the commodities it received through Lend-Lease to its state economic organizations and entered the resulting income in the budget as customs revenue. A similar practice seems to have been followed with respect to Lend-Lease munitions, which the defense ministries purchased with funds provided for this purpose by the government budget.

1948. The combined total of our estimates for items 4 and 5, amounting to 16.5 billion rubles, is the amount of budget receipts anticipated for 1948 from custom duties and from "income from the sale of goods ceded as compensation to the Soviet Union for losses caused by war action and by occupation of Soviet territory." See *Zasedaniia Verkhovnogo Soveta SSSR (chetvertaia sessiia) . . . 1948 g.,* p. 279. The latter budget category evidently refers to the sales to economic organizations, public institutions, and households of commodity deliveries made to the Soviet government on reparations account. The breakdown of this amount between custom duties in item 4 and government receipts on reparations account in item 5 is based on the ratio between these same two kinds of revenues in the 1947 budget plan: 6.9 rubles and 10.7 rubles, respectively. See *Zasedaniia Verkhovnogo Soveta SSSR (tret'ia sessiia) . . . 1947 g.,* p. 298. Account is taken, however, of the decline in Soviet imports which occurred during 1948.

6. ALLOWANCE FOR SUBSIDIZED LOSSES

As has been explained in the notes to Table 4-A, item 1c, Soviet data on the total profits of economic organizations (and therefore our own figures on retained profits, which follow from the Soviet data) are overstated. This is because of the failure to deduct losses of *glavki* covered by subsidies from the government budget, the unplanned losses of *glavki* covered by bank-credit creation, and the losses of economic organizations attached fully to the government budget. The "Allowance for subsidized losses" is intended to adjust the tabulation of charges in Table 4 for these three features. As is shown in Appendix Table 28, the "Allowance for subsidized losses" represents the total of their several magnitudes.

To refer first to the budget subsidies to economic organizations, the Russians are notably secretive on this subject. It has been necessary to rely here on the roughest of indirect estimates. According to Soviet budgetary practice in the years studied, subsidies to economic organizations (*dotatsiia*) were included along with a number of other outlays under the general budget heading "Financing the National Economy" (*finansirovanie narodnogo khoziaistva*). Essentially the procedure here is to break down this broad budget category and to estimate budget subsidies while doing so.

Besides subsidies, the budget appropriation for "Financing the National Economy" comprises:

(i) Funds made available to finance the fixed-capital investments of enterprises. According to the classification scheme usually used in Soviet financial sources, these funds include: (a) funds for financing fixed capital generally; (b) appropriations for "extra-limit" outlays, i.e., small investments not listed

---

APPENDIX TABLE 28

ALLOWANCE FOR SUBSIDIZED LOSSES BY CATEGORY,
1940, 1944, AND 1948

(*Billions of rubles*)

ITEM	1940	1944	1948
1. Budget subsidies to economic organizations	8.0	12.0	44.0
2. Unplanned losses of *glavki* financed by bank credit	1.0	1.0	1.0
3. Budget appropriations for operating losses of economic organizations attached to government budget: MTS only	5.0	3.0	8.0
4. Total	14.0	16.0	53.0

---

by title in the annual plan for capital works and accordingly not subject to the approval of the Union and Republican governments; (c) appropriations for capital repairs not charged as a current expense.

(ii) Funds to finance investments in the enterprise's "own" working capital, i.e., the part of the enterprise's working capital permanently assigned to it, as distinct from investments financed through bank loans.

(iii) Appropriations for the current expenses of enterprises attached fully to the government budget, e.g., the MTS.

(iv) Funds to finance investments in commodity stockpiles.

(v) Various other outlays, including expenditures for geological prospecting, conservation measures, antipest measures in agriculture, veterinary services, industrial resettlement, some outlays for scientific research and training of personnel of certain economic organizations, etc.

As was indicated above, we are attempting here to ascertain the amount of subsidies by breaking down the total of "Financing the National Economy" as between this and other outlay categories. It may now be explained that we are actually interested in a somewhat broader concept than is given by the budget category *dotatsiia*. In Bergson's calculations for 1937, subsidies are taken to include, in addition to the outlays so classified in the Soviet government budget, certain appropriations to compensate procurement agencies for premiums paid to farmers for above-quota deliveries of agricultural produce. Full details on the budget classification for 1937 were lacking. It was assumed that such appropriations were classified in the Soviet budget not under "subsidies" but under another heading, "operational outlays" (*operatsionnye raskhody*). This latter heading also includes outlays on geological prospecting, conservation, and the like. For the years 1940, 1944, and 1948, details of the budget classification are still lacking. Furthermore, it will become clear that the difference in concepts could hardly be important in practice in view of the limitations of our calculations. But if only for the sake of conceptual clarity we shall be concerned here, as in *Soviet National Income,* with budget subsidies in a sense comprehending the compensation for premium payments as well as "subsidies," so-called.

While only the compensation for premiums to farmers are reclassified in *Soviet National Income* and in the present calculations for 1940, 1944, and 1948, there is reason to think that the same treatment might possibly have been in order for certain other outlays as well. For example, the "operational outlays" are believed to include certain premiums to forestry workers. According to the concept of subsidies that must be of interest here, it is clear that such premiums too may properly be so classified. No attempt will be made here, however, to broaden the category "subsidies" further to include such items.

Regarding the outlay items included in "Financing the National Economy," see *Soviet National Income,* pp. 114 ff.; N. Kaplan, *Capital Investments in the Soviet Union, 1924–1951.*

The breakdowns derived for "Financing the National Economy" for the different years studied are shown in Appendix Table 29. The reasons for referring to the 1949 plan as well will appear later. Soviet sources are rarely explicit regarding the precise meaning of data cited on capital investments. It is believed that in the table "fixed capital" is exclusive of "extra-limit" outlays and also of capital repairs. At the same time, these latter items, along with stockpiling and geological prospecting and the like, fall under "Other, exclusive of subsidies."

During the years studied, the MTS are believed to have been the only economic organizations of consequence attached fully to the government budget. So far as there were outlays for the current expenses of other such organizations, however, these too fall under "Other, exclusive of subsidies." As will appear, we calculate the funds going to finance the current expenses of the MTS as the difference between (i) the total appropriation to the MTS and (ii) the appropriations to finance MTS investments in "fixed capital." Insofar as the data on "fixed capital" are exclusive of "extra-limit" outlays and capital repairs, the current expenses are correspondingly overstated by these sums. Furthermore, the appropriations probably also include some "operational outlays," so that, depending on the concept, the current expenses may be considered as being overstated on this account too. This does not matter especially for present purposes, but it does make a difference when we proceed subsequently to calculate the accounting losses of the MTS.

In Appendix Table 29 are presented data on the breakdown of "Financing the National Economy" not only for the economy as a whole but also for individual sectors. As will appear, the breakdowns for individual sectors contribute materially to the calculation of the magnitude of subsidies for the economy as a whole only for the year 1948. We have also inserted corresponding breakdowns for 1940 and 1944, however, primarily because they are needed in this study in various other connections.

The data in the table were obtained as follows:

1940. All sectors:

1. Total expenditures for "Financing the National Economy." From Plotnikov, 1948 ed., p. 207.

2..Fixed capital. This is calculated on the assumption that the government budget provided 67.5 percent of the total investment in fixed capital, given as 32 billion rubles in the notes to item 1 of Appendix Table 33. The assumed relative share of budget outlays in these expenditures is the one planned for 1940, according to Zverev, *Gosudarstvennye biudzhety Soiuza SSR, 1938–1945 gg.,* p. 77.

3. Working capital. This is calculated from the information that the government budget supplied 49.3 percent of the increase in "own" working capital in 1940. See Zverev, *Planovoe khoziaistvo,* No. 2, 1949, p. 45. According to Appendix Table 33, the increase in "own" working capital amounted to 7.6 billion rubles.

4. Current expenses of the MTS. See below, the notes to *1940. Industry; Agriculture, etc.*

6. Other, exclusive of subsidies; 7. Subsidies. The total for these two categories together, i.e., item 8, is obtained as a residual, i.e., as the difference between items 1 and 5. As to the breakdown between the two categories, this is a rather arbitrary calculation based mainly on the following information:

(i) According to Appendix Table 33, "extra-limit" outlays totaled 6 billion rubles in 1940. According to Zverev, *Gosudarstvennye biudzhety Soiuza SSR, 1938–1945 gg.,* p. 79, the plan for 1940 called for the budget to finance 70 percent of the "extra-limit" outlays of that year. Assuming that this percentage was realized, the budget appropriation would have amounted to 4.2 billion rubles.

(ii) According to the plan for 1940 (*ibid.*) the budget was to finance 1.4 billion rubles of capital repairs in that year.

APPENDIX TABLE 29

BUDGET EXPENDITURES FOR FINANCING THE NATIONAL ECONOMY, 1940, 1944, 1948, AND 1949 (PLAN)

(Billions of rubles)

ITEM	1940				1944			
	ALL SECTORS	INDUSTRY	AGRICULTURE	OTHER SECTORS	ALL SECTORS	INDUSTRY	AGRICULTURE	OTHER SECTORS
1. Total expenditures for "Financing the National Economy"	58.3	28.6	12.2	17.5	53.7	30.1	7.2	16.4
2. Fixed capital	21.6	12.5	1.1	8.0	20.6	15.1	.8	4.7
3. Working capital	3.8	3.0	.5	.3	2.0	2.0	...ᵃ	...
4. Current expenses of MTS	7.1	...	7.1	...	3.8	...	3.8	...
5. Total, (2) through (4)	32.5	15.5	8.7	8.3	26.4	17.1	4.6	4.7
6. Other, exclusive of subsidies	17.8	8.6	1.5	7.7	15.3	6.0	1.1	8.2
7. Subsidies	8.0	4.5	2.0	1.5	12.0	7.0	1.5	3.5
8. Total, (6) plus (7)	25.8	13.1	3.5	9.2	27.3	13.0	2.6	11.7

ᵃ ... = negligible.

APPENDIX TABLE 29 (*Continued*)

BUDGET EXPENDITURES FOR FINANCING THE NATIONAL ECONOMY, 1940, 1944, 1948, AND 1949 (PLAN)

(*Billions of rubles*)

ITEM	1948						1949 (*Plan*)					
	ALL SECTORS	INDUS-TRY	AGRI-CULTURE	TRANS-PORT, COMMUNI-CATIONS	TRADE	OTHER SECTORS	ALL SECTORS	INDUS-TRY	AGRI-CULTURE	TRANS-PORT, COMMUNI-CATIONS	TRADE	OTHER SECTORS
1. Total expenditures for "Financing the National Economy"	147.5	94.1	20.5	14.3	4.1	14.5	152.5	75.5	32.7	14.7	6.5	23.1
2. Fixed capital	57.2	39.7	4.2	7.2	.6	5.5	79.8	52.8	9.0	9.0	.6	8.4
3. Working capital	10.7	8.9	1.4	.3	...	.1	10.1	8.5	1.2	.3	...	.1
4. Current expenses of MTS	10.0	...	10.0	...	...	...	14.0	...	14.0	...	...	...
5. Total, (2) through (4)	77.9	48.6	15.6	7.5	.6	5.6	103.9	61.3	24.2	9.3	.6	8.5
6. Other, exclusive of subsidies	25.6	11.7	2.4	2.9	2.1	6.5	39.6	n.a.[b]	n.a.	n.a.	n.a.	n.a.
7. Subsidies	44.0	33.8	2.5	3.9	1.4	2.4	9.0	n.a.	n.a.	n.a.	n.a.	n.a.
8. Total, (6) plus (7)	69.6	45.5	4.9	6.8	3.5	8.9	48.6	14.2	8.5	5.4	5.9	14.6

[b] n.a. = information not available.

(iii) According to Voznesenskii, *Voennaia ekonomika* . . . , p. 154, "state material reserves" increased by 3.6 billion rubles in the year and a half before the German attack. In 1940, then, stockpiling may have been of the order of 2 billion rubles.

(iv) Given the foregoing, our calculation of "Other, exclusive of subsidies" as being 17.8 billion rubles allows for "operational outlays" on geological prospecting, industrial research, and personnel training, etc. of about 10 billion rubles. According to *Soviet National Income,* p. 129, "operational outlays" and the like, exclusive of compensation for agricultural premium payments, amounted to 8.55 billion rubles in 1937. Presumably, the total "operational outlays" increased from 1937 to 1940 in connection with the increase in money wages, which amounted to about one-third. Beyond this, there probably was some increase in industrial research and labor-training activities financed under this heading in connection with the mounting defense preparations. On the other hand, very likely outlays were pared on such dispensable measures as agricultural melioration and the like, which had been important in 1937.

As is shown in Appendix Table 28, we estimate subsidies, together with unplanned losses financed by bank credit and budget appropriations for the accounting losses of the MTS, at 14.0 billion rubles in 1940. The corresponding figure derived by Bergson for 1937 was 8.0 billion rubles. In view of the general increase in money wages by one-third from 1937 to 1940, our estimate for 1940 does not seem especially implausible, though perhaps it is on the high side.

According to A. Bergson and L. Turgeon, *Prices of Iron and Steel Products in the Soviet Union, 1928–1950: a Summary Report,* Soviet steel prices were stable from 1937 through 1939, but there was an increase in 1940 amounting to 30.5 percent in the case of ordinary steel and 12.9 percent in the case of quality steel. If prices generally increased in about the same proportion as money wages, subsidies of course would have increased by only about one-third.

1940. Industry; Agriculture; Other sectors:

1. Total expenditures for "Financing the National Economy." See Plotnikov, 1948 ed., p. 207.

2. Fixed capital. According to Voznesenskii, "Khoziaistvennye itogi 1940 goda i plan razvitiia narodnogo khoziaistva SSSR na 1941 god," *Bol'shevik,* No. 3–4, 1941, p. 50, the 1941 goal for fixed-capital investments in industry, 30.6 billion rubles, surpasses the 1940 level by 71 percent. This means that fixed-capital investments in industry in 1940 amounted to 17.89 billion rubles. According to Zverev, *Gosudarstvennye biudzhety Soiuza SSR, 1938–1945 gg.,* p. 77, the plan for 1940 called for the government budget to provide 69.6 percent of the funds for investments in industrial fixed capital in 1940. It is assumed that this goal was realized. In the case of agriculture, the figure on fixed-capital investment is obtained as the sum of (i) fixed-capital investments in MTS, given as .66 billion rubles in *Shestaia sessiia Verkhovnogo Soveta SSSR . . . 1940 g.,* p. 174; and (ii) fixed-capital investments in state farms and other enterprises of the USSR People's Commissariat of Agriculture, estimated as .40 billion rubles, from data in *ibid.,* pp. 425–43, and in Zverev, *Gosudarstvennye biudzhety Soiuza SSR, 1938–1945 gg.,* pp. 75 ff. Fixed-capital investments in sectors other than industry and agriculture are calculated as a residual.

3. *Working capital.* The budget appropriation for "own" working capital for the whole economy has already been taken to be 3.8 billion rubles. According to *ibid.,* p. 19, industry received in 1938 77.68 percent of the government budget appropriation for working capital for the whole economy. It is assumed that this was also its share in 1940. The figure for agriculture is a guess and that for other sectors is calculated as a residual.

4. *Current expenses of MTS.* This is the difference between the budget appropriation to the MTS, given as 7.79 billion rubles in Suchkov, *Dokhody . . . ,* p. 113, and the budget investment in MTS, cited above as .66 billion rubles.

6. *Other, exclusive of subsidies; 7. Subsidies.* The total for the two categories together is calculated as a residual, i.e., as the difference between items 1 and 5. As to the breakdown, this is a rather arbitrary calculation. Account is taken of: (i) the calculations in *Soviet National Income,* p. 129, according to which "operational outlays" (exclusive of compensation for agricultural premium payments) amounted in 1937 to 1.8 billion rubles in industry, 1.9 billion rubles in agriculture, and nearly 6.0 billion rubles in other sectors; (ii) the probability that there was a sizable shift in "operational outlays" to industry by 1940; (iii) the probability that budget appropriations for capital repairs, though perhaps not for "extra-limit" outlays, were concentrated to a great extent in industry; (iv) the fact that appropriations for stockpiling are believed to fall exclusively under "Other sectors"; and (v) the fact previously mentioned that some expenditures listed in the case of industry and other sectors under "Other, exclusive of subsidies" may in the case of agriculture fall under "Current expenses of the MTS."

Account is also taken of the calculations in *Soviet National Income,* p. 129, of the disposition of subsidies, including the accounting losses of the MTS, in 1937, i.e., 4.5 billion rubles to agriculture; 2.5 billion rubles to industry; and 1.0 billion rubles to other sectors. The corresponding figures calculated here for 1940 are 4.5, 7.0, and 1.5 billion rubles. Very possibly this represents too high a figure for agriculture compared with industry and other sectors.

But it is believed the overstatement is more likely to be in the accounting losses of the MTS than in the subsidies that are of immediate concern. The 1.0 billion rubles of subsidies to "Other sectors" in 1937 are divided evenly between compensation to procurement agencies for agricultural premiums and subsidies, so-called, to transport. There is no information in Soviet sources to indicate that premium payments changed from 1937 to 1940.

Transportation rates, including rates for water transport, the main recipient of subsidies in this field in 1937, were increased substantially in 1939 and 1940, and it may be that losses in this area were eliminated. This apparently was a principal objective of the rate change. On the other hand, there have probably been limited losses in other sectors, particularly housing. On the change in transportation rates, see K. T. Bunkin, *Uluchshit' kommercheskuiu rabotu rechnogo transporta,* pp. 32–33.

1944. All sectors:

1. Total expenditures for "Financing the National Economy." See Plotnikov, 1948 ed., p. 303.

2. Fixed Capital. On the basis of *ibid.,* p. 307, the government budget is taken here to have financed 75 percent of the total investments in fixed capital undertaken in the economy generally in 1944. According to Appendix Table 33, such investments totaled 27.4 billion rubles.

3. Working capital. This is a planned figure from Zverev, *Gosudarstvennye biudzhety Soiuza SSR, 1938–1945 gg.,* p. 133.

4. Current expense of MTS. See below, the notes to *1944. Industry; Agriculture, etc.*

6. Other, exclusive of subsidies; 7. Subsidies. The total for the two categories together is calculated as a residual, i.e., as the difference between items 1 and 5. The breakdown between the two categories is rather arbitrary. Appropriations for "extra-limit" outlays must have been very small during the war, and presumably there was little if any investment in stockpiling as of 1944. On the other hand, rising wage rates should have tended to raise service components of "operational outlays," so the total expenditures on "Other, exclusive of subsidies" may well have approached the 1940 level. At the same time, the indications are that the prices of industrial goods were held stable during the war. In the case of munitions, costs may have declined in the course of time despite wage increases, but probably losses elsewhere, and hence also subsidies, increased.

On the wartime developments regarding prices and costs, see Voznesenskii, *Voennaia ekonomika . . . ,* pp. 113, 127; Bergson and Turgeon, *Prices of Iron and Steel Products . . . ;* P. Belov, "Ekonomicheskaia pobeda SSSR v velikoi Otechestvennoi voine," *Voprosy ekonomiki,* No. 5, 1950.

1944. Industry; agriculture; other sectors:

1. Total expenditures for "Financing the National Economy." For agriculture, this is from Plotnikov, 1948 ed., p. 320. For industry and other sectors, the figures cited represent the preliminary data given in *Odinnadtsataia sessiia Verkhovnogo Soveta SSSR . . . 1945 g.,* p. 14. The data in this source are raised somewhat here to make the total for all sectors, 49.0 billion rubles, correspond to that in Appendix Table 29, 53.7 billion rubles.

2. Fixed capital. Estimated from planned figures in Zverev, *Gosudarstvennye biudzhety Soiuza SSR, 1938–1945 gg.,* p. 133.

3. Working capital. We arbitrarily assume that appropriations to sectors other than industry are negligible.

4. Current expenses of MTS. This is the difference between the budget appropriation to the MTS, given as 4.3 billion rubles in Plotnikov, 1948 ed., p. 320, and the appropriation for investments in the MTS, taken to be .5 billion rubles. The latter figure is based on the budget appropriation for investments in agriculture generally, cited above as .8 billion rubles.

6. Other, exclusive of subsidies; 7. Subsidies. The total for the two categories for each of the different sectors is calculated as a residual, i.e., as the difference between 1 and 5. The breakdown as between subsidies and "other, exclusive of subsidies" is more or less arbitrary. Account is taken of the prewar breakdown and of the considerations mentioned above in the discussion of subsidies for all sectors in 1944.

1948 and 1949 (Plan). All sectors:

1. Total expenditures for "Financing the National Economy." For both years, this is from Zverev, *Planovoe khoziaistvo,* No. 2, 1949, p. 42.

2. Fixed capital. For both years, *ibid.,* p. 43.

3. Working capital. The 1949 figure is given in *ibid.,* p. 45. The 1948 figure is a planned goal given in Zverev, *Gosudarstvennyi biudzhet SSSR na 1948 god,* p. 22.

4. Current expenses of MTS. See below, the notes to *1948 and 1949 (Plan). Industry; Agriculture; etc.*

6. Other, exclusive of subsidies; 7. Subsidies. The total outlay in the two categories together is calculated as a residual, i.e., as the difference between 1 and 5. The point of departure for the breakdown as between subsidies and other outlays is a statement in Zverev, *Planovoe khoziaistvo,* No. 2, 1949, p. 43. Referring to the planned budget appropriation for "state subsidies" (*gosudarstvennaia dotatsiia*) for 1949, Zverev informs us that this category "is reduced in comparison with the previous year by 5.3 times." We interpret this to mean that subsidies in 1948 were 5.3 times those planned for 1949, i.e.,

$$S_{48} = 5.3\, S_{49} \quad \dots\dots\dots\dots\dots\dots\dots\dots\dots\dots\dots\dots\dots \text{(a)}$$

Provisionally and for reasons explained below, we assume also that the item "Other, exclusive of subsidies" was to be increased by 50 percent from 1948 to 1949, i.e.,

$$1.5 \ R_{48} = R_{49} \dotfill (b)$$

We have, then, two equations and four unknowns. But two more equations are given at once by the fact that the total of subsidies and "Other than subsidies" is known for each year, i.e.,

$$R_{48} + S_{48} = 69.6 \text{ billion rubles} \dotfill (c)$$
$$R_{49} + S_{49} = 48.6 \text{ billion rubles} \dotfill (d)$$

Accordingly, the following values are indicated for the various unknowns:

$$S_{48} = 42.6 \text{ billion rubles}$$
$$S_{49} = \ \ 8.0 \text{ billion rubles}$$
$$R_{48} = 27.0 \text{ billion rubles}$$
$$R_{49} = 40.6 \text{ billion rubles}$$

In Appendix Table 29, the figures for subsidies have been raised somewhat above the foregoing, and those for "Other, exclusive of subsidies" have been reduced correspondingly to allow for the probable omission from the budget category "subsidies" of compensation paid to procurement agencies for premiums paid to farmers for above-quota deliveries.

Coming now to the assumption of a 50 percent increase in "Other, exclusive of subsidies" from 1948 to 1949, this happens to be about the amount by which investments in fixed capital in the whole economy were to increase. See Zverev, *Planovoe khoziaistvo,* No. 2, 1949, p. 43. It is believed that this increase in investments in fixed capital is primarily a result of the drastic increase in industrial prices that went into effect in January, 1949. The item "Other, exclusive of subsidies" comprises many investment-type activities; for this reason, the increase in money outlays for this item may well have corresponded to that in fixed-capital investments.

On the other hand, the amount of the increase is still conjectural. Accordingly, it is interesting to consider the implications of an alternative assumption, say, that "Other, exclusive of subsidies" was to increase by only 25 percent. In this case the subsidies in 1948 come to 36 billion rubles, compared with the estimate of 43 billion rubles derived above.

In Appendix Table 29 we present data for 1948 and 1949 (Plan) on the components of the budget category "Financing the National Economy" not only for all economic sectors taken together, but also for individual sectors. The derivation of these data on individual sectors is explained subsequently. Of interest here are some implications as to the magnitude of subsidies for all sectors together.

Consider item 8 in the table. This includes subsidies and "Other, exclusive of subsidies." Referring to this item, then, the following changes were planned for 1949, in comparison with 1948:

	BILLION RUBLES
Industry	−31.3
Agriculture	+3.6
Transportation; Communications	−1.4
Trade	+2.4
Other	+5.7

We indicated, above, reasons for believing that "Other, exclusive of subsidies" increased substantially for all sectors taken together. Presumably it also increased in most, if not all, the individual sectors taken separately. Accordingly, the decreases in item 8 shown above, totaling 32.7 billion rubles (i.e., 31.3 + 1.4), probably were due exclusively to decreases in subsidies. This total may be compared with the decrease in subsidies calculated from equations (a) through (d): 34.6 billion rubles.

While this comparison is somewhat reassuring regarding the magnitude of our estimate, it suggests that the actual decrease in subsidies may have been greater than is shown by equations (a) through (d). Only 1.9 billion rubles are allowed by our calculation for further decreases in subsidies in industry and transport and all decreases in other sectors that are offset by increases in "Other, exclusive of subsidies." On the other hand, Zverev makes it clear (*Planovoe khoziaistvo*, No. 2, 1949, p. 43) that the decreases in subsidies must have been more or less confined to industry and transport, while subsidies on some scale were to continue in other sectors.

On the question of the magnitude of subsidies, reference may also be made to the data set forth subsequently in Appendix Table 33 on various components of investment in 1948. Thus, "extra-limit" outlays for the whole economy are taken to be 12 billion rubles, and those for capital repairs, 14 billion rubles. These figures are highly arbitrary. Furthermore, little is known about the share of these outlays financed by the government budget. On the other hand, the figures do not appear inconsistent with the total, i.e., 25.6 billion rubles, assigned to these items, together with "operational outlays," stockpiling, etc., in Appendix Table 29.

Finally, reference may be made to some budget data for 1948 for the RSFSR, the largest of the union republics. According to *Pravda*, May 25, 1949, p. 2, the total subsidies paid out of the budget of the RSFSR in 1948 amounted to 2.54 billion rubles. This constituted 26 percent of the RSFSR budget item, "Financing the National Economy." Our estimate of 43 billion rubles of subsidies for the whole USSR constitutes 29 percent of the USSR budget item, "Financing the National Economy."

1948 and 1949 (Plan). Industry; agriculture; etc. The data for individual economic sectors on the budget expenditures on "Financing the National Economy"; investments in fixed capital; and, for the year 1949 (Plan), investments in "own" working capital are from Zverev, *Planovoe khoziaistvo,* No. 2, 1949, pp. 42–45. Budget outlays for investments in "own" working capital in the different sectors in 1948 are estimated on the assumption that the total outlays for all sectors, calculated previously as 10.7 billion rubles, are distributed by sectors in the same proportions as in the 1949 (Plan). The 1949 figure on the current expenses of the MTS is estimated from data in *ibid.,* p. 48, and *Pravda,* March 11, 1949, p. 3. The 1948 figure is the difference between the total budget appropriation to MTS, taken as 12.0 billion rubles, and budget investments in the MTS, taken as 2.0 billion rubles. The total budget appropriation to MTS for 1948 is estimated on the assumption that a little less than two-thirds of the budget appropriation in 1948 for financing all agriculture, 20.47 billion rubles (Zverev, *Planovoe khoziaistvo,* No. 2, 1949, p. 42), was earmarked for MTS. For 1940 the MTS share is two-thirds of the total budget expenditures for financing agriculture. A somewhat smaller proportion is assumed for 1948, since the size of the tractor park, as well as the extent of MTS operations, was still less than prewar in 1948. The 1951 budget plan gave the MTS appropriation as 17 billion rubles. Considering price changes and the greater volume of MTS activities after 1948, this figure appears consistent with our estimate of 12.0 billion rubles for 1948. The budget investments in the MTS are estimated here on the basis of the budget investments in agriculture generally, which amounted to 4.2 billion rubles. See Appendix Table 37.

The total for "Other, exclusive of subsidies" and "Subsidies," taken together, is calculated as a residual, i.e., as the difference between items 1 and 5. The breakdown as between the two categories takes as a point of departure the calculation made earlier, according to which subsidies in industry must have decreased by at least 31.3 billion rubles and in transportation by at least 1.4 billion rubles from 1948 to 1949 (Plan). This means that the subsidies in these two sectors in 1948 must have amounted to at least these two sums respectively. At the same time, we have calculated that subsidies, as recorded in the pertinent budget category, amounted to 42.6 billion rubles in 1948 for all sectors. Accordingly, after the subsidies just attributed to industry and transport are deducted, there is a residual of 9.9 billion rubles still to be allocated. We assume that this residual was evenly distributed among all sectors other than trade. We have taken subsidies as totaling 44.0 billion rubles in 1948, including, in addition to the amount recorded as such in the budget, a sum of 1.4 billion rubles that is supposed to represent compensation to procurement agencies for premiums paid to farmers for above-quota deliveries. In Appendix Table 29 we classify these latter payments under "trade."

On the sector allocation of subsidies, reference may be made to Zverev, *Planovoe khoziaistvo,* No. 2, 1949, p. 43.

As was explained at the outset of this section, the "Allowance for subsidized losses" in Table 4 is supposed to represent, in addition to budget subsidies, the unplanned losses of *glavki* financed by bank credit and the accounting losses of economic organizations attached fully to the government budget. We come now to these latter two categories.

To refer first to the unplanned losses of *glavki* financed by bank credit, we arbitrarily assume that these totaled 1.0 billion rubles in all years. According to the Soviet profits data below, the Russians were notably successful in fulfilling their profits goals in the years studied. The possibility still is open that *glavki* in the red and not covered by these Soviet profits data may have suffered large unplanned losses, but this does not appear especially likely. While the profits goal for 1948 was overfulfilled, some *glavki* in the red not covered by the profits figures may still have suffered unplanned losses. For this reason we have maintained the same allowance for unplanned losses in 1948 as in previous years.

The Soviet profits data referred to are as follows:

	1940	1944	1948
Planned profits (bil. rubles)	33.3	27.3	34.8
Realized profits (bil. rubles)	31.8	24.4	35.3

The figures for 1944 and 1948 are for state enterprises only; those for 1940 are for cooperatives as well. All figures on realized profits are from Appendix Table 25. The planned figure for 1940 is from Zverev, *Gosudarstvennye biudzhety Soiuza SSR, 1938–1945 gg.,* p. 69; that for 1944 is from Zverev, *Gosbiudzhet SSSR na 1944 god,* p. 14; and that for 1948 is from Appendix Table 26.

To the writers' knowledge, the MTS were the only economic organizations of any consequence that were attached fully to the government budget in the period studied. The earnings of the MTS are derived from the collective farms for services performed by contract, and consist mainly of payments in kind. Accounting losses arise because of the bookkeeping method of valuing the payments in kind. The collective farms deliver these payments for MTS services to the state procurement organization, which then credits the MTS account in terms of the nominal prices it itself pays for obligatory deliveries. See TSU, *Slovar'-spravochnik . . . ,* 1944 ed., p. 107.

In Appendix Table 29 we already have compiled data on the current expenses of the MTS. The figures in Appendix Table 28 on the budget appropriations for the operating losses of the MTS represent the difference between the operating expenses of the MTS and their accounting income, taken as 2.0 billion rubles in 1940, .8 billion rubles in 1944, and 1.9 billion rubles in 1948. These latter figures are obtained as follows:

1940. From Suchkov, *Dokhody . . . ,* p. 113.

1944. This is estimated on the basis of data in Plotnikov, 1948 ed., concerning aggregate MTS income in 1945 (p. 269) and in some of the war years (p. 347).

1948. Reference is to the planned amount of MTS income in 1948, as given in *Zasedaniia Verkhovnogo Soveta SSSR (chetvertaia sessiia) . . . 1948 g.,* p. 278. This figure is taken as comprehensive of all MTS income on the basis of information in L. S. Galimon, *Dokhody mashinno-traktornykh stantsii,* pp. 8 and 63.

It should be noted that the "current expenses of the MTS" to which reference is made in the foregoing calculation of the accounting losses of the MTS is not quite the category that might be appropriate for this purpose. On the one hand, because of the nature of the calculation of "current expenses" as the difference between total budget appropriations and appropriations for investments in fixed capital, this category may include "extra-limit" outlays and possibly even capital repairs. On the other hand, it is believed that the budget appropriations to the MTS, and hence "current expenses" as computed, do not include any allowance for depreciation. See the notes to Table 4-A, item 8, that follow below.

8. DEPRECIATION

As a part of the prevailing *khozraschet* system, economic enterprises in the USSR, like their counterparts in Western countries, include among their expenses a charge for depreciation on capital. The amount is calculated according to rates fixed by law. An interesting feature is the control over funds created in this way. The practice is simply to transfer periodically to the banking system funds corresponding to the depreciation charge. In part the funds are reserved there for the use of the enterprise itself, for capital repairs, and in part they are put at the disposal of the Ministry for the financing of investment in that agency generally.

On the other hand, as has been explained elsewhere, some economic enterprises, most importantly the MTS, do not operate under the *khozraschet* system as generally applied. Rather they are attached fully to the government budget, and are financed in the same way as a government agency. Understandably, then, the system of depreciation accounting just described does not apply to these enterprises. Depreciation may still be charged as an expense for purposes of compiling an income statement. Whether or not this is done is not entirely clear from Soviet sources; but such a charge is probably made in the case of the MTS. But, no counterpart fund is established for capital repairs; these, like all other outlays, are financed simply from the government budget.

The *khozraschet* system as generally operative does not apply to the collective farm either, and here too an exception must be made concerning Soviet practice on depreciation accounting. No depreciation charge is made

APPENDIX TABLE 30

DEPRECIATION CHARGES BY TYPE OF CAPITAL,
1940, 1944, AND 1948
(*Billions of rubles*)

ITEM	1940	1944	1948
1. Economic organizations, other than MTS and collective farms	10.6	9.0	12.0
2. MTS and collective farms	1.5	1.0	1.5
3. Privately owned housing	.6	.5	.6
4. Total	12.7	10.5	14.1

for purposes of compiling an income statement, and accordingly no counterpart funds are established for capital repairs. The latter are financed, along with capital investments generally, from the "indivisible funds."

The charge for depreciation in Table 4, to come now to the question of immediate concern, comprises three categories: (i) depreciation recorded in the books of all enterprises other than the MTS and collective farms; (ii) a corresponding allowance for depreciation on the capital of the MTS and collective farms; and (iii) an allowance for depreciation on privately owned housing.

Or rather this was the aim. Because of limitations in the underlying information, the figures derived on the different categories, which are compiled in Appendix Table 30, are more or less arbitrary. To refer first to the depreciation recorded in the books of enterprises other than the MTS and collective farms, the figures are obtained as follows:

1940. According to data in Zverev, *Gosudarstvennye biudzhety Soiuza SSR, 1938–1945 gg.,* p. 79, economic organizations were supposed to undertake in 1940 some 5.21 billion rubles in capital repairs "on account of depreciation allocations" (*za schet amortizatsionnykh otchislenii*). Zverev is referring here to the practice just described of financing capital repairs out of funds established as a counterpart to the charge of depreciation expense. At the same time, according to a decree of 1938, the amounts of both the depreciation charge and the allocation to capital repairs for industrial ministries (commissariats as of 1938) were fixed as follows (see *Sobranie postanovlenii . . . SSSR,* No. 1, January 8, 1938, p. 1; also F. Gaposhkin, "Kapital'nyi remont v 1938 godu," *Planovoe khoziaistvo,* No. 9, 1938, pp. 55–56):

| | PERCENT OF FIXED CAPITAL | |
COMMISSARIAT	*Allowance for depreciation*	*Allowance for capital repairs*
Heavy Industry	5.6	2.4
Machinery Industry	5.5	2.2
Defense Industries	5.5	2.6
Timber Industry	6.0	3.0
Light Industry	5.5	3.6
Food Industry	6.0	2.8

For purposes of estimating the total recorded charges for depreciation for economic enterprises other than the MTS and collective farms, we assume that on the average for all such organizations the allocations for capital repairs were to amount to 49.12 percent of the charges for depreciation. This is the relation obtaining on the average for industrial ministries only; i.e., the unweighted average of the allowances tabulated above for capital repairs, 2.8 percent, comes to 49.12 percent of an unweighted average of the corresponding allowances for depreciation, 5.7 percent.

Our figure of 10.6 billion rubles for the book value of 1940 depreciation allowances is in general accord with the amount of depreciation allowances projected for the entire period of the Third Five Year Plan, 1938–42, amounting to 47.7 billion rubles. Some 26.0 billion rubles were allotted for capital repairs. See Gosplan, *Tretii piatiletnii plan . . . ,* pp. 115, 120.

Note: At a late stage in our calculations, we came across the following more definite information on the depreciation recorded in the books of Soviet enterprise. According to D'iachenko, *Finansy i kredit SSSR,* p. 397, n. 1, this was planned to amount to 9.15 billion rubles in 1940.

1944. We assume that recorded depreciation charges of economic organizations other than the MTS and collective farms totaled nearly the same as in 1940. As a result of the wartime destruction, the total capital stock on hand in 1944 must have been a good deal less than in 1940, but the capital expansion undertaken during the war probably was relatively costly. While, as has been noted previously (p. 183), the prices of industrial goods were fairly stable during the war, construction costs must have risen with increasing wages. In any event, the capital goods added during the war must have been higher priced than those on hand in 1940. Accordingly, the book value of the capital stock may not have been far below the prewar figure.

Of interest here is an item of information in Sh. Ia. Turetskii, *Vnutri-promyshlennoe nakoplenie v SSSR*, p. 105: Recorded charges for depreciation in industry increased from 2.2 percent of the total costs of production in 1940 to 2.9 percent in 1943. Presumably this increase was due mainly to the wartime shifts in the structure of industrial production, but the possibility is suggested that in some measure it was due to the factor mentioned above, namely, the increase in the average price of industrial capital on hand.

1948. This figure is something of a guess, but it finds some support in data on the sources and disposition of Soviet investment funds in Zverev, *Planovoe khoziaistvo*, No. 2, 1949, pp. 41–43. According to these data, some 9.0 billion rubles of investments in fixed capital in 1948 were financed from the funds of the enterprise, as distinct from budgetary funds. Furthermore, the plan called for 3.9 billion rubles to be financed from profits. The principal remaining source of such investments is depreciation funds, so the amount of these going to fixed capital investments may have amounted to some 5.0 billion rubles. As has been indicated above, depreciation funds are also used in the USSR to finance capital repairs. Before the war, about half the depreciation funds were devoted to this purpose. Assuming the division might have been more favorable to capital repairs in the reconstruction period, a total current depreciation charge of 12.0 billion rubles does not seem implausible.

This figure is also in accord with the known facts concerning the postwar recovery of the Soviet stock of fixed capital. Probably the stock of fixed capital in 1948 was not much below that of 1940 in physical terms. On the average the prices of capital goods on hand in 1948 were presumably well above those of the earlier year.

Coming now to the depreciation on the MTS and collective farms, the indications are that before the war these organizations may have held about one-tenth as much fixed capital as all other economic organizations taken together. See TSUNKHU, *Sotsialisticheskoe stroitel'stvo SSSR*, p. xxxi; Kaplan, *Capital Investments in the Soviet Union, 1924–1951*, p. 58. On the assumption that the agricultural capital might be subject to a higher depreciation rate than that in the economy generally, we take the depreciation charge for the MTS and collective farms for the year 1940 to be 15 percent of that for the rest of the economy. The corresponding figures for 1944 and 1948 are taken to be 11 and 13 percent respectively. This is to allow for the disproportional decline in agricultural capital during the war and the presumably still disproportionately low level of this capital thereafter.

The figures in Appendix Table 30 for depreciation on privately owned housing are similarly rough. Account is taken of data in Kobalevskii, *Organi-zatsiia ekonomika zhilishchnogo khoziaistva SSSR*, p. 107, on the value of privately owned urban housing in 1936, and of data in Appendix Table 10 and the accompanying notes on the urban and rural housing fund in the years studied. It is assumed that per square meter rural housing was worth one-half that in urban localities. Also, all privately owned housing is taken to depreciate at the rate of 2 percent per annum.

In the foregoing, we took as our desideratum, so far as the capital of economic enterprises other than the MTS and collective farms is concerned, the determination of the total depreciation charges actually recorded in the books of Soviet economic enterprise. Furthermore, we attempted to estab-lish a more or less comparable figure for the MTS and the collective farms. We believe this procedure is correct. In the USSR, as in many other coun-tries, depreciation seems generally to be charged on the basis of original cost. Because of rising prices, this necessarily means an understatement from the economic standpoint. Also, it is more than doubtful that the legal rates allow sufficiently for the intensive use. This aspect was especially important during the war. But for the time being the concern is only to compile a list of charges which exhaust the Soviet value product at prevailing prices. For this purpose, it is clear that the book charges for depreciation are the ones to consider, no matter how erroneous.

On the other hand, we shall be concerned at a later point with the validity of the Soviet prices for purposes of national income valuation. In this con-nection, consideration necessarily will have to be given among other things to the validity of the book charges for depreciation.

A word or two may be in order about several other matters. For one thing, the "Imputed net rent of owner-occupied dwellings" included among house-hold incomes in Table 3 actually represents something of a gross figure rather than a true net figure. The owner-occupied housing simply is valued at the rental rates prevailing for government housing. While these rates undoubt-edly are low from any economic standpoint, the inclusion now of a separate allowance for depreciation on owner-occupied housing represents in a sense a form of double-counting. See the notes to Table 3-A, item 4.

The same may be said for the MTS, for as has been indicated, the allow-ance for subsidized losses may not take account of the depreciation on MTS capital. On the other hand, a probable offset is the improper inclusion in these losses of some capital investments, particularly "extra-limit" outlays, etc. See the notes to Table 4-A, item 6.

Finally, while estimated from Soviet data, the agricultural production expenses deducted from the gross harvest in our calculation of net income in kind are believed to include an allowance for depreciation on agricultural capital. The fact that the collective farms themselves do not seem to make such a charge for purposes of compiling an income statement might suggest the contrary.

In the preceding paragraphs, reference has been made at various points to Soviet practice regarding depreciation accounting. In this connection, use has been made of the following sources: TSU, *Slovar'-spravochnik* . . . , 1944 ed., pp. 47–48; *ibid.*, 1948 ed., pp. 71–72, 232–33; I. D. Laptev (ed.), *Uchenye zapiski,* Issue 13, p. 46; S. V. Shol'ts, *Kurs sel'skokhoziaistvennoi statistiki,* chap. x; Kaplan, *Capital Investments in the Soviet Union, 1924–1951,* pp. 17 ff.

10. TRANSFER RECEIPTS

10a. Net savings of households

For all years this is taken from Table 3-B, item 6.

10b. Direct taxes

For all years this is taken from Table 3-B, item 7.

B. OUTLAYS

1. COMMUNAL SERVICES

1a. Health care

Under the prevailing system of socialized medicine, health care in the USSR is the object of expenditures not only by government agencies but also to a limited extent by various other organizations, principally the trade unions. As is indicated in Appendix Table 31, the attempt has been made here to take into account expenditures from all sources. At the same time, we deduct capital outlays which are included in these expenditures as recorded in the budget. These are classified below under "Gross investment . . . ."

As to the figures compiled on these different features, those on expenditures by nongovernmental organizations are rather arbitrary. We take as a point of departure calculations in the notes to Appendix Table 14, item 1, according to which expenditures of social insurance funds for purposes other than for payment of pensions and allowances amounted to 2.00 billion rubles in 1940, .72 billion rubles in 1944, and 3.48 billion rubles in 1948. These expenditures are mainly, although not exclusively, of a sort properly included under "health care," e.g., maintenance of rest homes, sanitariums, etc. We raise these figures arbitrarily to allow for expenditures for health care from sources other than social insurance funds.

According to data in *Soviet National Income,* pp. 40, 119, and Plotnikov, 1948 ed., p. 223, expenditures by economic and social organizations accounted for 30 percent of all expenditures for health care in 1937. The figures compiled here indicate lower figures for later years, especially 1944, and may understate this feature. On the other hand, the 1937 figure may well be too high.

The figures on the government budget appropriations and capital outlays in Appendix Table 31 are obtained as follows:

1940. 1. Government budget appropriations for health care. From *ibid.,* p. 329.

APPENDIX TABLE 31

CALCULATION OF TOTAL CURRENT OUTLAYS
FOR PUBLIC HEALTH, 1940, 1944, AND 1948
(*Billions of rubles*)

ITEM	1940	1944	1948
1. Government budget appropriations for health care	9.04	10.20	19.64
2. Expenditures for health care by economic and social organizations	2.50	1.00	5.00
3. Total expenditures for health care	11.54	11.20	24.64
4. Less: Capital outlays	.40	1.00	1.50
5. Total current outlays for public health	11.14	10.20	23.14

1940. 4. Capital outlays for public health. On the basis of data in the 1941 plan, it is estimated that capital outlays for health care and education (i.e., for the construction of hospitals, schools, etc.) amounted to about one billion rubles, of which approximately 40 percent were for public health. See *Gosudarstvennyi plan . . . na 1941 god,* p. 485.

1944. 1. Government budget appropriations for health care. From Plotnikov, 1948 ed., p. 329.

1944. 4. Capital outlays for public health. An arbitrary estimate.

1948. 1. Government budget appropriations for health care. From Zverev, *Planovoe khoziaistvo,* No. 2, 1949, p. 48.

1948. 4. Capital outlays for public health. On the basis of data on capital expenditures in 1948 (*ibid.*) and in the 1941 plan (*Gosudarstvennyi plan . . . na 1941 god,* p. 485), it is estimated that total capital outlays for public health and education amounted to 4 billion rubles in 1948, of which 1.5 billion rubles were expended in the field of public health.

1b. Education

As appears in Appendix Table 32, this represents outlays for education both by the government and by nongovernmental organizations. At the same time, a variety of items which are included in these outlays as recorded in Appendix Table 32 are taken into account elsewhere in our calculations and accordingly must be deducted here. Reference is to stipend payments, which appear as a transfer receipt of households and presumably as expenditures under the different household outlays; tuition scholarships, which are treated similarly; outlays for education covered by tuition payments, which are included under household consumption; and capital outlays, which are to be taken into account subsequently under "Gross investment . . . ."

APPENDIX TABLE 32

CALCULATION OF TOTAL OUTLAYS FOR EDUCATION
NOT COVERED ELSEWHERE, 1940, 1944, AND 1948
(*Billions of rubles*)

ITEM	1940	1944	1948
1. Government budget appropriations for education	22.49	20.66	55.09
2. Expenditures for education by economic and social organizations	4.50	3.00	11.00
3. Total outlays for education	26.99	23.66	66.09
4. Less: Outlays covered elsewhere			
(i) Stipends	2.43	2.14	3.00
(ii) Tuition scholarships and payments	.20	.30	.60
(iii) Capital outlays for education	.60	1.50	2.50
(iv) Total outlays covered elsewhere	3.23	3.94	6.10
5. Total outlays for education not covered elsewhere	23.76	19.72	59.99

In Appendix Table 32, the figures on stipends and tuition scholarships and payments are from Appendix Tables 15 and 20. According to data in *Soviet National Income*, pp. 40, 119, and in Plotnikov, 1948 ed., p. 146, expenditures for education by nongovernmental organizations in 1937 amounted to 27.7 percent of the expenditures by government organizations. We arbitrarily assume that the corresponding figures in 1940, 1944, and 1948 were respectively 20, 15, and 20 percent. The data on government budget appropriations and capital outlays are obtained as follows:

1940. 1. Government budget appropriations for education. From Plotnikov, 1948 ed., p. 329.

1940. 4 (iii). Capital outlays for education. See notes to Appendix Table 31, item 4.

1944. 1. Government budget appropriations for education. The same as for 1940.

1944. 4 (iii). Capital outlays for education. An arbitrary estimate.

1948. 1. Government budget appropriations for education. From Zverev, *Planovoe khoziaistvo,* No. 2, 1949, p. 48.

1948. 4 (iii). Capital outlays for education. See Appendix Table 31, item 4.

In the foregoing, we took the government budget appropriation for "education" (*prosveshchenie*) to represent the government expenditures in this area. It should be noted that the pertinent heading in the Soviet government budget comprises, in addition to outlays for the support of schools, libraries, and the like, funds for a variety of other activities, including scientific research, the press, the theater, and other cultural activities. In the postwar period, this item presumably also includes research on atomic energy. Furthermore, data concerning educational outlays by economic and social organizations no doubt embrace similarly diverse activities, including not only vocational training but also, say, the "Red Corner." On the scope of activities supported by government budget outlays for "education," see Rovinskii, *Gosudarstvennyi biudzhet SSSR,* 1951 ed., chap. xiii.

1c. Other

These are arbitrary figures intended to allow for aspects that may not be covered by 1a and 1b, e.g., outlays for physical culture; administrative expenses of the party and trade unions over and above amounts financed by dues.

2. GOVERNMENT ADMINISTRATION

These figures are taken directly from the government budgets of the respective years. The budget appropriations for "government administration" (*gosudarstvennoe upravlenie*) are for the maintenance of all higher and local organs of state authority, except the NKVD and its successors, the MVD and MGB, and of the defense departments. The organs of government include the supreme and local soviets; the courts and the state prosecutor; the Council of Ministers, its commissions and committees; the Ministry of Foreign Affairs and the diplomatic corps; and all the ministries in charge of the various branches of the national economy, as well as those responsible for social and cultural measures. In the case of agencies administering the economy, i.e., departments of ministries (*glavki*), these are generally supported out of appropriations to the superior ministries, but many supply and procurement departments operate on a *khozraschet* basis, and accordingly are more or less self-financing. Furthermore, some agencies which might conventionally be considered government organs probably are supported out of government appropriations to "Financing the National Economy," under the heading "operational outlays" rather than government "administration." For example, this is believed to be so in the case of agencies administering the weather service and geodetics, resettlement, and weights, measures, and standards.

We record elsewhere the expenditures of the NKVD (now MVD-MGB). As is noted subsequently, this agency, in addition to its concern with internal security generally, performs a variety of other activities normally classified as government functions.

The sources of finance for the Communist Party apparatus are not mentioned in Soviet budget sources. The Party's expenditures may exceed its income from dues and other revenues, such as from the sale of publications, and accordingly it may receive allocations from the budget, but under which expenditure item is not known.

On the agencies supported by the budget appropriations for "government administration," see *Soviet National Income,* pp. 14, 23 ff.; Rovinskii, *Gosudarstvennyi biudzhet SSSR,* 1939 ed., p. 339; *ibid.,* 1951 ed., chap xii; Narkomfin SSSR, *Otchet ob ispolnenii gosudarstvennogo biudzheta SSSR za 1935 god; Vos'maia sessiia Verkhovnogo Soveta SSSR . . . 1941 g.,* pp. 498 ff.

The figures which we cite for outlays on government administration are from the following sources:

1940. D'iachenko, *Finansy i kredit SSSR,* p. 182; and Plotnikov, 1948 ed., p. 226.

1944. Ibid., p. 340.

1948. Pravda, March 11, 1949, p. 3.

3. NKVD (MVD AND MGB)

These figures represent the government budget appropriations which were made in 1940 to the People's Commissariat of Internal Affairs (NKVD) and in 1944 and 1948, to its successors, the Ministry of Internal Affairs (MVD) and the Ministry of State Security (MGB). The precise scope of these appropriations is not entirely clear. In addition to its main concern, internal security, the NKVD performs a variety of other activities such as fire protection, civil registration, forest guards, automobile inspection, and inspection of weights and measures. Presumably these are generally included under the budget appropriation in question, though possibly some such outlays are listed elsewhere, particularly under "operational expenditures" in "financing the national economy." Of course, in Western countries the internal security and the other activities alike would all normally be classified with other government activities recorded in Table 4-B, item 2.

As part of its internal security activities, the NKVD also maintains quasi-military detachments performing such services as military police, POW guards, convoy escorts, etc. In other countries such services usually fall to the military establishment proper, and in national economic accounts such as ours would be classified below in Table 4-B, item 4, "Defense."

The figure cited here for 1940 is known to be exclusive of an appropriation for "various construction work of the NKVD" and in general it is believed that capital construction outlays are included under "Financing the National Economy" rather than under the main budget heading referring to NKVD appropriations. Such capital construction properly finds its way in our accounts in Table 4-B, item 5, "Gross investment . . . ."

On the scope of the activities of the NKVD, see S. S. Studenikin, *Sovetskoe administrativnoe pravo;* I. I. Evtikhiev and V. A. Vlasov, *Administrativnoe pravo SSSR;* and V. Gsovski, *Soviet Civil Law.*

The data on government budget appropriations to the NKVD are obtained as follows:

1940. Shestaia sessiia Verkhovnogo Soveta SSSR . . . 1940 g., pp. 248, 450.

1944. According to *Desiataia sessiia Verkhovnogo Soveta SSSR . . . 1944 g.,* p. 249, "expenditures on the maintenance of organs of government administration" in the union and union-republican governments amounted to 10.7 billion rubles. It is indicated that this includes the appropriation to the MVD and MGB. We have recorded elsewhere the total budget outlays for government administration as 7.4 billion rubles. This includes not only the outlays of union and republican governments but also those of local organs, but it is exclusive of outlays of the MVD and MGB. On the basis of information in A. M. Aleksandrov, *Finansy i kredit SSSR,* pp. 217–21, and in Rovinskii, *Gosudarstvennyi biudzhet SSSR,* 1949 ed., pp. 47 and 55, we estimate that 56 percent of the appropriation of 7.4 billion rubles, or 4.1 billion rubles, went to support union and republican organs. Deducting this latter sum from the 10.7 billion rubles going to these organs and the MVD and MGB together, we calculate that the appropriation for the latter alone was 6.6 billion rubles.

1948. According to *Zasedaniia Verkhovnogo Soveta SSSR (chetvertaia sessiia) . . . 1948 g.,* p. 281, "expenditures on the maintenance of organs of government administration" in the union and republican governments amounted to 33.1 billion rubles. Again, this includes outlays of the MVD and MGB, and, as before, we calculate the latter as a residual in the amount of 25.8 billion rubles. The budget outlays for government administration, including local as well as union and republican organs but not the MVD and MGB, have already been recorded at 13.1 billion rubles. We take the share of union and republican organs in this total to be 56 percent, or 7.3 billion rubles.

4. DEFENSE (AS RECORDED IN BUDGET)

This represents the budget appropriation to the military establishment, i.e., in 1940 and 1944, to the People's Commissariats of Defense and Navy; in 1948, to the Ministry of the Armed Forces.

It does not seem advisable to try here to compare the scope of this budget appropriation with that of comparable appropriations in budgets of other countries. On the other hand, something ought to be said about what is and what is not included. The appropriations cover outlays of the military establishment for the procurement of munitions end-items, the maintenance of military installations, and the pay and subsistence of troops. Much, if not all, military construction, i.e., construction of bases, camps, etc., probably is also included.

Munitions production, as distinct from munitions procurement, is the responsibility not of the military establishment but of various other ministries specializing in this task, e.g., as of 1948, the Ministries of the Aircraft Industry, Shipbuilding, etc. Accordingly, munitions production is recorded as an outlay of the military establishment only at the time of procurement, while stocks held by the defense production ministries are omitted from the expenditures of the military establishment. It is not known whether any munitions stocks are held by still other agencies; if so, these too would be omitted.

Expenditures for the construction of new munitions plants are classified not as appropriations to the military establishment but as outlays under "Financing the National Economy." Under this heading, they are included in appropriations to the defense production ministries.

What has been said of munitions and defense plant construction generally, it is believed, applies among other things to atomic weapons and atomic weapon plant construction. Very possibly stockpiles of atomic weapons in the USSR, as in the United States, are held by agencies other than the defense ministries. If so, the stockpiling of these weapons would not be included in defense appropriations, as shown in the budget. This, however, is presumably not a factor to reckon with in the period under consideration. Outlays on military research, including atomic research, may in some measure be included under the budget appropriation for education rather than under that for the defense ministries.

As has been noted already, the NKVD is engaged in some activities which, in other countries, would generally be performed by the military establishment as such. Accordingly, the budget appropriation to the latter is correspondingly restricted.

Some premilitary training is given in common schools, and as such is financed by budget appropriations to education. Paramilitary training is provided by various "voluntary" societies as assistance to the armed forces; these societies were recently merged into a single organization, DOSAAF.

It is not known how the Russians have accounted in their budget for requisitions and occupation charges levied since the war in Eastern Europe and Germany. No doubt these in some part do not show up in the budget at all, and accordingly are also omitted from the recorded outlays of the military establishment. It is not known either how the Russians account for military assistance to the satellites.

Finally, military pensions are included in the budget as outlays for "social-cultural measures" rather than being included under the appropriations to the military establishment.

In our national economic accounts, additions to military stockpiles not held by the defense ministries and defense plant construction are included under "Gross investment." Defense activities and activities in support of defense included in the Soviet budget headings "education" and "NKVD" are correspondingly classified in our accounts. Military pensions are included under the transfer incomes of households.

The facts on the scope of the budget appropriations to defense must be gleaned primarily from available information on the government budget generally, as set forth, for example, in Rovinskii, *Gosudarstvennyi biudzhet SSSR*, 1951 ed. On various special aspects, reference may be made also to *Izvestiia*, August 26, 1950, p. 3; *Odinnadtsataia sessiia Verkhovnogo Soveta SSSR . . . 1945 g.*, p. 84; *Sbornik rukovodiashchikh materialov i konsul'tatsii po stroitel'stvu*, No. 8, 1949.

The figures we cite for the defense appropriations are from the following sources:

1940. Plotnikov, 1948 ed., p. 216.

1944. Ibid., p. 303.

1948. Pravda, March 11, 1949.

5. GROSS INVESTMENT, INCLUDING INVESTMENTS IN FIXED CAPITAL, INVENTORY ACCUMULATIONS, ADDITIONS TO STOCKPILES, ETC.

This is calculated as a residual, i.e., as the difference between the sum of all incomes and the sum of all outlays other than gross investment. We have attempted, with varying success, however, to account for the computed residual in terms of the available information on the different types of investment included.

In Appendix Table 33 are shown data the writers have compiled for a number of different categories of investment that are included in gross investment computed as a residual, particularly:

1. Investments in fixed capital, other than "extra-limit" outlays and capital repairs. The figure cited for 1940 is calculated from data in Voznesenskii, *Bol'shevik*, No. 3–4, 1941, p. 37; that for 1944 is from Plotnikov, 1948 ed., p. 306; that for 1948 is from *Pravda*, March 11, 1949. In calculating the figure for 1940 we deducted from a figure of 38.0 billion rubles given by Voznesenskii for investments in fixed capital, 6.0 billion rubles of "extra-limit" outlays which, according to him, are included in the former figure. It is believed that these "extra-limit" outlays, representing investments not listed by title in the annual plan for capital works and accordingly not subject to the approval of union and republican governments, are also excluded from the figures on fixed-capital investment cited for other years. The data for all years also exclude capital repairs not charged as current expense. On the other hand, they may include military construction previously classified in this study as "Defense." Probably this latter item was important in 1940. On the scope of the Soviet data on investments in fixed capital cited here, see Kaplan, *Capital Investments in the Soviet Union, 1924–1951*, pp. 117 ff., 133 ff., 211. The figure cited here for 1944, 27.4 billion rubles, has been given preference over that cited by Kaplan, 29.0 billion rubles, since it comes from a later source.

APPENDIX TABLE 33

INVESTMENTS BY TYPE, 1940, 1944, AND 1948

(*Billions of rubles*)

ITEM	1940	1944	1948
1. Investments in fixed capital, other than "extra-limit" outlays and capital repairs	32.0	27.4	66.2
2. "Extra-limit" outlays	6.0	. . .	12.0
3. Capital repairs	5.0	5.0	14.0
4. Investments in "own" working capital	7.6	4.0	17.1
5. Collective farm investments			
(i) Retained income in kind	. . .[a]	2.0	4.0
(ii) Other	5.5	5.8	8.0
(iii) Total	5.5	7.8	12.0
6. Other investments	6.6	11.7	28.8
7. All types	62.7	55.9	150.1

[a] . . . = negligible.

2. *"Extra-limit" outlays.* The figure cited for 1940 is from Voznesenskii, *Bol'shevik*, No. 3–4, 1941, p. 37; that for 1948 is a "very rough" estimate derived in Kaplan, *Capital Investments in the Soviet Union, 1924–1951*, pp. 133 ff. It is not believed that "extra-limit" outlays were of any importance in 1944. See *ibid.*

3. *Capital repairs.* According to *Shestaia sessiia Verkhovnogo Soveta SSSR . . . 1940 g.*, p. 78, the goal for capital repairs for 1940 was 6.6 billion rubles. The indications are that this goal was not fulfilled. The figures for 1944 and 1948 are estimates derived in Kaplan, *Capital Investments in the Soviet Union, 1924–1951*, pp. 133 ff.

4. *Investments in "own" working capital.* The figure for 1940 is calculated

from data in Zverev, *Gosudarstvennye biudzhety Soiuza SSR, 1938–1945 gg.*, pp. 80, 108. Zverev gives two different figures on the goal for the total working capital of economic organizations for January 1, 1941: 71.1 billion rubles (p. 80) and 68.4 billion rubles (pp. 107–8). But apparently the smaller figure refers to "government" economic organizations only and does not cover cooperatives. On the other hand, the indicated underfulfillment in the goal for government organizations, 2.7 billion rubles, is taken here to apply equally to the goal for all economic organizations, including cooperatives. Our figure of 7.6 billion rubles for investments in "own" working capital in 1940 is derived from this information together with Zverev's statement (p. 80) that working capital (apparently in all economic organizations) was planned to increase by 10.3 billion rubles in 1940.

For 1944, we have already taken the budget appropriation for "own" working capital to be 2.0 billion rubles. See Appendix Tables 29. Also, in 1940 the budget financed about one-half of all investments in "own" working capital. See the notes to Appendix Table 29, item 3. We assume the same relation obtained in 1944. The 1948 figure is the goal of the annual plan for that year. See Zverev, *Gosudarstvennyi biudzhet SSSR na 1948 god,* p. 22.

5. Collective farm investments. The figures on retained income in kind are explained above in Appendix A, notes to Table 3-A, item 1d. The figures on other collective farm investments for 1940 and 1944 are derived on the following basis: According to Appendix A (notes to Appendix Table 3) and Appendix B (notes to Appendix Table 24) there were in operation in 1940 some 236,300 collective farms, and in 1944, some 190,722. According to Anisimov, *Pobeda . . .* , p. 83, the average collective farm invested 23,200 rubles in 1940 and 30,500 rubles in 1944. Anisimov, it is believed, refers to fixed-capital investments, and accordingly these outlays are over and above the retained income in kind, which presumably would consist mainly of seed and fodder funds, work-in-process, etc.

The figure on other collective farm investments in 1948 is an estimate of fixed-capital investments for that year, based on the following: (i) According to *Zakon o piatiletnem plane vosstanovleniia i razvitiia narodnogo khoziaistva SSSR na 1946–1950 gg.,* p. 38, collective farms were to invest in fixed capital in the period of the plan some 38 billion rubles. (ii) According to N. N. Rovinskii (ed.), *Organizatsiia finansirovaniia i kreditovaniia kapital'nykh vlozhenii,* p. 19, collective farm investments in fixed captial amounted to 14 billion rubles in the two-year perior, 1946 and 1947.

On collective farm investments, see also Kaplan, *Capital Investments in the Soviet Union, 1924–1951,* pp. 133 ff.

In Appendix Table 33 we assume by implication that collective farm investments are not covered by "investments in fixed capital . . ." as understood in item 1. On this, see *ibid.,* pp. 29 ff. and 133 ff.

In addition to the foregoing five categories of investment, reference is made in Appendix Table 33 to "Other investments." This is calculated as a balance. It represents the difference between total investment calculated as a residual in Table 4 and the amount of investment accounted for by the five enumerated categories. In trying on this basis to appraise the calculation of investment as a residual, hower, consideration must be given to several additional categories of investment that are still to be reckoned with:

6 (*i*). *Investments in working capital financed by bank-credit creation.* Reference was made above to the "own" working capital of the Soviet firm, which is financed partly through budgetary grants and partly from the enterprise's own resources. In addition to this "own" working capital, the enterprise also possesses working capital financed through bank loans. Furthermore, while these loans must be repaid, the amount outstanding has tended to increase in the course of time, so that in effect there are investments in working capital financed through bank loans as well as through government grants and the enterprise's own resources. According to data in *Soviet National Income,* p. 121, investments in working capital totaled 15 billion rubles in 1937. Of this probably about 8.5 billion rubles were financed from budgetary grants and the enterprise's own resources, while 6.5 billion rubles were financed by bank credit.

No data are at hand on the investments in working capital financed through bank credit in the years studied. Some idea of their magnitude in 1940, however, may be gathered from the fact that the outstanding loans of the State Bank increased from 45.0 billion rubles on January 1, 1939, to 55.0 billion rubles on January 1, 1941. See M. V. Condoide, *The Soviet Financial System,* p. 40. In other words, the investments must have totaled 10.0 billion rubles in the years 1939 and 1940 taken together. Also, there is reason to think that in 1948 the bank-financed investments in working capital must have been especially large, possibly comparable with the planned goal of 17.1 billion for investment in "own" working capital. This is in view of the notably large budget surplus of that year. We comment on this aspect subsequently. See Appendix C, notes to Table 7-B, item 9.

The figures cited here on bank-financed investments in working capital, and also those cited previously on investments in "own" working capital, are believed to represent funds made available to Soviet economic enterprise for the expansion of working capital, including not merely physical assets but also cash and unused bank balances. Accordingly, they cannot be taken to indicate a corresponding increase in physical assets. Only the latter, of course, is of concern here.

6 (*ii*). *Investments in commodity stockpiles.* According to Voznesenskii, *Voennaia ekonomika . . . ,* p. 154, "state materials reserves" increased by 3.6 billion rubles in the year and a half before the German attack. Voznesenskii no doubt is referring to the stockpiles of foodstuffs and raw materials

which the government maintains for strategic and other purposes, and the implication is that investments in such stockpiles in 1940 might have been of the order of two billion rubles. There surely was little investment in commodity stockpiles in 1944; possibly there was some disinvestment. Stockpiling may well have assumed sizable proportions again in 1948, in view of the need to replenish reserves depleted in wartime. According to Ia. Kronrod, "Natsional'nyi dokhod SSSR," *Bol'shevik,* No. 8, 1950, p. 61, the Fourth Five Year Plan called for 6 percent of the national income to be devoted to "building up reserves" in 1950, as compared with only 3 percent in 1937. If anything like this goal were realized in 1948, the stockpiling of course would have come to a substantial sum. Even 3 percent of the national product would have come to 11.6 billion rubles. The national product is taken here to be 387.3 billion rubles in 1948. This is in terms of the Soviet concept, according to which services generally are omitted. See *Soviet National Income,* pp. 143 ff.

6 (*iii*). *Gold production.* According to A. Gerschenkron, *Economic Relations with the USSR,* pp. 36–37, the Russians produced about 175 billion dollars worth of gold a year before the war. This would have come to nearly one billion rubles at the then prevailing official rate of exchange. The indications are that the Russians continued gold production on some scale during the war, but the production then and also in postwar years is not known.

6 (*iv*). *Net foreign balance.* The Russians had in 1937 a net foreign balance on commodity account of 387 million rubles at the official rate of exchange. In 1938 there was a net deficit on commodity account of 91 million rubles. See A. Baykov, *Soviet Foreign Trade,* Appendix Table I. There was again a deficit amounting to 34 million rubles in 1940. See Voznesenskii, *Voennaia ekonomika* . . . , p. 73. As of 1944 trade consisted almost exclusively of Lend-Lease imports, which, as has already been explained, is treated provisionally in our accounts as having a zero value at the port of entry prior to Soviet custom charges. We treat likewise the reparations which had become important in 1948, but commercial trade again was sizable at that time. According to statistics compiled in the United Nations' Economic Commission for Europe, *Economic Survey of Europe in 1948,* Appendix C, Table XVI, the USSR had in 1948 a net export balance, exclusive of reparations, of about 163 million dollars. Soviet exports in 1948 were valued at 769 million 1948 dollars and imports, at 606 million 1948 dollars—all prices f.o.b. At the official rate of exchange, a net favorable balance on merchandise account of less than one billion rubles is indicated. No information is at hand on Russia's foreign balance on service account.

6 (*v*). *Expenditures on geological prospecting, conservation measures, etc.* Reference was made in the notes to Table 4-A, item 6, to the "operational outlays" included in the government budget under "Financing the National Economy." According to the logic of our calculations, some—though not all

—of the expenditures must be viewed here as still another element of investment. Reference is particularly to expenditures on geological prospecting, conservation measures, agricultural melioration, etc. Beyond this, the "operational outlays" include also compensation to procurement agencies for premiums paid to farmers for above-quota deliveries. As was explained in the notes to Table 4-A, item 6, these expenditures are treated here as subsidies. Also included are some expenditures on industrial research and personnel training, which presumably are allowed for in our tabulation of the disposition of the national product under "Education."

As to the magnitude of the investment components, in our calculation of subsidies we rather arbitrarily allowed for "operational outlays," exclusive of compensation to procurement agencies, of some 10 billion rubles in 1940.

In view of the rapid increase in defense production that occurred then, the expenditures on industrial research and personnel should have constituted an appreciable part of this sum. Probably "operational outlays" in 1944 were not very different from those of 1940, whereas those of 1948 should have been larger.

The foregoing tabulation of the different components of investment was supposed to provide a basis for appraising our calculation of investment as a residual. What is to be concluded in this regard? As was noted previously, the figure cited in Appendix Table 33 on investments in fixed capital probably includes military construction, which in our accounts has already been recorded under "Defense." For the year 1940, it is believed such construction may have amounted to several billion rubles. On the other hand, after due account is taken of this aspect and the limitations in our data generally, the implication seemingly is that investment calculated as a residual may be understated to a very limited extent in 1940. For 1944, investment calculated as a residual checks notably closely with investment calculated as a sum of its components. Accordingly, there is no basis for thinking the former figure errs significantly one way or the other. The data on the investment components for 1948 are inadequate for any satisfactory appraisal of the calculation of investment as a residual in that year. But it is believed that the former data are broadly consistent with the latter calculation.

7. TRANSFER OUTLAYS

7a. Pensions and allowances
See Table 3-A, item 8.

7b. Stipends and scholarships
See Table 3-A, item 9.

7c. Interest payments to households
See Table 3-A, item 10.

APPENDIX C: NOTES TO TABLE 7

A. REVENUES

1. DIRECT TAXES

The figures for all years are taken from Table 3-B, item 7.

2. NET BORROWING

2a. From households
For all years, this is from Table 3-B, item 6a.
2b. From economic organizations and financial system
For all years, item (3) (ii) of Appendix Table 21.

4. REVENUES OF SOCIAL INSURANCE BUDGET

The figures for all years are taken from Table 4-A, item 2a.

5. INDIRECT TAXES AND OTHER PAYMENTS OUT OF INCOMES BY ECONOMIC ENTER-
PRISES TO GOVERNMENT BUDGET

5a. Taxes on incomes of collective farms
For all years, from Table 4-A, item 3a.
5b. Payments from profits of state enterprises to government budget
For all years, from Table 4-A, item 3b.
5c. Taxes on incomes of cooperative organizations
For all years, from Table 4-A, item 3c.
5d. Turnover tax
For all years, from Table 4-A, item 3d.
5e. Miscellaneous
For all years, from Table 4-A, item 3e.

6. CUSTOM DUTIES; 7. GOVERNMENT RECEIPTS FROM SALE OF LEND-LEASE; REPARA-
TIONS

The figures for all years are taken from Table 4-A, items 4 and 5.

8. OTHER REVENUES

This represents the sum of a variety of items tabulated in Appendix
Table 34.

The figures on tuition receipts are from Appendix Table 20. In Appendix

B, pp. 173 ff., reference was made to the item in the Soviet budget "non-tax incomes and various levies." It was assumed there that some of these revenues represented charges on the population, and that for the rest they comprised in equal parts charges against the current income of economic organizations and budget revenues realized from capital transfers and from other sources. Item 2 in Appendix Table 34 represents the amount of the latter sort of revenue.

APPENDIX TABLE 34

"OTHER REVENUES" IN TABLE 7, 1940, 1944, AND 1948

(*Billions of rubles*)

ITEM	1940	1944	1948
1. Tuition receipts	.2	.3	.6
2. "Nontax incomes and various levies" assumed not to represent charges against current product	1.3	3.1	5.5
3. Other identified budget revenues assumed not to represent charges against current product	4.7	14.5	5.0
4. Residual budget revenues assumed not to represent charges against current product	1.9	4.2	6.0
5. Total	8.1	22.1	17.1

Item 3, "Other identified budget revenues . . ." comprises for the year 1940 a variety of items in the budget the nature of which is not clear in every case but all of which seem to fall outside the realm of charges against the current income of economic organizations, and accordingly outside the realm of charges included in Table 4. The items in question follow:

	BILLION RUBLES
Unexpended budget funds in State Bank on first of year	1.57
Unexpended appropriations for previous year returned to the budget	.30
Unexpended budget funds resulting from revaluation of raw materials and other commodities	.24
Payments of enterprises into the budget connected with the financing of additional inventories by bank credit	.62
Economies realized from curtailment of administration and auto transportation	1.95

The foregoing data are from *Shestaia sessiia Verkhovnogo Soveta SSSR . . . 1940 g.*, pp. 235-39. They represent budget forecasts rather than realized figures.

Still referring to item 3 in Appendix Table 34, this represents for the year 1944 a variety of donations made to wartime patriotic funds. As was explained in Appendix A, p. 163, reference has been found in Soviet sources to three types of patriotic funds: the defense fund, the Red Army fund, and the fund for reconstruction. According to *Desiataia sessiia Verkhovnogo Soveta SSSR . . . 1944 g.,* p. 247, the budget forecast for 1944 called for total contributions to these funds amounting to 17.8 billion rubles. The realized totals for defense and Red Army funds alone amounted to 3.3 billion rubles, and we have recorded this sum elsewhere as representing total contributions by households, as distinct from economic organizations, to patriotic funds generally; or at least the amounts contributed in cash rather than in kind. See Appendix Table 23. We record in Appendix Table 34 the difference between the total contributions to all funds, 17.8 billion rubles, and the assumed amount of household donations to such funds, 3.3 billion rubles. Presumably this represents contributions by economic organizations either in cash or in kind and possibly also some household contributions to the reconstruction fund. In recording the cash contributions by economic organizations here rather than under indirect taxes, we are assuming that such payments were not treated as a charge against current income. The contributions in kind may have taken the form of cattle, tractors, etc., and it will readily be seen are also properly classified here rather than under indirect taxes.

The Soviet source of the figure of 17.8 billion rubles refers explicitly only to the Red Army fund and to the reconstruction fund. Possibly we are in error in assuming here, as we have done, that the defense fund is also included. On the other hand, the cited figure is said to include not only donations to the Red Army and reconstruction funds but also "other incomes," the nature of which is not explained. These may represent the defense fund, in which case our interpretation is in order again. But they may represent still other revenues, and accordingly our treatment of these revenues as donations would represent still another source of error in our calculations.

Item 3 for the year 1948 consists of only one item appearing in the budget forecast for 1948, and representing certain revenues derived from the revaluation of inventories. See *Zasedaniia Verkhovnogo Soveta SSSR (chetvertaia sessiia) . . . 1948 g.,* p. 279.

Reference is made finally to item 4, "Residual budget revenues assumed not to represent charges against current product." A comparison of the total budget revenue as recorded in Soviet sources with the sum of revenue items that have been accounted for in our calculations to this point leaves a residual unaccounted for which amounts to 3.8 billion rubles in 1940, 8.5 billion rubles in 1944, and 12.1 billion rubles in 1948. We assume that one-half of this

APPENDIX TABLE 35

CALCULATION OF UNACCOUNTED FOR RESIDUAL
OF BUDGET REVENUES, 1940, 1944, AND 1948
(*Billions of rubles*)

ITEM	1940	1944	1948
1. Total budget revenue as recorded in Soviet sources	180.2	268.7	408.4
2. Less: Adjustments			
(i) Expenditures for debt retirement and lottery prizes classified as revenue offsets in Table 7	2.4	1.2	1.8
(ii) Budget income from MTS classified as expenditure offset in Table 7	2.0	.8	1.9
(iii) Total adjustments	4.4	2.0	3.7
3. Adjusted total budget revenue	175.8	266.7	404.7
4. Less: Accounted for revenues			
(i) Direct taxes	10.8	48.8	37.5
(ii) Net borrowing	9.8	32.6	22.1
(iii) Revenues of social insurance budget	8.5	9.0	16.2
(iv) Indirect taxes, etc., exclusive of share of unaccounted for residual previously allocated to miscellaneous indirect taxes	133.8	125.9	289.2
(v) Customs duties	2.9 ⎫		6.0
(vi) Government receipts from sale of Lend-Lease, reparations	...ᵃ ⎬	24.0	10.5
(vii) Tuition receipts	.2 ⎭	.3	.6
(viii) "Nontax incomes and various levies" assumed not to represent charges against current product	1.3	3.1	5.5
(ix) Other identified budget revenues assumed not to represent charges against current product	4.7	14.5	5.0
(x) Total	172.0	258.2	392.6
5. Budget residual	3.8	8.5	12.1

ᵃ ... = negligible.

residual represents charges against the current income of economic organizations and accordingly a charge to be included in Table 4. The other half is taken to represent revenues from transactions on capital account and the like.

The calculation of the budget residual is shown in Appendix Table 35. The basic data in this table are taken from the following sources:

1. Total budget revenue as recorded in Soviet sources:
1940. Plotnikov, 1948 ed., p. 181.
1944. Ibid., p. 259.
1948. Pravda, March 11, 1949.
2. Adjustments:
The figures for all years on debt retirement are from Appendix Table 21. Those for lottery winnings (this applies only to 1944) are from the same source as was used to calculate net lottery subscriptions in Appendix Table 23. The figures for the budget income of the MTS are those given in Appendix B, notes to Table 4-A, item 6.
4. Accounted for revenues:
All figures except those on items (iv), (vii), (viii), and (ix) are from Table 7. Data on item (iv) are from Appendix Table 27. Those on items (vii), (viii), and (ix) are from Appendix Table 34.

B. EXPENDITURES

1. INTEREST CHARGES ON DEBT

1a. To households
For all years, from Appendix Table 16.

1b. To savings banks and other organizations
1940. Estimated on the basis of the information and sources indicated in the notes to Appendix Table 21.
1944. Calculated from a rough estimate of the outstanding debt in the hands of organizations in 1944 as 20 billion rubles and an average interest rate of 2 percent.
1948. Calculated as a residual by subtracting the bond interest paid to the population, taken above as 1.4 billion rubles from the estimated carrying charge of 1.7 billion rubles for the debt outstanding in 1948. The outstanding debt is taken roughly as 62.5 billion rubles on the basis of data in the Soviet press, including *Pravda,* May 4 and 11, 1949.

2. PENSIONS AND ALLOWANCES, INCLUDING THOSE PAID BY THE SOCIAL INSURANCE SYSTEM

The figures for all years are from Table 3.

3. COMMUNAL SERVICES

3a. Health care, including capital construction
For all years, Appendix Table 31, item 1.

3b. Education, including students' stipends and capital construction
For all years, Appendix Table 32, item 1.

4. GOVERNMENT ADMINISTRATION

For all years, from Table 4.

5. NKVD (MVD-MGB)

For all years, from Table 4.

6. DEFENSE

The figures for all years are from Table 4.

7. FINANCING THE NATIONAL ECONOMY

The total outlays are those given in Appendix Table 29, less the gross
budgetary revenue from the MTS, as given in Appendix B, notes to Table
4-A, item 6, p. 159. The budget subsidies, including the net appropriations
for the operating expenses of the MTS over and above budgetary revenue
from these organizations, are taken from Appendix Table 28. The item
"Other" under "Financing the National Economy" is calculated as a
residual.

8. OTHER EXPENDITURES

This is calculated as the difference between the total budget expenditures
recorded in Soviet sources, after certain adjustments, and the total of all
expenditures accounted for in Table 7. The adjustments are the counterpart
of those made in Appendix Table 35 for total budget revenues recorded in
Soviet sources and are intended to make the Soviet totals comparable with
those obtained from Table 7. Soviet expenditure totals do not include the
indicated budget surplus shown in Table 7 and discussed subsequently,
but no adjustment is made for this; rather we simply omit the budget
surplus from the calculated sum of accounted-for expenditures which is
compared with the totals given in Soviet sources, after adjustment.

In Appendix Table 36, the figures on total budget expenditures as
recorded in Soviet sources are obtained as follows:

1940. From Plotnikov, 1948 ed., p. 207.

1944. From Zverev, *Gosudarstvennye biudzhety Soiuza SSR, 1938–1945
gg.,* p. 149.

1948. See *Pravda,* March 11, 1949, p. 2.

The adjustments are from Appendix Table 35. The figures on expenditures accounted for in Table 7 represent the sum of Table 7-B, items 1
through 7.

As just calculated, the category "Other expenditures" represents a variety
of items, including some expenditures classified in the Soviet budget as
outlays for "social-cultural measures," other than outlays for education,

health care, and pensions and allowances. These miscellaneous expenditures for "social-cultural measures" include administrative expenses of the social insurance system, outlays for certain physical-culture activities, etc., and are believed to have amounted to 2.3 billion rubles in 1940, .7 billion rubles in 1944, and 4.7 billion rubles in 1948.

APPENDIX TABLE 36

CALCULATION OF "OTHER EXPENDITURES" IN TABLE 7, 1940, 1944, AND 1948
(*Billions of rubles*)

ITEM	1940	1944	1948
1. Total budget expenditures as recorded in Soviet sources	174.4	263.0	368.8
2. Less: Adjustments			
(i) Expenditures for debt retirement and lottery prizes classified as revenue offset in Table 7	2.4	1.2	1.8
(ii) Budget income from MTS classified as expenditure offset in Table 7	2.0	.8	1.9
(iii) Total adjustments	4.4	2.0	3.7
3. Adjusted total expenditures	170.0	261.0	365.1
4. Less: Expenditures accounted for in Table 7, excluding indicated budget surplus	166.9	258.4	353.3
5. "Other expenditures"	3.1	2.6	11.8

9. INDICATED BUDGET SURPLUS

This is the difference between total budget revenues and total budget expenditures as recorded in Soviet sources. For the Soviet data on total budget revenues and expenditures, see Appendix Table 35 and Appendix Table 36.

At various points in this study we have assumed that the magnitude of the Soviet budget surplus might be indicative of various items, particularly the amount of cash dishoarding on the part of the population and the amount of investments in working capital by economic organizations that is financed by bank-credit creation. We shall try now to explain briefly this assumption.

To begin with, it is necessary to bear in mind that there are two different types of revenue and expenditure in the Soviet government budget. On the one hand, there are revenues representing charges against the national product and transfer receipts from households; and expenditures representing dispositions of the national product and transfer payments to households. These, in other words, are the revenues and expenditures that show up in Table 4. On the other hand, there are other revenues and expenditures such as the transactions on capital account and the like tabulated in Appendix Table 34.

Suppose for the moment that the budget surplus shown in Table 5 arose entirely from an excess of revenues of the former kind over expenditures of the former kind. It is readily seen that the surplus would have to mean one or another of various things, including chiefly: (i) bank-financed investments in working capital; (ii) a decrease in the bank balances of economic organizations; and (iii) cash dishoarding of the population. The reader can satisfy himself on this score by inspecting Table 4. Table 4 must balance, and if the government charges and transfer receipts exceed government dispositions of final product and transfer payments, the excess must be balanced elsewhere. Investment financed by bank credit which does not show up as a charge in Table 4 is one possible offset. Investments of enterprises out of previously accumulated balances is another; and cash dishoarding by households is still another. There might also be others, but the foregoing probably are the most important. In this connection it should be noted that bank-financed investments in working capital are the chief form of bank-financed investments in the USSR.

Suppose now that the surplus arises on accounts other than those showing up in Table 4. The nature of the Soviet budget revenue and expenditures which we have excluded from Table 4 is not altogether clear, but for the most part it is believed that they have no bearing one way or another on bank-financed investments in working capital and dishoarding by economic organizations and households. The revenues in question are those shown in Appendix Table 34. The expenditures are the balance of "Other expenditures" in Table 7, over and above the miscellaneous outlays for "social-cultural measures" referred to above, pp. 212–13.

To what extent are the Soviet budget surpluses of the first type, i.e., due to revenues and expenditures showing up in Table 4? From the data set forth in Table 7 and Appendix Table 34 and on pp. 212–13, it may be calculated that instead of a surplus there was, in 1940, a deficit of 1.5 billion rubles on account of budget revenues and expenditures recorded in Table 4. Similarly, in 1944 there was a deficit of 14.5 billion rubles on the same account. On the other hand, there was still a surplus of 27.2 billion rubles in 1948.

While hardly conclusive, these calculations seem to be broadly consistent with the following views, previously expressed, concerning household cash balances and bank-financed working capital:

(i) There was no appreciable change in household cash balances in 1940.

Bank-financed investments in working capital are known to have amounted to 10.0 billion rubles in 1939 and 1940 taken together.

(ii) Household cash balances increased by 14.6 billion rubles. The almost exact correspondence with the deficit cited above must be rated as a curious coincidence.

(iii) There was no change in household cash balances in 1948, but probably a very sizable expansion in bank-financed working capital.

The notably large surplus in 1948 actually might be taken to indicate a decrease in household balances as well as sizable bank-financed investments in working capital. Moreover, one must recall here the monetary reform of December, 1947. Under this reform the government restored the open market for consumers' goods after a lapse of nearly six years, and at the same time carried out a series of monetary measures designed to reduce the volume of liquid assets outstanding. Among other things there was an exchange of currency at the rate of ten old rubles for one new one.

Under the circumstances, the budget surplus may have been in part a measure to reduce further the cash balances of the households. The government may have wished to ensure and re-ensure that the effectiveness of the open market would not be impaired by household dishoarding.

On the other hand, the monetary reform itself already signified a draconian step in this direction, and one wonders whether there could still have been any excess household cash balances after its institution.

It is occasionally suggested that Soviet budget surpluses are not bona fide excesses of revenues over expenditures. Rather they represent concealed outlays of one sort or another. This is a possibility, but the writers see little ground for this belief. In view of the limited detail the Russians provide on their budget incomes and outlays, they presumably have opportunities enough for concealment without resorting to the introduction of a fictitious budget surplus. For example, they could easily conceal all sorts of expenditures under the broad budget heading "Financing the National Economy."

At the same time, the surpluses seem more readily understood in terms already indicated, namely, as the counterpart of bank-financed working capital and dishoarding by economic organizations and households. This relationship has an economic as well as an accounting character. In effect the surplus provides a fiscal means to absorb excess purchasing power released through bank-financed investments in working capital and dishoarding. Incidentally, the official Soviet explanation of the budget surplus seems to stress this feature. The surplus is said to "serve as a principal source for extending short-term credit to the national economy" and thus to promote monetary stability. (See *Pravda,* May 18, 1949, p. 2.)

APPENDIX D: CALCULATION OF INCIDENCE OF TURNOVER TAX, SUBSIDIES, ETC.

A. INCIDENCE OF TURNOVER TAX (TABLE 8)

The calculation of the incidence of the turnover tax by national product categories shown in Table 8 may best be explained by referring to the more detailed version shown in Appendix Table 37.

Columns 2, 5, 8. Value of product:

All figures other than those in parentheses are from Tables 3, 4, and 5. The figures in parentheses are obtained as follows:

6. *Communal services.* According to *Soviet National Income,* p. 134, these were divided evenly between outlays for commodities and outlays for services in 1937. We assume the same breakdown obtained in 1940 and 1948. For the year 1944 we assume that the share of services had risen to 65 percent. This is mainly to allow for a wartime increase in wage rates in comparison with commodity prices.

7. *Government administration;* 8. *NKVD.* According to *Soviet National Income,* p. 134, about 80 percent of each of these two categories consisted of outlays for services and 20 percent of outlays for commodities in 1937. We assume that the same breakdown obtained in 1940 and 1948, but again for the year 1944 we assume an increase in the share of services: in the present case, to 90 percent.

9. *Defense.* Outlays on munitions are calculated as a residual.

10. *Gross investment.* The figures on stockpiles are more or less arbitrary estimates which take into account the information in Appendix B, pp. 204 ff. The figures on fixed capital represent the total outlays on the following items as given in Appendix Table 33: "Investments in fixed capital, other than 'extra-limit' outlays, capital repairs"; "'Extra-limit' outlays"; "Capital repairs"; "Collective farm investments, other." The figures on other investments are calculated as a residual.

Columns 3, 6, 9. Turnover tax, assumed effective rate; Columns 4, 7, 10. Turnover tax:

These data are intended to represent the amount of the turnover tax levied on the specified categories of goods and services, either directly or indirectly, insofar as taxed materials are used in their production. The main steps in the calculation are as follows:

(i) We assume provisionally that no turnover tax is levied in the USSR on the following use categories:

	VALUE OF PRODUCT, BILLION RUBLES		
	1940	*1944*	*1948*
Retail sales to households in collective farm markets	35.0	50.0	48.0
Trade-union and other dues	1.6	1.8	3.1
Farm income in kind	54.0	31.0	56.0
Communal services: services	18.2	20.1	42.6
Government administration: services	5.4	6.7	10.5
NKVD: services	5.7	5.9	20.6
Defense: services	4.1	14.2	14.0
Collective farm investment in kind	. . .ª	2.0	4.0
Stockpiles	2.0	. . .	5.0
Total	126.0	131.7	203.8

ª . . . = negligible.

(ii) For reasons that will appear in a moment, it is necessary to calculate for each of the years studied the average effective turnover tax rate, understood as the ratio of the total amount of the tax collected to the amount of the national product subject to tax. The calculation is as follows:

	1940	*1944*	*1948*
Gross national product (bil. rubles)	458.0	487.4	811.2
Less: tax-free product (bil. rubles)	126.0	131.7	203.8
Gross national product subject to tax (bil. rubles)	332.0	355.7	607.4
Less: Military subsistence (bil. rubles)	8.0	31.0	19.0
Gross national product subject to tax, less military subsistence (bil. rubles)	324.0	324.7	588.4
Turnover tax revenue (bil. rubles)	105.9	94.9	247.5
Average effective turnover tax rate (turnover tax revenue ÷ gross national product subject to tax) (in percent)	32.7	29.2	42.1

The reason for deducting army subsistence from the gross national product in the foregoing calculation is to avoid double counting.

(iii) We assume provisionally that the following national product use categories are subject to the average effective turnover tax rate: army subsistence; communal services, commodities; government administration, commodities; NKVD, commodities; gross investment, other. Furthermore, for reasons to appear, we take the average turnover tax rate to be 1.0 percent for housing, etc.; 7.5 percent for defense, munitions; and 7.5 percent for gross investment, fixed capital.

CALCULATION OF INCIDENCE OF TURNOVER TAX BY NATIONAL PRODUCT USE CATEGORY, 1940, 1944, AND 1948

ITEM	1940			1944			1948		
	Value of product, billion current rubles	Turnover tax, assumed effective rate, percent	Turnover tax, billion rubles	Value of product, billion current rubles	Turnover tax, assumed effective rate, percent	Turnover tax, billion rubles	Value of product, billion current rubles	Turnover tax, assumed effective rate, percent	Turnover tax, billion rubles
(1)	(2)	(3)	(4)	(5)	(6)	(7)	(8)	(9)	(10)
1. Retail sales to households									
a. Government and cooperative shops and restaurants	162.0	52.5	85.1	113.2	59.7	67.6	305.2	62.5	190.7
b. Collective farm market	35.0	...ᵃ	...	50.0	...	...	48.0	...	...
c. Total	197.0	43.2	85.1	163.2	41.4	67.6	353.2	54.0	190.7
2. Housing; services	27.7	1.0	.3	21.9	1.0	.2	39.5	1.0	.4
3. Trade-union and other dues	1.6	...	...	1.8	...	...	3.1	...	...
4. Consumption of income in kind									
a. Farm income	54.0	...	...	31.0	...	...	56.0	...	...
b. Army subsistence	8.0	32.7	2.6	31.0	29.2	9.1	19.0	42.1	8.0
c. Total	62.0	4.2	2.6	62.0	14.7	9.1	75.0	10.7	8.0
5. Total outlays of households on goods and services	288.3	30.5	88.0	248.9	30.9	76.9	470.8	42.3	199.1

6. Communal services									
a. Commodities	(18.2)	32.7	6.0	(10.8)	29.2	3.2	(42.5)	42.1	17.9
b. Services	(18.2)	...	...	(20.1)	...	...	(42.6)	...	...
c. Total	36.4	16.5	6.0	30.9	10.4	3.2	85.1	21.0	17.9
7. Government administration									
a. Commodities	(1.4)	32.7	.5	(.7)	29.2	.2	(2.6)	42.1	1.1
b. Services	(5.4)	...	...	(6.7)	...	...	(10.5)	...	...
c. Total	6.8	7.4	.5	7.4	2.7	.2	13.1	8.4	1.1
8. NKVD									
a. Commodities	(1.4)	32.7	.5	(.7)	29.2	.2	(5.2)	42.1	2.2
b. Services	(5.7)	...	...	(5.9)	...	...	(20.6)	...	...
c. Total	7.1	7.0	.5	6.6	3.0	.2	25.8	8.5	2.2
9. Defense									
a. Army subsistence	8.0	32.7	2.6	31.0	29.2	9.1	19.0	42.1	8.0
b. Munitions	(44.6)	7.5	3.3	(92.5)	7.5	6.9	(33.3)	7.5	2.5
c. Services	4.1	...	(—)2.6	14.2	...	(—)9.1	14.0	...	(—)8.0
d. Total	56.7	5.8	3.3	137.7	5.0	6.9	66.3	3.8	2.5
10. Gross investment									
a. Farm investment of income in kind	...	...	...	2.0	...	...	4.0	...	...
b. Stockpiles	(2.0)	7.5	...	(...)	7.5	...	(5.0)	7.5	2.5
c. Fixed capital	(48.5)	7.5	3.6	(38.2)	7.5	2.9	(100.2)	7.5	7.5
d. Other	(12.2)	32.7	4.0	(15.7)	29.2	4.6	(40.9)	42.1	17.2
e. Total	62.7	12.1	7.6	55.9	13.4	7.5	150.1	16.5	24.7
11. Gross national product	458.0	23.1	105.9	487.4	19.5	94.9	811.2	30.5	247.5

a ... = negligible or not applicable.

(iv) The foregoing assumptions determine the incidence of the turn-over tax for all national product use categories exclusive of retail sales in government and cooperative shops and restaurants. This we calculate as a residual, i.e., as the difference between the total yield of the tax and the amount imputed to all other national product use categories.

(v) The question of the correct valuation of Soviet military services is to be examined separately. Accordingly, in calculating the incidence of the turnover tax, we assume provisionally that military money pay is adjusted so as to offset the change in the value of army subsistence and leave the total value of military services unaltered. Strictly speaking, what is derived in this way is not the incidence of the turnover tax, but the adjustments in different use categories to be made when taxes are eliminated and the value of military services is held constant. But this latter aspect is the one on which it seems in order to focus here.

In the calculation just outlined, we introduced a number of assumptions concerning the effective turnover tax rates on different national product use categories. These assumptions are essentially the same as those intro-duced in a calculation of the incidence of the turnover tax in 1937 in *Soviet National Income*, pp. 135 ff. In this work, Bergson based his assumptions mainly on a consideration of the schedule of turnover taxes on different commodities that prevailed at the time of his study. Reasons for thinking that the incidence of the turnover tax was much the same in the years 1940, 1944, and 1948 as in 1937 are found in a variety of sources, including particu-larly Narkomfin SSSR, *Stavki naloga s oborota po prodovol'stvennym tovaram;* Narkomfin SSSR, *Stavki naloga s oborota po promtovaram;* Narkomfin SSSR, *Alfavitnyi perechen' promtovarov po stavkam naloga s oborota i biudzhetnykh natsenok;* Narkomfin SSSR, Upravlenie Gosdo-khodov, *Spravochnik po stavkam naloga s oborota . . . na promtovary;* Narkomfin SSSR, Upravlenie Gosdokhodov, *Spravochnik po stavkam naloga s oborota . . . po prodovol'stvennym tovaram; Sobranie postanov-lenii . . . SSSR,* Nos. 7, 12, 16, 1940; No. 2, 1941; A. Gordin, "Sistema biudzhetnykh platezhei i ukreplenie khozrascheta," *Planovoe khoziaistvo,* No. 6, 1939, pp. 136–48; *Finansy SSSR za XXX let,* p. 177; Suchkov, *Do-khody . . . ,* chap. ii; Suchkov, *Gosudarstvennye dokhody SSSR,* chap. iv.

Also, for the year 1940, reference may be made to the following data on the planned turnover tax collections from different administrative sectors of the economy:

	TURNOVER TAX, PLANNED YIELD, 1940, BILLION RUBLES
Commissariats of coal, electric power, iron and steel, and basic industries, exclusive of oil	2.880
Commissariat of oil industry	9.098
Commissariats of textiles and other light industries	16.201
Commissariats of food processing industries	45.032
Commissariat of agricultural procurements	28.798
Commissariat of trade	2.511
Industrial and consumers cooperatives	2.195
Other	1.894
Total	108.609

The foregoing data are compiled from *Shestaia sessiia Verkhovnogo Soveta SSSR ... 1940 g.*, pp. 425–27.

The total planned yield for 1940, 108.6 billion rubles, may be compared with the amount of the tax actually collected, 105.9 billion rubles. At the same time, the distribution of the tax by administrative sector seems broadly consistent with that calculated in Appendix Table 37 by national product use category. In this connection it should be noted that probably an appreciable part of the taxes paid by basic industrial commissariats was levied directly or indirectly on consumers' goods, i.e., as taxes on fuel and power used in consumers' goods production and as taxes on finished products, such as kerosene, radios, housewares, etc. In Appendix Table 37 these taxes fall on retail trade. The bulk of the taxes on the commissariat administering agricultural procurements would be classified similarly in Appendix Table 37.

Finally, interest attaches also to the following statement in *Pravda,* March 12, 1949: "Over 93 percent of all revenues from the turnover tax is provided by enterprises of the Ministry of Procurements and the Ministries of Food, Meat, Dairy, Light and Oil Industries." This is about the same as the share paid by these industries in 1940, and again seems broadly consistent with the incidence of the turnover tax calculated in Appendix Table 37 for the year 1948.

B. INCIDENCE OF SUBSIDIES (TABLE 9)

As with the data on the incidence of the turnover tax, those on the incidence of subsidies are intended to represent the amounts accruing to different use categories indirectly through the consumption of affected raw materials, etc., as well as directly in the disposition of the final product. The calculation of the incidence of subsidies in this sense may best be explained by reference to Appendix Table 38.

INCIDENCE OF SUBSIDIES BY NATIONAL PRODUCT USE CATEGORY, 1940, 1944, AND 1948

(Billions of rubles)

ITEM	1940		1944		1948	
1. Retail sales to households						
a. Government and cooperative shops and restaurants	6.4		4.8		13.5	
b. Collective farm market	...ᵃ		...		...	
c. Total		6.4		4.8		13.5
2. Housing; services		...		...		...
3. Trade-union and other dues		...		...		...
4. Consumption of income in kind						
a. Farm income	...		...		...	
b. Army subsistence	.3		1.3		.8	
c. Total		.3		1.3		.8
5. Total outlays of households on goods and services		6.7		6.1		14.3
6. Communal services						
a. Commodities	.7		.5		1.9	
b. Services	...		...		...	
c. Total		.7		.5		1.9
7. Government administration						
a. Commodities					.1	
b. Services					...	
c. Total		.1		.1		.1
8. NKVD						
a. Commodities					.2	
b. Services					...	
c. Total						.2
9. Defense						
a. Army subsistence	.3		1.3		.8	
b. Munitions	2.8		6.0		7.6	
c. Services	(−).3		(−)1.3		(−).8	
d. Total		2.8		6.0		7.6
10. Gross investment						
a. Farm investment of income in kind	...		...		...	
b. Stockpiles	.1		...		.7	
c. Fixed Capital	3.0		2.5		22.7	
d. Other	.6		.8		5.5	
e. Total		3.7		3.3		28.9
11. Gross national product		14.0		16.0		53.0

ᵃ ... = negligible or not applicable.

In this table, the data on total subsidies are taken from Appendix Table 28 and (as is indicated there) include, in addition to budget subsidies to economic organizations operating on a *khozraschet* basis, the budget appropriations to cover the net operating losses of the MTS, and the unplanned losses of *glavki* financed by bank credit. The allocation of these totals by use categories proceeds as follows:

(i) In view of their nature the following use categories may be taken as exempt from subsidies:

> Trade-union and other dues
> Communal services, services
> Government administration, services
> NKVD, services
> Defense, services

Also, it seems in order to treat in the same way the following additional categories:

> Retail sales to households, collective farm market
> Housing; services
> Consumption of farm income in kind
> Investment of farm income in kind

As will appear, the collective farm market sales and the two categories of farm income in kind make use of subsidized farm products. But for the present purposes we believe nothing will be lost if we proceed provisionally on the assumption that such subsidies nevertheless accrue exclusively to other use categories, especially to goods sold in state shops and restaurants. The question of the proper value to be attached to collective farm sales may then be examined separately at a later point. The value of farm income in kind in any event is derived from the values attached to other use categories. In the case of "Housing; services," we are disregarding here a probably small amount of subsidy allowed directly by the state in this sector as well as sums accruing indirectly through the use of some subsidized industrial materials and fuel.

(ii) For reasons that will appear in a moment the remaining use categories are broken down into two broad groups as follows:

Group I

> Defense, munitions
> One-half the investment in stockpiles
> Gross investment, fixed capital
> One-half of gross investment, other

Group II

Retail sales, government and cooperative shops and restaurants
Army subsistence
Communal services, commodities
Government administration, commodities
NKVD, commodities
One-half the investment in stockpiles
One-half of gross investment, other

For reasons that will become clear, we list army subsistence here only once, rather than twice as it appears in our accounts.

(iii) From previous calculations, we have the following breakdown of the total subsidies by economic sector:

	SUBSIDIES, BILLION RUBLES		
	1940	1944	1948
Industry	5.5	8.0	34.8
Agriculture	7.0	4.5	10.5
Transportation; communications			3.9
Trade	1.5	3.5	1.4
Other			2.4
Total	14.0	16.0	53.0

These data are taken from Appendix Tables 28 and 29. Budget appropriations for operating losses of the MTS are included here under subsidies to agriculture; losses financed through bank-credit creation are included here under subsidies to industry.

(iv) We assume that the subsidies paid to different economic sectors accrue to our two groups of use categories in the following proportions:

	SHARE IN TOTAL SUBSIDIES, PERCENT	
	Group I	Group II
Industry	90	10
Agriculture	10	90
Transportation; communications; trade; other	40	60

This is a rule-of-thumb allocation. We take into account here the generally known facts about Soviet subsidy policy, particularly the exclusive concern in the case of industry with heavy industrial products rather than consumers' goods. Reference has been made, too, to the input-output table set forth in N. Kaplan *et al., A Tentative Input-Output Table for the USSR, 1941 Plan.*

(v) We arbitrarily allocate subsidies among the use categories in each group in proportion to the value of product disposed of, as shown in Appendix Table 37.

(vi) As in the calculation of the incidence of the turnover tax, we assume provisionally that the value of military services, including army subsistence, is constant.

C. INCIDENCE OF REVALUATION OF COLLECTIVE FARM MARKET SALES (TABLE 10)

The revaluation is understood in the following sense:

(i) Collective farm market prices fall to the level of state and cooperative retail shop prices before all adjustments. While not subject to turnover taxes and subsidies, collective farm market prices in addition decline proportionately to retail prices in state and cooperative shops when turnover taxes and subsidies are eliminated.

(ii) Procurement prices for farm produce are increased in order to compensate farmers for the loss in income due to the cut in collective farm market prices.

(iii) To simplify the calculation it is assumed that the total money cost of seed, etc., used on the farm is unchanged throughout.

(iv) Provisionally, the value of military services, including subsistence as presently recorded, is constant. See above, p. 220.

The calculation of the incidence of the revaluation of collective farm market prices may best be explained by reference to Appendix Table 37. The data in the table are obtained as follows:

(i) In calculating the incidence of subsidies in Section B of this appendix we introduced certain assumptions concerning among other things the incidence of agricultural subsidies. The result is the following allocation of such subsidies by national product use categories:

	PERCENT		
	1940	1944	1948
State and cooperative retail trade	73.6	62.0	69.1
Army subsistence	3.6	17.0	4.3
Communal services, commodities	8.3	5.9	9.6
Government administration, commodities	.6	.4	.6
NKVD, commodities	.6	.4	1.2
Defense, munitions	4.5	6.7	2.1
Gross investment, stockpiles	.6	. . .[a]	.7
Gross investment, fixed capital	4.8	2.8	6.4
Gross investment, other	3.4	4.9	5.9
Total	100.0	100.0	100.0

[a] . . . = negligible.

INCIDENCE OF REVALUATION OF COLLECTIVE FARM MARKET SALES BY NATIONAL PRODUCT USE CATEGORY

(Billions of rubles)

ITEM	1940		1944		1948	
1. Retail sales to households						
a. Government and cooperative shops and restaurants	15.3		28.3		18.7	
b. Collective farm market	(−)20.8		(−)45.7		(−)27.0	
c. Total		(−)5.5		(−)17.4		(−)8.3
2. Housing; services		...ᵃ		...		...
3. Trade-union and other dues		...		...		...
4. Consumption of income in kind						
a. Farm income	...		...		...	
b. Army subsistence	.8		7.7		1.2	
c. Total		.8		7.7		1.2
5. Total outlays of households on goods and services		(−)4.7		(−)9.7		(−)7.1
6. Communal services						
a. Commodities	1.7		2.7		2.6	
b. Services	...		...		...	
c. Total		1.7		2.7		2.6
7. Government administration						
a. Commodities	.1		.2		.2	
b. Services	...		...		...	
c. Total		.1		.2		.2
8. NKVD						
a. Commodities	.1		.2		.3	
b. Services	...		...		...	
c. Total		.1		.2		.3
9. Defense						
a. Army subsistence	.8		7.7		1.2	
b. Munitions	.9		3.1		.6	
c. Services	(−).8		(−)7.7		(−)1.2	
d. Total		.9		3.1		.6
10. Gross investment						
a. Farm investment of income in kind	...		...		...	
b. Stockpiles	.1		...		.2	
c. Fixed capital	1.0		1.3		1.7	
d. Other	.7		2.2		1.6	
e. Total		1.8		3.5		3.5
11. Gross national product		...		...		...

ᵃ ... = negligible or not applicable.

Minor discrepancies here between the indicated totals and calculated sums of items are due to rounding.

(ii) Evidently the increase in procurement prices needed to compensate farmers for the cut in collective farm prices would affect the different use categories in the same proportions as an increase due to the removal of subsidies.

(iii) Taking the level of prices in state and cooperative shops as 100 percent, we assume that the level of prices in collective farm markets in the years studied was as follows:

1940	150
1944	800
1948	110

The ratio for 1940 is a rule-of-thumb estimate based mainly on information in unpublished sources, the authors of which prefer to remain anonymous.

In Appendix A, p. 157, we have assumed that collective farm market prices in 1944 might have been some 850 percent of those of 1940. In assuming that they were 800 percent of the state and cooperative shop prices in 1944 we take into account various sources of information indicating that state and cooperative shop prices rose very little during the war. According to Voznesenskii, *Voennaia ekonomika* . . . , p. 128, state shop prices in 1943 were 100.5 percent of the "prewar level." The "prewar level" referred to by Voznesenskii here may be that of June, 1941. On the basis of the price quotations in the *Monthly Labor Review,* February, 1941, p. 4746; May, 1941, pp. 1294–95; and July, 1947, p. 28, it appears that state shop prices in June, 1941, might have been about 10 percent above the average for the year 1940.

The state and cooperative shop prices just referred to for the year 1944 are ration prices. Strictly speaking, for present purposes reference probably ought to be made to the average of these together with the so-called commercial shop prices. But while the latter, like the collective farm market prices, were extremely high, the total volume of trade involved even in current prices was very small. According to *Sovetskaia torgovlia za XXX let,* p. 129, the total turnover in commercial shops amounted to 6 billion rubles in 1944. This was about 5 percent of all state and cooperative trade in that year. Accordingly, the average of ration and commercial prices together must have been very little above the ration prices alone.

The assumption regarding the ratio of collective farm market prices to state shop prices in 1948 is based on diverse information in the Soviet press and elsewhere. See particularly V. Moskvin, "Sovetskaia torgovlia v tret'em godu piatiletki," *Bol'shevik,* No. 15, 1948, p. 33.

(iv) Collective farm market sales are made both to households and institutions. But the latter are quite limited, and we shall not err much if we disregard them. Accordingly, collective farm market sales to households represent the total income derived by farmers from collective farm market sales. Since the value of seed, etc., is taken to be constant, variations in collective farm market sales represent variations in the value of farm services.

(v) Let k represent the relative decline in state and cooperative retail shop prices after all adjustments. Then we have the following relation:

$$m = (R - 1 + k)\frac{1}{R}$$

Here m is the relative decline in collective farm market prices after all adjustments and R represents the initial ratio of collective farm market prices to state and cooperative retail shop prices. Furthermore, the net reduction in the value of retail sales in state and cooperative shops after all adjustments must equal the difference between, on the one hand, the amount of the turnover tax, in excess of subsidies, borne by these sales initially, and, on the other, the share of the additional compensatory increase in procurement values that is absorbed by sales in state and cooperative shops. Hence,

k × retail sales in state and cooperative shops =
turnover taxes on such sales — subsidies on such sales —
α × m × collective farm market sales.

Here α is the share of the increase in procurement values that falls on retail sales in state and cooperative shops. The product of m and collective farm market sales represents the decline in such sales after all adjustments and hence also represents the aggregate amount of the compensatory increase called for in procurement values.

Substituting in the foregoing equation data previously compiled, we have the following three relations:

k_{40} × 162.0 billion rubles = 85.1 billion rubles — 6.4 billion rubles — .736 $(1.5 - 1 + k_{40}) \frac{1}{1.5}$ × 35.0 billion rubles.

k_{44} × 113.2 billion rubles = 67.6 billion rubles — 4.8 billion rubles — .620 $(8.0 - 1 + k_{44}) \frac{1}{8.0}$ × 50.0 billion rubles.

k_{48} × 305.2 billion rubles = 190.7 billion rubles — 13.5 billion rubles — .691 $(1.1 - 1 + k_{48}) \frac{1}{1.1}$ × 48.0 billion rubles.

Solving,
$$k_{40} = .391 \text{ or } 39.1 \text{ percent}$$
$$k_{44} = .305 \text{ or } 30.5 \text{ percent}$$
$$k_{48} = .519 \text{ or } 51.9 \text{ percent}$$

Also, for the relative decline in collective farm market prices, we have the following magnitudes:

$$m_{40} = .594 \text{ or } 59.4 \text{ percent}$$
$$m_{44} = .913 \text{ or } 91.3 \text{ percent}$$
$$m_{48} = .563 \text{ or } 56.3 \text{ percent}$$

Accordingly, for the decline in the value of collective farm sales we have:

1940: .594 × 35.0 billion rubles = 20.8 billion rubles
1944: .913 × 50.0 billion rubles = 45.7 billion rubles
1948: .563 × 48.0 billion rubles = 27.0 billion rubles

In Appendix Table 39 these latter magnitudes are recorded opposite collective farm market sales to represent the incidence of the revaluation on this use category. Under our assumptions the compensatory increase in procurement values corresponds to the decline in the value of collective farm market sales, while the incidence of the revaluation on other use categories represents their pro rata share of this compensatory increase. Accordingly, the incidence of the revaluation on other use categories is now calculated on the basis indicated above, pp. 225 ff.

(vi) By implication, we have assumed in the foregoing that farm income in kind along with various other use categories is unaffected by the revaluation of collective farm market sales. At the same time, it will be recalled that we took farm income in kind to be constant previously when calculating the incidence of turnover taxes and subsidies. Considering that the concern here is to revalue national income for all these aspects taken together, it is readily seen that this treatment of farm income in kind is in order. In the initial calculation of national income in current rubles, farm income in kind is valued at the average of prevailing procurement and collective farm market prices, net of turnover taxes and gross of subsidies. Evidently these are also the prices that prevail for farm produce after the elimination of taxes and subsidies. Furthermore, in terms of their effects on farm income, the decrease in collective farm market prices and the compensatory increase in procurement prices are equivalent magnitudes, so the average of realized farm prices is still unchanged after the revaluation of collective farm market sales. Accordingly, no change is called for in farm income in kind.

APPENDIX E: THE TERRITORIAL COVERAGE
OF SOVIET STATISTICS FOR 1940

THE CHANGES that have taken place in the international boundaries of the USSR during the past ten years give rise to a question concerning the coverage of Soviet statistical data relating to the years since 1939: To what extent have these boundary changes been taken into account in the official statistics for these years? Since the data are usually published without any explanation of this matter, the question needs investigation. The purpose of this Appendix is to examine the available evidence on the territorial coverage of Soviet statistics for the pertinent years, and to consider the implications of the evidence for our national product accounts.

In speaking of territorial changes in the years since 1939, a distinction is in order between those of a temporary nature due to the fortunes of war and those of a permanent character sanctioned by treaty or otherwise. We have already commented in the text, pp. 7, 29 ff., on the problem posed regarding the scope of Soviet wartime statistics by territorial changes of the former kind. We focus here exclusively on changes of the latter kind. These changes, all of which occurred in 1939–40 and 1944–45, have been listed in Table 1, p. 6.

As can be seen from this table, the territorial changes which occurred in 1944–45 were quite small, resulting in a net population gain of no more than one million persons.[1] For our purposes, then, these changes may safely be ignored. The inclusion or exclusion of these territories would have no appreciable effect on aggregate data for the Soviet economy as a whole. On the other hand, the territories incorporated in the USSR during 1939–40 did involve significant magnitudes, including a population gain of some 12.5 percent. To what extent have these changes been taken into account in the official data for the years studied in our national income calculation?

This question might be explored separately for each of the three years

[1] This population gain changes to a net loss of about 1 million persons if account is taken of the wartime population movements. Some 2 million persons are estimated to have left the territories which belonged to the USSR before the war or were subsequently incorporated in the USSR. See Kulischer, p. 274.

considered. It is believed, however, it will suffice if instead we focus only on the year 1940. On the one hand, it turns out that in their prewar statistical releases for the year 1940 the Russians already had done much to allow for the boundary changes, whereas postwar releases for the same year probably embody revisions to take into account such boundary changes as were not previously covered. Accordingly, there is at once a presumption that the figures for 1944 (except for areas held by the Germans) and for 1948 are entirely comprehensive. On the other hand, diverse releases make it abundantly clear that this is in fact the case for the statistics relating to postwar years generally.[2]

1940 statistics in prewar sources. We shall consider first the coverage of the data for 1940, published in prewar Soviet sources. On this there is the following evidence:

(i) *Budgetary data.* It is known that the data on the government budget for 1940 take into account at least the incorporation of the Polish provinces in 1939 and probably also some of the additional areas acquired in 1940. In the course of the discussions of the projected 1940 budget before the Supreme Soviet of the USSR in March-April, 1940, the deputies from the Byelorussian and Ukrainian Republics (the two republics to which the Polish territories had been annexed) devoted a good portion of their speeches to the financial work being carried on in the "newly incorporated Western regions," and showed in some detail what portions of the respective republics' budgets for 1940 were allocated to these new areas.[3] The acquisition of the Finnish provinces was ratified at the same session of the Supreme Soviet, a new Karelo-Finnish Soviet Socialist Republic being created. Its budget, apparently, had not been prepared in time for this session, but the Council of People's Commissars was charged with its preparation and directed to allot the necessary funds out of its own Reserve Account.[4]

As for the remaining territories acquired during 1940 (Bessarabia, Northern Bukovina, Latvia, Lithuania, Estonia), these were not provided for in the projected budget for 1940, since their incorporation in the USSR did not take place until the succeeding (Seventh) Session of the Supreme Soviet in August, 1940. Their budgets were fully covered for the first time in the consolidated government budget for 1941. However, their inclusion, in part at least, in the realized budget statistics for 1940, published in February, 1941, is likely. The People's Commissar of Finance, A. G. Zverev, in his report to the Supreme Soviet on the fulfillment of the budget for

---

[2] See, for example, the Fourth Five Year Plan in *Pravda*, March 16, 1946.

[3] *Shestaya sessiia Verkhovnogo Soveta SSSR . . . 1940 g.*, pp. 210–16, 320–23, 378–81, 399–404.

[4] *Ibid.*, p. 503.

1940, made several references to the fiscal work that has been carried on in these areas during the last half of 1940.[5]

(ii) *Official plan data.* An impression of the speed and energy with which Soviet statistical agencies extended their coverage into the newly acquired areas can be derived from an examination of the 1941 Soviet national economic plan, a 750-page statistical document consisting of several hundred supplements to an official government decree enacted January 17, 1941.[6] These statistical supplements are marked "Not for publication" and were evidently intended for use within Soviet planning circles. Presumably they were compiled by the Central Statistical Administration at various times prior to January 17, 1941, most probably during the last months of 1940. What is of interest here is the fact that, with relatively few exceptions, the coverage of these statistical compilations is comprehensive of most of the territories newly acquired by the USSR in 1939–40; more specifically, the plan data for the various economic sectors (industry, agriculture, transport, trade, etc.) are in almost every case *inclusive* of the former Polish provinces (incorporated in the Ukrainian and Byelorussian Soviet Republics in November, 1939), the former Finnish provinces (formed into the Karelo-Finnish Soviet Socialist Republic in March, 1940), and the former Rumanian provinces (formed into a Moldavian Soviet Republic in August, 1940). At the same time, most of the statistical supplements which constitute the 1941 plan document explicitly *exclude* from their coverage the three Baltic states Latvia, Lithuania, and Estonia, which were incorporated in the USSR as Soviet Republics in August, 1940. The plan document does, however, contain a section devoted to the development of economic regions, which includes a detailed compilation of 1941 plan statistics for industry, agriculture, and social services in the three Baltic republics; in other words, even for these most recently acquired territories a considerable amount of statistical coverage had been achieved by the beginning of 1941. Notable omissions from this coverage are the data on retail trade, wage bill, and costs of production. The plan document provides no data on retail trade for the Baltic republics,[7] and only very sparse statistics on the labor force, wage bill, and production costs in these regions.

[5] *Pravda,* February 26, 1941. Additional information on the budgets and fiscal developments in the newly incorporated areas during 1940 and 1941 is contained in Plotnikov, 1948 ed., pp. 236–39.

[6] The decree is referred to in the document as decree No. 127 of the Council of People's Commissars of the USSR and of the Central Committee of the All-Union Communist Party (Bolsheviks), of January 17, 1941. See *Gosudarstvennyi plan . . . na 1941 god.*

[7] In a subsequently published report on the 1941 Plan delivered by N. Voznesenskii, Chairman of the State Planning Commission to the 18th Party Conference, the total retail trade figure contained in the plan document was revised upward, presumably to take account of the previously omitted Baltic republics. See *Pravda,* February 19, 1941.

(iii) *Agricultural data.* In the prewar years, during the appropriate seasons, reports on progress in spring and fall sowing were published regularly in the Soviet press every five to ten days. The reports contain data on the acreage sown to spring and fall crops for the whole USSR, broken down by republics and *oblasts* (provinces). A survey of these reports for 1940 and 1941 reveals that data for the former Polish provinces as well as for the Karelo-Finnish and Moldavian republics appear for the first time in the fall sowing report in *Pravda* on August 31, 1940, and were then reported regularly thereafter. Reports on the Baltic republics did not appear in that year, but were included for the first time in the spring sowing statistics in *Pravda* on May 22, 1941, and were then reported regularly thereafter. From this, we are left with the impression that the 1940 data on sown area and harvest probably take into account at least the incorporation of the largest part of the areas acquired during 1939–40 (i.e., all areas except the Baltic republics). This impression is further supported by the official figure on the grain-sown area for 1940, 110.9 million hectares, made public by Voznesenskii in his Party Conference report in February, 1941.[8] This figure represents an increase of 10 percent over 1939. But prior to 1939 the trend in grain-sown area was consistently downward. The higher acreage figure for 1940, then, must be a reflection of a larger territorial coverage.

1940 statistics in postwar sources. So far we have considered only the coverage of 1940 statistics published in *prewar* Soviet sources, i.e., data for 1940 published during 1940 and 1941. Our conclusion is that these statistics already take account of most of the newly incorporated territories. Much of the presently available information relating to 1940, however, was not published by the Russians until after the war, and in postwar years many previously published figures for 1940 have been revised. Again, these data are almost invariably presented without any indication as to their territorial coverage. There appears to be at least some evidence, however, to suggest that the more recent figures are comprehensive, and that an attempt has been made to revise the earlier official data to allow for territorial changes not previously taken into account. The evidence on this is as follows:

(i) Normally, in Soviet fiscal accounting practice, the final figures covering revenues collected and expenditures disbursed under the consolidated government budget of the USSR do not become available until a full year after the close of any fiscal year. In other words, the final budgetary figures for 1940 would have become available only in 1942. The 1940 budget data released in 1941, therefore, must be considered as preliminary and were in fact presented as such. Because of the war situation, no budgetary figures at

[8] *Ibid.*

all were published in 1942. Postwar sources, on the other hand, do contain revised data on the 1940 government budget, and these almost certainly represent final, rather than preliminary, figures. A comparison of these final figures with the preliminary statistics published in 1941 reveals that in almost every case the revision is upwards. Thus total revenues are given as 180.2 billion rubles in postwar sources, as against 178.1 billion in prewar sources. Total expenditures are shown as 174.4 billion rubles in postwar sources, as against 173.3 billion in prewar sources. Comparable revisions have been made in the major component categories.[9] These revisions may have been designed, at least in part, to take into account such territorial gains as were not previously included in the prewar data.

(ii) The upward revision of prewar statistics in postwar sources was not confined to budgetary data alone. The practice was followed also with respect to nonfiscal data. The following examples, all released by the same authoritative source (N. Voznesenskii, former chairman of the State Planning Commission), will illustrate the point:

	FIGURES FOR 1940 FROM	
	Voznesenskii report of 1941[10]	*Voznesenskii book of 1947*[11]
Gross industrial output (bil. 1926–27 rubles)	137.5	138.5
Railway freight turnover (bil. ton-km.)	409.0	415.0
National Income (bil. 1926–27 rubles)	125.5	128.0
Workers and employees (millions)	30.4	31.2
State and coop. retail trade (bil. 1940 rubles)	174.5	175.1

(iii) An explicit statement on the territorial coverage of postwar Soviet data relating to 1940 was contained in a Soviet review of an article in the London *Economist,* discussing the Fourth Five Year Plan. The Soviet critic claims that, contrary to the assertion of the *Economist,* the statistics on production of industry and agriculture in 1940 and 1950 given in the Fourth Five Year Plan "refer to one and the same territory, i.e., including the territory incorporated in the Soviet Union after September 17, 1939,"[12] and that the figure of 30.4 million individuals in the labor force also "includes the wage earners and salaried workers of the territories incorporated in the USSR in 1939–40."[13]

[9] The figures are from *Pravda,* February 26, 1941, and Plotnikov, 1948 ed., pp. 181 ff.

[10] *Pravda,* February 19, 1941.

[11] *Voennaia ekonomika* . . . , pp. 11–13.

[12] E. Granovskii, "Kritika i bibliografiia—Angliiskii 'Ekonomist' o novoi stalinskoi piatiletke," *Mirovoe khoziaistvo i mirovaia politika,* No. 3, 1947, p. 102.

[13] *Ibid.,* p. 108. Apparently, however, this figure did not take into account all the territorial changes, since it was later revised upward to 31.2 million in Voznesenskii's 1947 book (see above).

Implication for the 1940 national product accounts. What are the implications of the evidence presented above for our 1940 national product accounts?

In general, as has been indicated, the Soviet data used in our calculations for 1940 appear to include at least the major part of the areas added to the territory of the USSR as the result of the boundary revisions of 1939–40. Even the data from prewar sources are believed to be generally inclusive of at least the former Polish, Finnish and Rumanian provinces, which represent more than two-thirds of the areas incorporated in the USSR in 1939–40. Almost all of the figures for 1940 used in our calculations, however, are taken directly from, or based on information in, postwar Soviet publications. Accordingly, upward revisions of the earlier official data made to allow for boundary changes are taken into account.

Quite possibly, there are some minor deficiencies, nevertheless, in one or two of the items included in the tables. Notable among these may be the comprehensive wage fund for the national economy, appearing in the household account as an income item. In postwar Soviet statistics a small upward revision appears in the number of wage earners and salaried workers for 1940; to the writers' knowledge, no postwar revision of the 1940 wage fund has been published, and the figure used is based on a 1941 source. If, as we suspect, this prewar figure does not include all of the new territories, our nonfarm money income figure may be understated by at most 3 percent. Any remaining deficiencies in our data that could be attributed to inadequate territorial coverage, it is believed, are likely to be of the order of 1 percent. In no case could the margin of error due to boundary changes exceed 5 percent.

PUBLICATIONS CITED

ABBREVIATIONS

FZMK	Fabrichno-zavodskie i Mestnye Komitety (Factory and Local Committees)
glavk	glavnoe upravlenie (central administration)
Gosplan	Gosudarstvennyi Planovoi Komitet SSSR (State Planning Committee of the USSR). Formerly Gosudarstvennaia Planovaia Komissiia (State Planning Commission)
Gosstrakh	Gosudarstvennoe strakhovanie (State Insurance)
khozraschet	khoziaistvennyi raschet (economic accounting)
MGB	Ministerstvo Gosudarstvennoi Bezopasnosti, SSSR (Ministry of State Security of the USSR)
MTS	mashinno-traktornaia stantsiia (machine-tractor station)
MVD	Ministerstvo Vnutrennikh Del SSSR (Ministry of Internal Affairs of the USSR)
Narkomfin	Narodnyi Komissariat Finansov SSSR (People's Commissariat of Finances of the USSR)
NKVD	Narodnyi Komissariat Vnutrennikh Del SSSR (People's Commissariat of Internal Affairs of the USSR)
SNK	Sovet Narodnykh Komissarov SSSR (Council of People's Commissars of the USSR)
Soviet National Income	A. Bergson, Soviet National Income and Product in 1937, New York, 1953
TSK VKP(b)	Tsentral'nyi Komitet, Vsesoiuznaia Kommunisticheskaia Partiia (bol'shevikov) Central Committee of the All-Union Communist Party [Bolsheviks]
TSU	Tsentral'noe Statisticheskoe Upravlenie (Central Statistical Administration)
TSUNKHU	Tsentral'noe Upravlenie Narodno-khoziaistvennogo Ucheta (Central Administration of National Economic Accounting)

PUBLICATIONS CITED, TOGETHER WITH
TRANSLATIONS OF RUSSIAN TITLES

Aleksandrov, A. M. Finansy i kredit SSSR (Finance and Credit in the USSR). Moscow, 1948.

Anisimov, N. I. Pobeda sotsialisticheskogo sel'skogo khoziaistva (The Victory of Socialist Agriculture). Moscow, 1947.

—— Sel'skoe khoziaistvo SSSR za 30 let (The Agriculture of the USSR for 30 Years). Moscow, 1947.

—— "Velikaia sila kolkhoznogo stroia" (The Great Strength of the Collective Farm System), *Sputnik agitatora,* No. 19–20, 1944.

Barker, G. R. "Soviet Labor," *Bulletins on Soviet Economic Development* (University of Birmingham, England), No. 6, June, 1951.

Baykov, A. The Development of the Soviet Economic System. New York, 1947.

—— Soviet Foreign Trade. Princeton, N.J., 1946.

Belov, P. "Ekonomicheskaia pobeda SSSR v velikoi Otechestvennoi voine" (The Economic Victory of the USSR in the Great Patriotic War), *Voprosy ekonomiki,* No. 5, 1950.

Bergson, A. "The Fourth Five Year Plan: Heavy versus Consumers' Goods Industries," *Political Science Quarterly,* June, 1947.

—— "A Problem in Soviet Statistics," *Review of Economic Statistics,* November, 1947.

—— (ed.). Soviet Economic Growth: Conditions and Perspectives. Evanston, Ill., 1953.

—— Soviet National Income and Product in 1937. New York, 1953.

—— "Soviet National Income and Product in 1937," seriatim, Part I, "National Economic Accounts in Current Rubles," *Quarterly Journal of Economics,* Vol. 64, No. 2, May, 1950; and Part II, "Ruble Prices and the Valuation Problem," *ibid.,* No. 3, August, 1950.

—— The Structure of Soviet Wages. Cambridge, Mass., 1946.

—— and R. Bernaut. Prices of Basic Chemical Products in the Soviet Union, 1928–1950. RM-920, The RAND Corporation, Santa Monica, Calif., 1952 (unpublished).

—— J. H. Blackman, and A. Erlich. "Postwar Economic Reconstruction and Development in the U.S.S.R.," *Annals of the American Academy of Political and Social Science,* May, 1949.

Bergson, Abram, and L. Turgeon. Prices of Iron and Steel Products in the Soviet Union, 1928–1950: a Summary Report. RM-802, The RAND Corporation, Santa Monica, Calif., 1951 (unpublished).

Blackman, J. "Transportation," in A. Bergson (ed.), Soviet Economic Growth.

Bodrov, M. "Narodnye sberezheniia v SSSR" (National Savings in the USSR), *Bol'shevik,* No. 3–4, 1941.

Bogolepov, M. I. The Soviet Financial System. London, 1945.

Bol'shevik.

Broner, D. L. Kurs zhilishchnogo khoziaistva (Course on Housing Economy). Moscow, 1948.

—— Ocherki ekonomiki zhilishchnogo khoziaistva Moskvy (Essays on the Economics of Moscow's Housing Economy). Moscow, 1946.

Bulletins on Soviet Economic Development (University of Birmingham, England).

Bunkin, K. T. Uluchshit' kommercheskuiu rabotu rechnogo transporta (Improve Commercial Work of River Transport). Moscow, 1940.

Buzyrev, V. M. Vosstanovitel'nye raboty i ikh finansirovanie (Reconstruction Work and Its Financing). Moscow, 1945.

Chapman, J. Retail Prices in the USSR, 1937–48. RM-707-1, The RAND Corporation, Santa Monica, Calif., 1953 (unpublished).

Cherniavskii, U., and S. Krivetskii. "Pokupatel'nye fondy naseleniia i roznichnyi tovarooborot" (Purchasing Power of the Population and the Retail Turnover), *Planovoe khoziaistvo,* No. 6, 1936.

Chernyi, G. "Kolkhoznaia torgovlia i finansovoe khoziaistvo v kolkhozakh" (Collective Farm Trade and the Financial Economy of Collective Farms), *Sotsialisticheskoe sel'skoe khoziaistvo,* No. 2, 1949.

Chuvikov, V. "O nedelimykh fondakh kolkhozov" (Concerning the Indivisible Funds of the Collective Farms), *Sotsialisticheskoe sel'skoe khoziaistvo,* No. 4, 1948.

—— "Raspredelenie dokhodov v kolkhozakh i avansirovanie kolkhoznikov" (The Distribution of Income in Collective Farms and Payments on Account to Collective Farmers), *Kolkhoznoe proizvodstvo,* No. 8–9, 1945.

Condoide, M. V. The Soviet Financial System. Columbus, Ohio, 1952.

Current Digest of the Soviet Press.

Dadugin, A. P., and P. G. Kagarlitskii. Organizatsiia i tekhnika kolkhoznoi bazarnoi torgovli (Organization and Techniques of Collective Farm Market Trade). Moscow, 1949.

Degtiar, D. Zabota sovetskogo gosudarstva ob uluchshenii material'nogo polozheniia trudiashchikhsia (The Concern of the Soviet Government for the Improvement of the Material Situation of the Workers). Moscow, 1946.

Demidov, S. F. Razvitie sel'skogo khoziaistva v poslevoennoi piatiletke (Development of Agriculture in the Postwar Five Year Plan). Moscow, 1946.

Desiataia sessiia Verkhovnogo Soveta SSSR . . . 1944 g.; Stenograficheskii otchet (Tenth Session of the Supreme Soviet of the USSR . . . 1944; Verbatim Report). Moscow, 1944.

D'iachenko, V. P. Finansy i kredit SSSR (Finance and Credit in the USSR). Moscow, 1940.

Dukel'skii, D. "Uluchshit' rabotu Sel'khozbanka po privlecheniiu nedelimykh fondov kolkhozov" (Toward Improving the Operation of the Agricultural Bank with Respect to Attracting the Indivisible Funds of Collective Farms), Sovetskie finansy, No. 3, 1947.

Eason, W. "Population and Labor Force," in A. Bergson (ed.), Soviet Economic Growth.

Ely, L. B. The Red Army Today. Harrisburg, Pa., 1949.

Evseev, P. V. Kooperativnaia i mestnaia promyshlennost' v poslevoennoi piatiletke (Cooperative and Local Industry in the Postwar Five Year Plan). Moscow, 1948.

—— "Reservy uvelicheniia vypuska tovarov shirokogo potrebleniia v mestnoi i kooperativnoi promyshlennosti" (Reserves of Growth in the Output of Goods of Mass Consumption in Local and Cooperative Industry), Planovoe khoziaistvo, No. 4, 1948.

Evtikhiev, I. I., and V. A. Vlasov. Administrativnoe pravo SSSR (Administrative Law of the USSR). Moscow, 1946.

Farnsworth, H. C., and V. P. Timoshenko. World Grain Review and Outlook, 1945. Stanford, Calif., 1945.

Finansy SSSR za XXX let (Finances of the USSR for 30 Years). Moscow, 1947.

Galenson, W. "Industrial Labor Productivity," in A. Bergson (ed.), Soviet Economic Growth.

Galimon, L. S. Dokhody mashinno-traktornykh stantsii (Incomes of Machine-Tractor Stations). Moscow, 1948.

Gaposhkin, F. "Kapital'nyi remont v 1938 godu" (Capital Repairs in 1938), Planovoe khoziaistvo, No. 9, 1938.

Gerschenkron, A. Economic Relations with the USSR. New York, 1945.

Gogol', B. I. Sovetskaia torgovlia i ee rol' v narodnom khoziaistve (Soviet Trade and Its Role in the National Economy). Moscow, 1948.

Gordin, A. "Sistema biudzhetnykh platezhei i ukreplenie khozrascheta" (The System of Budgetary Payments and the Strengthening of Economic Accounting), Planovoe khoziaistvo, No. 6, 1939.

—— "Zaimy v sotsialisticheskom gosudarstve" (Bond Loans in the Socialist State), Planovoe khoziaistvo, No. 7, 1940.

Gosplan. Narodnokhoziaistvennyi plan na 1936 god (National Economic Plan for 1936). 2d ed., Moscow, 1936.

—— Tretii piatiletnii plan razvitiia narodnogo khoziaistva Soiuza SSR (1938–42 gg.) (proekt) (Third Five Year Plan of Development of the National Economy of the USSR 1938–42. Draft). Moscow, 1939.

Gosplan and TSU. "Ob itogakh vypolneniia chetvertogo (pervogo poslevoennogo) piatiletnego plana SSSR na 1946–1950 gody" (On the Results of Fulfilling the Fourth [First Postwar] Five Year Plan of the USSR, 1946–50), *Voprosy ekonomiki,* No. 5, 1951.

Gosudarstvennyi plan razvitiia narodnogo khoziaistva SSSR na 1941 god (State Plan for the Growth of the National Economy of the USSR for 1941). This volume was issued officially as an appendix to a decree of the Council of People's Commissars and the Central Committee of the Communist Party, January 17, 1941. It has been reissued by the American Council of Learned Societies.

Granditskii, P. A. Kolkhoz "Borets" (The Borets Collective Farm). Moscow, 1946.

Granick, D. Plant Management in the Soviet Industrial System. Doctoral dissertation, Columbia University, 1951. Published, New York, 1954.

Granovskii, E. "Kritika i bibliografiia—Angliiskii 'Ekonomist' o novoi stalinskoi piatiletke" (Critique and Bibliography—The English *Economist* on the New Stalin Five Year Plan), *Mirovoe khoziaistvo i mirovaia politika,* No. 3, March, 1947.

Grossman, G. "Efforts toward Monetary Stability in the USSR." An unpublished study.

Gsovski, V. "Elements of Soviet Labor Law," United States Department of Labor, Bureau of Labor Statistics, *Bulletin No. 1026,* Washington, 1951.

—— Soviet Civil Law. Ann Arbor, Mich., 1948.

Gurevich, S., and S. Partigul. Novyi pod"em narodnogo khoziaistva SSSR v poslevoennoi piatiletke (The New Advance of the National Economy of the USSR in the Postwar Five Year Plan). Moscow, 1949.

Holzman, F. D. "The Burden of Soviet Taxation," *American Economic Review* (forthcoming).

Hutt, W. H. "Two Studies in the Statistics of Russia," *The South African Journal of Economics,* March, 1945.

Izvestiia (News).

Jasny, N. "Labor and Output in Soviet Concentration Camps," *Journal of Political Economy,* October, 1951.

—— Soviet Prices of Producers' Goods. Stanford, Calif., 1952.

Kaplan, N. "Capital Formation and Allocation," in A. Bergson (ed.), Soviet Economic Growth.

—— Capital Investments in the Soviet Union, 1924–1951. RM-735, The RAND Corporation, Santa Monica, Calif., 1952 (unpublished).

—— J. H. Blackman, H. Heymann, Jr., A. D. Redding, N. Rodin. A Tentative Input-Output Table for the USSR, 1941 Plan. RM-924, The RAND Corporation, Santa Monica, Calif., 1952 (unpublished).

Karnaukhova, E. S. Kolkhoznoe proizvodstvo v gody Otechestvennoi voiny (Collective Farm Production in the Years of the Patriotic War). Moscow, 1947.

Kerr, W. The Russian Army. New York, 1944.

Klimov, A. "Sovetskaia potrebitel'skaia kooperatsiia na sovremennom etape" (Soviet Consumers' Cooperation at the Present Stage), *Voprosy ekonomiki*, No. 6, 1948.

Kobalevskii, V. L. Organizatsiia i ekonomika zhilishchnogo khoziaistva SSSR (Organization and Economics of Soviet Housing). Moscow, 1940.

Kolkhoznoe proizvodstvo (Collective Farm Production).

Koshelev, F. Stalinskii ustav—osnovnoi zakon kolkhoznoi zhizni (The Stalin Charter—the Basic Law of Collective Farm Life). Moscow, 1947.

Kosiachenko, G. "Povyshenie material'nogo i kul'turnogo urovnia zhizni naroda v novoi piatiletke" (Raising the Material and Cultural Level of the People's Life in the Five Year Plan), *Planovoe khoziaistvo*, No. 2, 1946.

Kozev, N. Sotsialisticheskaia sistema khoziaistva i ee prevoskhodstvo nad kapitalisticheskoi sistemoi khoziaistva (The Socialist Economic System and Its Superiority over the Capitalist Economic System). Moscow, 1949.

Krasnopolskii, A. S. "O prirode sovetskogo gosudarstvennogo sotsial'nogo strakhovaniia" (On the Nature of Soviet State Social Insurance), *Sovetskoe gosudarstvo i pravo*, No. 6, 1951. A translation of this article appears in *The Current Digest of the Soviet Press*, Vol. III, No. 46, December 29, 1951, pp. 3 ff.

Kravis, I. B., and J. Mintzes. "Food Prices in the Soviet Union, 1936–50," *Review of Economics and Statistics*, May, 1950.

Kronrod, Ia. "Natsional'nyi dokhod SSSR" (National Income of the USSR), *Bol'shevik*, No. 8, 1950.

Kulischer, E. M. Europe on the Move—War and Population Changes, 1917–47. New York, 1948.

Kutyrev, S. M. Analiz balansa dokhodov i raskhodov khoziaistvennoi organizatsii (Analysis of the Balance of Incomes and Outlays of the Economic Organization). Moscow, 1948.

Kuz'minov, I. "Nepreryvnyi pod"em narodnogo khoziaistva SSSR—zakon sotsializma" (The Uninterrupted Increase in the National Economy of the USSR Is the Law of Socialism), *Voprosy ekonomiki*, No. 6, 1951.

Laptev, I. D. (ed.). Uchenye zapiski (Learned Notes). Issue 13, Moscow, 1951.

Lever, P. R. The State Labor Reserve System of the Soviet Union. Certificate essay, Russian Institute, Columbia University, May, 1948.

Lifits, M. M. (ed.). Ekonomika sovetskoi torgovli (Economics of Soviet Trade). Moscow, 1950.

—— "Razvitie sovetskoi torgovli v poslevoennyi period" (Development of Soviet Trade in the Postwar Period), *Voprosy ekonomiki,* No. 7, 1951.

—— Sovetskaia torgovlia (Soviet Trade). Moscow, 1948.

Lorimer, F. The Population of the Soviet Union: History and Prospects. Geneva, 1946.

Margolin, N. S. Balans denezhnykh dokhodov i raskhodov naseleniia (Balance of the Money Income and Outlays of the Population). Moscow, 1940.

—— "Nekotorye voprosy balansa denezhnykh dokhodov i raskhodov naseleniia" (Some Problems of the Balance of the Money Income and Outlays of the Population), *Planovoe khoziaistvo,* No. 4, 1949.

—— Voprosy balansa denezhnykh dokhodov i raskhodov naseleniia (Problems of the Balance of the Money Income and Outlays of the Population). Moscow, 1939.

Mar'iakhin, G. L. Nalogi i sbori s naseleniia i kolkhozov (Taxes and Fees on the Population and Collective Farms). Moscow, 1946.

Mikolenko, Ia. F., and A. N. Nikitin. Kolkhoznoe pravo (Collective Farm Law). Moscow, 1946.

Ministerstvo Kommunal'nogo Khoziaistva RSFSR (Ministry of Communal Economy of the RSFSR). Zhilishchnye zakony (Housing Laws). Moscow, 1947.

Ministerstvo Vysshego Obrazovaniia SSSR (Ministry of Higher Education of the USSR). Vysshaia shkola (The Higher School). Moscow, 1948.

Mirovoe khoziaistvo i mirovaia politika (World Economics and World Politics).

Monthly Labor Review.

Moskvin, V. "Sovetskaia torgovlia v tret'em godu piatiletki" (Soviet Trade in the Third Year of the Five Year Plan). *Bol'shevik,* No. 15, 1948.

Narkomfin, SSSR. Alfavitnyi perechen' promtovarov po stavkam naloga s oborota i biudzhetnykh natsenok (Alphabetic List of Industrial Commodities by Rates of the Turnover Tax and Budget Surcharges). Moscow, 1938.

—— Otchet ob ispolnenii gosudarstvennogo biudzheta SSSR za 1935 god (Account on the Fulfillment of the Government Budget of the USSR for 1935). Moscow, 1937.

—— Spravochnik po stavkam naloga s oborota i biudzhetnoi raznitse po prodovol'stvennym tovaram (Handbook of Turnover Tax Rates for Food Products). Moscow, 1944.

—— Stavki naloga s oborota po prodovol'stvennym tovaram (Turnover Tax Rates on Food Products). Moscow, 1937.

—— Stavki naloga s oborota po promtovaram (Turnover Tax Rates on Industrial Goods). Moscow, 1937.

—— Upravlenie Gosdokhodov (Administration of State Revenues). Spravochnik po stavkam naloga s oborota . . . na promtovary (Handbook of Turnover Tax Rates . . . on Industrial Goods). Moscow, 1944.

Nesmii, M. "Finansovoe khoziaistvo kolkhozov" (Financial Economy of Collective Farms), *Planovoe khoziaistvo*, No. 8, 1939.

New York *Herald Tribune*.

New York *Times*.

Nikolaev, M. V. Bukhgalterskii uchet (Accounting). Moscow, 1936.

Nosyrev, S. "Ustav sel'skokhoziaistvennoi arteli i finansovoe khoziaistvo kolkhozov" (Charter of the Agricultural Artel and the Financial Economy of Collective Farms), *Sovetskie finansy*, No. 1, 1947.

Odinnadtsataia sessiia Verkhovnogo Soveta SSSR . . . 1945 g.; Stenograficheskii otchet (Eleventh Session of the Supreme Soviet of the USSR . . . 1945; Verbatim Report). Moscow, 1945.

Pavlov, P. M. O planovykh khoziaistvennykh rychagakh sotsialisticheskogo gosudarstva (Concerning the Planned Economic Levers of the Socialist Government). Leningrad, 1950.

Planovoe khoziaistvo (Planned Economy).

Plotnikov, K. N. Biudzhet sotsialisticheskogo gosudarstva (Budget of the Socialist Government). Leningrad, 1948.

—— Biudzhet sovetskogo gosudarstva (Budget of the Soviet Government). Moscow, 1945.

Pravda (Truth).

Prokopovicz, S. N. *Quarterly Bulletin of Soviet-Russian Economics*.

Redding, A. D. "Reliability of Estimates of Unfree Labor in the U.S.S.R.," *Journal of Political Economy*, August, 1952.

Results of the Fulfillment of the Five-Year Plan of the USSR for 1946–1950, Supplement to *USSR Information Bulletin* (Embassy of the USSR), Washington, D.C., no date.

Riauzov, N., and N. Titel'baum. Kurs torgovoi statistiki (Course on Trade Statistics). Moscow, 1947.

RKKA (Raboche-krest'ianskaia Krasnaia Armiia), Upravlenie Voennykh Vozdushnyk Sil (Workers' and Peasants' Red Army, Administration of the Air Force). Tsennik-spravochnik po material'noi chasti VVS

RKKA, Chast' III (Price Handbook for Material of the VVS RKKA, Part III), Moscow, 1940.

Rothstein, A. Workers in the Soviet Union. London, 1942.

Rovinskii, N. N. Gosudarstvennyi biudzhet SSSR (State Budget of the USSR). Moscow, 1939, 1944, 1949, and 1951.

—— (ed.). Organizatsiia finansirovaniia i kreditovaniia kapital'nykh vlozhenii (Organization of Financing and Credit for Capital Investment). Moscow, 1951.

Sbornik rukovodiashchikh materialov i konsul'tatsii po stroitel'stvu (Collection of the Leading Articles and Notes concerning Construction).

Schechtman, J. B. European Population Transfers, 1939–45. New York, 1946.

Schwartz, H. "Prices in the Soviet War Economy," *American Economic Review,* December, 1946.

—— Russia's Soviet Economy. New York, 1950.

—— "Soviet Labor Policy, 1945–1949," *Annals of the American Academy of Political and Social Science,* May, 1949.

Shabad, T. "Political-Administrative Divisions of the USSR, 1945," *The Geographic Review,* No. 2, 1946.

Shepilov, D. "Kolkhoznyi stroi SSSR" (Collective Farm System of the USSR), *Problemy ekonomiki,* No. 1, 1941.

Shestaia sessiia Verkhovnogo Soveta RSFSR (Sixth Session of the Supreme Soviet of the RSFSR). Moscow, 1945.

Shestaia sessiia Verkhovnogo Soveta SSSR . . . 1940 g.; Stenograficheskii otchet (Sixth Meeting of the Supreme Soviet of the USSR . . . 1940; Verbatim Report). Moscow, 1940.

Shol'ts, S. V. Kurs sel'skokhoziaistvennoi statistiki (Course in Agricultural Statistics). Moscow, 1945.

Smilga, A. "Finansy sotsialisticheskogo gosudarstva" (Finances of the Socialist State), *Problemy ekonomiki,* No. 2, 1937.

Sobranie postanovlenii i rasporiazhenii pravitel'stva Soiuza Sovetskikh Sotsialisticheskikh Respublik (Collection of the Laws and Decrees of the Government of the USSR).

Sotsialisticheskoe sel'skoe khoziaistvo (Socialist Agriculture).

Sotsialisticheskoe zemledelie (Socialist Agriculture).

Sovet Ministrov SSSR (Council of Ministers of the USSR). O gosudarstvennom plane vosstanovleniia i razvitiia narodnogo khoziaistva SSSR na 1947 god (On the State Plan for the Restoration and Development of the National Economy of the USSR in 1947). Moscow, 1947.

Sovetskaia torgovlia za XXX let (Soviet Trade for 30 Years). Moscow, 1947.

Sovetskie finansy (Soviet Finance).

Sovetskoe gosudarstvo i pravo (Soviet Government and Law).

Sovnarkom SSSR (Council of People's Commissars). O vypolnenii posta-

novleniia SNK SSSR i TSK VKP(b) ot 21 avgusta 1943 goda, "O neotlo-
zhnykh merakh po vosstanovleniiu khoziaistva v raionakh, osvobo-
zhdennykh ot nemetskoi okkupatsii" (On Fulfilling the Resolution of the
Council of People's Commissars and Central Committee of the Communist Party of August 21, 1943, "Concerning Emergency Measures
Connected with the Reconstruction of Areas Liberated from German
Occupation"). Moscow, 1944.

Sputnik agitatora (The Agitator's Companion).

Statistical Year-book of the League of Nations, 1940/41. Geneva, 1941.

Stines, N. C., Jr. Cooperatives in Soviet Industry. Monograph of the Foreign
Service Institute, Department of State, May, 1950.

Studenikin, S. S. Sovetskoe administrativnoe pravo (Soviet Administrative
Law). Moscow, 1945.

Suchkov, A. K. Dokhody gosudarstvennogo biudzheta SSSR (Income of
the State Budget of the USSR). Moscow, 1945.

—— Gosudarstvennye dokhody SSSR (Government Incomes of the USSR).
Moscow, 1949.

Sukharevskii, B. Sovetskaia ekonomika v velikoi Otechestvennoi voine
(Soviet Economics in the Great Patriotic War). Moscow, 1945.

Survey of Current Business.

Trud (Labor).

TSU. Slovar'-spravochnik po sotsial'no-ekonomicheskoi statistike (Diction-
ary Handbook of Socio-economic Statistics). Moscow, 1944, 1948.

TSUNKHU. Chislennost' i zarabotnaia plata rabochikh i sluzhashchikh
v SSSR (Number and Wages of Workers and Employees in the USSR).
Moscow, 1936.

—— Sotsialisticheskoe sel'skoe khoziaistvo Soiuza SSR (Socialist Agriculture of the USSR), reprinted in *Planovoe khoziaistvo,* No. 7, 1939.

—— Sotsialisticheskoe stroitel'stvo SSSR (Socialist Construction of the
USSR). Moscow, 1936.

—— Sotsialisticheskoe stroitel'stvo Soiuza SSR, 1933–1938 gg. (Socialist Construction of the USSR, 1933–1938). Moscow, 1939.

Turetskii, Sh. Ia. Vnutripromyshlennoe nakoplenie v SSSR (Intraindustry
Accumulation in the USSR). Moscow, 1948.

United Nations, Economic Commission for Europe. Economic Survey of
Europe in 1948. Geneva, 1949.

—— Economic Survey of Europe in 1951. Geneva, 1952.

United States Bureau of the Census. Statistical Abstract of the United States:
1952. Washington, D.C., 1952.

United States Department of Agriculture. *Foreign Agricultural Circular.*

United States Department of Commerce. International Reference Service.

—— National Income, 1951 Edition. Washington, D.C., 1951.

United States Department of Commerce. *Russian Economic Notes.*

Valler, L. B. Sberegatel'noe delo v SSSR (Savings-Bank Affairs in the USSR). Moscow, 1950.

Vladimirov, P. "Za rentabel'nuiu rabotu predpriiatii" (Toward the Profitable Operation of Enterprises), *Voprosy ekonomiki,* No. 8, 1948.

Voprosy ekonomiki (Problems of Economics).

XVIII S"ezd VKP(b) (Eighteenth Congress of the All-Union Communist Party of Bolsheviks). Moscow, 1939.

Vos'maia sessiia Verkhovnogo Soveta SSSR . . . 1941 g.; Stenograficheskii otchet (Eighth Meeting of the Supreme Soviet of the USSR . . . 1941; Verbatim Report). Moscow, 1941.

Voznesenskii, N. A. "Khoziaistvennye itogi 1940 goda i plan razvitiia narodnogo khoziaistva SSSR na 1941 god" (Economic Results of 1940 and the Plan of Development of the National Economy of the USSR in 1941), *Bol'shevik,* No. 3-4, 1941.

—— Piatiletnii plan vosstanovleniia i razvitiia narodnogo khoziaistva SSSR na 1946–1950 gg. (Five Year Plan of Reconstruction and Development of the National Economy of the USSR for 1946–1950). Moscow, 1946.

—— Voennaia ekonomika SSSR v period Otechestvennoi voiny (War Economy of the USSR in the Period of the Great Patriotic War). Moscow, 1947.

V pomoshch FZMK (In Assistance to Factory and Local Committees). Journal of the All-Union Central Council of Trade Unions.

"Za dal'neishii pod"em sel'skogo khoziaistva" (For a Further Rise of Agriculture), *Bol'shevik,* No. 5, 1948.

Zakon o piatiletnem plane vosstanovleniia i razvitiia narodnogo khoziaistva SSSR na 1946–50 gg. (Law concerning the Five Year Plan of Reconstruction and Development of the National Economy of the USSR, 1946–50). Moscow, 1946.

Zasedaniia Verkhovnogo Soveta RSFSR (vtoraia sessiia), . . . 1948 g. (Sittings of the Supreme Soviet of the RSFSR [Second Session] . . . 1948). Moscow, 1948.

Zasedaniia Verkhovnogo Soveta SSSR (tret'ia sessiia) . . . 1947 g. (Sittings of the Supreme Soviet of the USSR [Third Session] . . . 1947). Moscow, 1947.

Zasedaniia Verkhovnogo Soveta SSSR (chetvertaia sessiia) . . . 1948 g. (Sittings of the Supreme Soviet of the USSR [Fourth Session] . . . 1948). Moscow, 1948.

"Za skoreishee vosstanovlenie i pod"em sel'skogo khoziaistva" (Toward the Most Rapid Reconstruction and Advance of Agriculture"), *Bol'shevik,* No. 4, 1947.

"Znamenatel'nye itogi tret'ego goda poslevoennoi piatiletki" (Significant

Results of the Third Year of the Postwar Five Year Plan), *Bol'shevik,* No. 2, 1949.

Zverev, A. G. "Biudzhet mirnogo khoziaistvennogo i kul'turnogo stroitel'stva" (Budget of Peacetime Economic and Cultural Construction), *Planovoe khoziaistvo,* No. 2, 1951.

—— Gosbiudzhet SSSR na 1944 god (State Budget of the USSR for 1944). Moscow, 1944.

—— Gosudarstvennye biudzhety Soiuza SSR, 1938–1945 gg. (State Budgets of the USSR, 1938–1945). Moscow, 1946.

—— "Gosudarstvennyi biudzhet chetvertogo goda poslevoennoi stalinskoi piatiletki" (State Budget in the Fourth Year of the Postwar Stalin Five Year Plan), *Planovoe khoziaistvo,* No. 2, 1949.

—— "Gosudarstvennyi biudzhet zavershaiushchego goda poslevoennoi stalinskoi piatiletki" (State Budget of the Last Year of the Postwar Stalin Five Year Plan), *Planovoe khoziaistvo,* No. 4, 1950.

—— O gosudarstvennom biudzhete SSSR na 1947 god (On the State Budget of the USSR in 1947). Moscow, 1947.

—— O gosudarstvennom biudzhete SSSR na 1948 god (On the State Budget of the USSR in 1948). Moscow, 1948.

OTHER VOLUMES OF RAND RESEARCH

PUBLISHED BY MCGRAW-HILL BOOK COMPANY, NEW YORK

Leites, Nathan. *The Operational Code of the Politburo* (1950).

Janis, Irving L. *Air War and Emotional Stress* (1950).

Mead, Margaret. *Soviet Attitudes toward Authority* (1950).

Selznick, Philip. *The Organizational Weapon in Bolshevik Strategy and Tactics* (1952).

McKinsey, J. C. C. *Introduction to the Theory of Games* (1952).

Shanley, F. R. *Weight-Strength Analysis of Aircraft Structures* (1952).

Williams, J. D. *The Compleat Strategyst, a Primer on the Theory of Games of Strategy* (1954).

PUBLISHED BY THE FREE PRESS, GLENCOE, ILLINOIS

Goldhamer, Herbert, and Andrew W. Marshall. *Psychosis and Civilization* (1953).

Garthoff, Raymond L. *Soviet Military Doctrine* (1953).

Leites, Nathan. *A Study of Bolshevism* (1953).

Leites, Nathan, and Elsa Bernaut. *The Ritual of Liquidation, Communists on Trial* (1954).